Praise for *All the Gold Stars*

"If you've been doing 'everything right' for as long as you can remember, and can't quite figure out why you're so exhausted, or bored, or unmotivated, or just *over it*—this book will change your life. Rainesford Stauffer gives us permission—and the language!—to imagine a different way forward."

—Anne Helen Petersen, author of *Can't Even: How
Millennials Became the Burnout Generation*

"*All the Gold Stars* is a probing, challenging, and deeply thoughtful exploration of what it means to find compassion for ourselves and pursue the lives we want without self-punishment. Drawing on her own experiences as well as dozens of interviews, Rainesford Stauffer writes with both clarity and care, considering the function and purpose of ambition from multiple angles while inviting readers to imagine how it may be redirected to aid and nourish us and our communities. If you, like so many born or made strivers, are engaged in the work of reevaluating your relationship to ambition and achievement, this is a wonderful book to keep you company as you do so."

—Nicole Chung, author of *A Living Remedy*

"As a firstborn daughter (read: recovering perfectionist), self-employed writer, and mother, I needed to read this very book at this very moment. *All the Gold Stars*, ironically, is a brilliant achievement."

—Maggie Smith, author of *You Could Make
This Place Beautiful* and *Keep Moving*

"A timely, important literary reckoning with the toll ambition takes on all of us, and how to reclaim our fire and fortitude in an age of burnout."

—Amber Tamblyn, author of *Listening in the Dark:
Women Reclaiming the Power of Intuition*

"*All the Gold Stars* is a lively read about a little-discussed problem that's leaving millions of us exhausted and unhappy: Americans work far too hard, far more hours than workers in other wealthy nations. With insightful analysis and excellent examples, Rainsford Stauffer explains the two main reasons why we work so much. First, forever seeking the next gold star, Americans push themselves too hard in their quest for more money and success. Second, too many companies push their workers too hard and demand too much as they seek to maximize their profits. This book sounds an important alarm—it's time to work less and enjoy life more."

—Steven Greenhouse, author of *Beaten Down, Worked
Up: The Past, Present, and Future of American Labor*

"As a chronic seeker of external validation and a collector of gold stars since kindergarten, this book was a balm for my weary, approval-seeking soul. Rainesford Stauffer has a rare gift for blending rigorous research and journalism with tender and empathetic storytelling. This is a must-read for try-hards, strivers, and other ambitious people whose candle has burnt out on both ends."

—Nora McInerny

"In *All the Gold Stars*, Rainesford Stauffer looks at our societal conversations around ambition and success for young people, and deftly unravels the myriad of ways those conversations preach a cruel and unyielding message to the inheritors of this society: deny the limits of your humanity to get ahead. Stauffer speaks with those deeply affected by this warped messaging and writes a new narrative for us. One that includes an acknowledgment of our humanness, our need for play, and a more compassionate path to a better future. Read this book, and expand your imagination beyond what is, and toward what could be."

—Ashley C. Ford, Writer and Host

"Everything in [this] book connects the personal, the political, and the structural. . . . [Stauffer] gives the reader a lot of inspiration. . . [providing] ideas and hope and direction in how we think about the insidiousness of the [capitalist] philosophy in the United States, how we go forward with other people."

—*Yes! Magazine*

"The author calls for a wholesale reimagining of ambition: rather than adopting a go-it-alone attitude, readers should assign greater value to relationships and friendships, as true success can't be achieved solo. Stauffer is most convincing when she explores the intersection of ambition and injustice, as when she trenchantly critiques the ways student loans and academic tracking systems such as Advanced Placement classes reinforce racial inequalities. . . . Stauffer takes on a fascinating social question."

—*Publishers Weekly*

All the Gold Stars

Gold Stars

REIMAGINING
AMBITION
AND THE WAYS
WE STRIVE

Rainesford Stauffer

hachette
BOOKS

New York

To all our younger selves, who were striving so hard.

Hachette Go, an imprint of Hachette Books
Hachette Book Group
1290 Avenue of the Americas
New York, NY 10104
HachetteGo.com
Facebook.com/HachetteGo
Instagram.com/HachetteGo

First Edition: June 2023

Hachette Books is a division of Hachette Book Group, Inc.

The Hachette Go and Hachette Books name and logos are trademarks of Hachette Book Group, Inc.

The Hachette Speakers Bureau provides a wide range of authors for speaking events. To find out more, go to www.hachettespeakersbureau.com or call (866) 376-6591.

Hachette Go books may be purchased in bulk for business, educational, or promotional use. For information, please contact your local bookseller or Hachette Book Group Special Markets Department at: special.markets@hbgusa.com.

The publisher is not responsible for websites (or their content) that are not owned by the publisher.

Print book interior design by Amy Quinn.

Library of Congress Control Number: 2022950577

ISBNs: 9780306830334 (hardcover), 9780306830358 (ebook)

Printed in the United States of America

LSC-C

Printing 1, 2023

Contents

I'll Go First:
An Introduction

It rushed me every time I met a down-to-the-wire deadline; when I popped out of the shower to scribble a sentence that was never as good as busting through the shower curtain with shampoo dripping from my hair led me to believe; when I *finally* landed on a new idea and felt a half second of relief that I hadn't used them all up: ambition, what I thought of as the sum of all my parts—the best and most broken thing about me. More than glory, ambition felt like the pursuit of goodness. More than success, striving felt like my best shot at safety.

If you've ever celebrated an achievement over the glittery clink of a flute of Martinelli's or Vueve, basked in the fleeting warmth of your boss's praise for a job well done, or experienced a sweet exhale of thinking maybe, just maybe, with this win you'd earned a break, you know it: the gold star. They cling to us—literally—from elementary school onward, appearing as sparkly stickers, good grades, and pizza parties celebrating the ableist concept of perfect attendance. Then those symbols of excellence shape-shift into grown-up versions, organizing life into neat rows of accomplishment made for an Instagram grid or chirpy "what do you do" sound bites, degrees that were supposed to be worth the debt, job titles we're giddy to announce on LinkedIn, marriages at the "right" age, and the abstract concept of timelines. Whatever direction you turn, there's something to strive for; whatever you dreamed up can be outmatched by new dreams.

Somehow, ambition felt *alluring* to me, a quality I should aspire to have. It felt generative—every taste of it produced hunger, every achievement put down one brick leading to the next. I could time my life by goals and map a trail of aspirations. I could feel the flood of relief awash in my mind when a teacher, a boss, and, if we're being honest, a random kind stranger on the internet thought I'd done a good job. I could outwork loneliness by constantly giving myself something new to look forward to, forever looking ahead. Rather than deriving my self-worth, passion, and identity from *outcomes* of work—GPA, job titles, or awards—my attachment to ambition came in the form of *being ambitious* itself. I lit up not at accolades or accomplishments but at the acknowledgment that came with them: *Such a hard worker. Always going above and beyond.* When I faltered personally, the act of being ambitious felt like a saving grace.

As a perpetually anxious, average student, ambition was my way of scoring points that weren't coming on Scantrons: a good listener, good at overdoing her homework, good at the act of hard work even if the work produced little. As a young adult juggling multiple jobs and trying to earn my way into self-worth via bylines, timelines, and going it alone, I had big goals, even if I couldn't tell you what they were and sometimes my biggest, secret goal was to stop trying so hard. I handed over pieces of me to sketchy bosses who had me working 39.5 hours per week to avoid granting health insurance, which turned out to be a dire trade-off as the gut issues doctors had dismissed for years as a "nervous stomach" enshrined my newest ambition of creating maps of public bathrooms in every city I traversed. As my physical and mental health demanded my attention, I attempted to work around them, to patch holes in myself, my life plan, the anxious gut feeling that maybe I didn't know what I wanted after all with gold stars—like playing against myself in a buzzer-beater during March Madness: me in the crowd, watching myself, and only I stood to lose.

By my late twenties, my pile of career goals, my tendency to interpret "you did a good job" as "you are a good person," my messy-at-best physical and mental health were all stacked up like wobbly Jenga pieces. And ambition—well, I couldn't find it. The dazzling quality that made me feel like my aspirations were written in the stars vanished right when I needed it to carry me. At the intersection of a physical and mental health crisis, what burst forth from me wasn't *I'm burnt out, I need help, I'm lost, I'm not holding it together anymore* but rather a confession: I'm not ambitious anymore.

The Glimmer Catches Everything

    1 a: an ardent desire for rank, fame, or power
       With her talent and fierce ambition, she became a very
        successful actress.
     b: desire to achieve a particular end

2: the object of ambition
Her ambition is to start her own business.

—*Merriam-Webster*

a strong wish to achieve something
—*Cambridge Dictionary*

a particular goal or aim: something that a person hopes
to do or achieve
—*Britannica Dictionary*

Ambition evades a single, all-encompassing definition and exists instead as a virtue and a vice, a compliment and an insult, a framework for stepping into your own power, and a way to question what power is at all. Ambition is stuffed with different meanings individually, different implications systemically, communally, and politically, and fluctuates between being a personal ideology, a motivational speech, and a death sentence, depending on who and where and when you are in time. Because the idea of ambition is so loaded—and has been, throughout history—there is no means to strive for it in one way without falling short in another.

At the time, I thought I'd lost my ambition—but the question that lingered was why ambition felt so bound up in my sense of self, my sense of *control,* that it was the loss I pointed to first. The problem, as I identified it, wasn't that I was sick physically and receiving no answers or that my mind refused to trust itself; the problem I articulated was that I couldn't *keep going* the way I had been.

On the surface, I thought I understood ambition. Hard work, check. Big goals, check. Motivation, check. I'd heard about how ambition was warped by gender stereotypes, the mentality that men were inherently more ambitious than women and that women were punished or shamed by people who considered them too ambitious. I'd run into instances myself: the stilted first date where the man sitting across from me eye-rolled my dreams and—unprompted—compared my published pieces to the hypothetical article he *thought* about writing for *Golf* magazine. Or the contradictory advice I received: the boss who told me to quit being quiet and learn to be cutthroat while another encouraged me not to come on "too strong" or use too many exclamation points. (You'll pry 'em from my cold, dead laptop.)

There is a lot of *too* in ambition: too much, too little. We shame people for being *too ambitious* yet judge them for not being ambitious *enough*. And most of the time this occurs without any acknowledgment of what ambition even is, let alone where it comes from, how it might change, and the resources needed to have it to begin with. Some research supporting the thesis that ambition effects career success states that central to most definitions of ambition is the "aspirational nature" of it—a motivational process "oriented toward the attainment of outcomes."[1] The outcomes part feels most crucial, and most ambiguous, because shouldn't outcomes—goals or dreams—vary by person? Other research, focused on expectations of achievement in youth in the United States, underscored that "expressions of ambition and likely future achievements are informed by the social structural positions that individuals inhabit."[2] With that framing, ambition is shaped by cultural, structural, and institutional forces. Sure, I might be undergoing an isolated ambition identity crisis, but I suspected there was more to it than that.

Ambition Never Quit

The past few years especially—during a pandemic, ongoing recession, an insurrection, and intersecting crises in public health, education, childcare, caregiving, work and labor—have underscored what many people have known for a long time: America's systems of worth, stability, and achievement are broken.

During a pandemic in which approximately 600 million people globally have been sickened and more than 6 million have died to date, there was a fleeting period in which many were asked to pause, while the already overworked and underpaid (now labeled "essential") continued to work and risk their lives.[3] We blinked, and it was "back to normal," surging COVID case numbers and mass death be damned—back to the office or bust. Disparities in work and the economy disproportionately impact Black, Latinx, Indigenous, and immigrant workers,[4] while disabled and chronically ill people watched the application of and the conversation around accessibility of work and public spaces fade again. Without paid leave, universal basic income, flexible work schedules, or universal health care, people struggled to get by on their own.[5] People who were single and/or lived alone grappled with intense isolation and, in some cases, the expectation that, because of the assumption that they had nothing to do besides work, they'd be glad to pick up the extra (unpaid) slack. Personal crises compounded on top of structural ones; most people were given the resources and time to grapple with neither. *Grieve through it; strive through it* was structurally reinforced by how much didn't change at all.

A more generous reading of the period so many would refer to as "postpandemic"—a term I will not use because we are not, in fact, postpandemic at the time of writing—is that the relationship to hustling and achieving was reconsidered. This was a time for reckoning with what mattered to us—for reestablishing what often got lost in the swirl of Slack notifications and last-minute schedule changes. Banana bread was baked, after all! But if we looked a little closer, the usual metrics of achievement and success churned on, everlasting even when school and work went virtual for some, even as people grieved, and even as so many sought to protect their families and communities amid a dismal federal response. Even when the achievements themselves were technically no longer possible, the impulse to funnel energy and effort into them remained. The goals weren't there; they were ghosts. And our efforts were gestures toward the next save point even as our surroundings flickered, as everything went dark.

Performance reviews happened. Aside from temporary breaks from letter grades, which weren't applied everywhere and to everyone, the need for good grades, impressive résumés, and high test scores remained. Parents and caregivers were expected to parent as if they weren't workers, and work as if they weren't caregivers—both roles being full-time jobs. People showed up to work in person—voluntarily or by company decree—even as cases surged and mask mandates were removed. Excel sheets, "circling back," and team-building Zooms were to be handled with the same attention and care as figuring out how to quarantine according to changing guidelines and rationed sick days, if you had them to begin with.

I'm immensely privileged—I'm white, my work was remote prepandemic, and I'm not singlehandedly responsible

for caring for another person, to name a few advantages—
and the outrageousness of the expectation struck even me. I
received two calls simultaneously during the first few weeks
of March 2020: one was from my dad, telling me he'd taken
my mom—who he thought was having a heart attack but
actually had COVID—to the emergency room, only to be
turned away and told to come back when she fully couldn't
breathe, when her lips were blue. The other was from my
manager at my then part-time job I felt lucky to have hung
on to that long, wondering why I was a minute late to a
Zoom meeting if I was truly at home "doing nothing."

Then came the so-called Great Resignation, in which
workers exited their jobs for reasons ranging from inequitable,
unsafe working conditions, low pay, and lack of childcare to
seeing the moment as the narrow window to start over and
find work that felt more meaningful or, at least, more tena-
ble. Quitting itself was publicly deemed ambitious, like someone was actively choosing to give up and pour their energy
toward something better. But "choosing" is the key word. For
every person who could quit, there were numerous people who
didn't have the option to walk away from an abusive boss, a
low-paying role, or a job with no boundaries. Meanwhile, the
so-called end of ambition was presented as an abdication of
overwork, a rejection of tying one's whole self to work and
instead committing to live slower and more simply, to watch
more sunsets—as at least one article pointed out.

But I thought of all the stories the so-called end of ambition didn't touch: people expected to keep going onward,
upward, sky's the limit, when they were already running on
empty. I thought of passions put on the backburner because
life got in the way and what happened to *those* ambitions. I

thought of how one's goals or dreams might change and how that was spun as a betrayal—a lack of commitment or maturity rather than recommitting to oneself. I thought of people who had sacrificed and strained and striven to earn society's gold stars, only to wonder what the hell it was all for in the end. But the real-time sorting of who our definition of ambition was made for—and who it destroyed—betrayed a bigger truth: we were still supposed to be ambitious as the world around us, and the rewards on offer, burned.

Even as we decry hustle culture and denounce grind life, ambition, it seemed to me, had avoided that sort of reconsideration. In and of itself, popular conceptions of ambition and what's considered worthy of aspiration assume a certain level of able-bodied privilege, financial prowess, and personal freedom to make choices, to *have* choices. The thing about dreams is that the opportunity to have them has never been equally applied. So much of the gospel of "being ambitious" is cemented in the idea that there is always a little something *more*. More we could be. More we could aspire to. More out there for us. In some ways, both good and bad, that feels like the most succinct definition of ambition: *more*.

I picked at my own relationship with ambition in the absentminded way I'd pick a scab. Suddenly, ambition was in all the cheery talk I heard in job interviews ("We're looking for a self-starter!"). It was in my relationships with loved ones, negotiating whose goals were going to be the ones life was organized around and what it meant to split that down the middle. It popped up as I reported stories on the toxicity of pay-your-dues culture. Maybe I was just seeing it like gold glitter, all over everything despite my best efforts to rid myself of it after feeling I'd lost my get-up-and-go, my second gear, my belief that ambition would sustain me. Or maybe it really *did* just touch that much—work, school, relationships, life. But what bounced to the forefront, time and again, was that so many of us were reconfiguring what we were ambitious *about*.

It's Complicated . . .

The pandemic might've been one visible, drastic change to ambition, but the past couple of years were really only one of multiple makeovers that ambition has undergone. Or rather, ways it has been blown up and rebuilt. While the concept of ambition predates capitalism, capitalism created new versions, funneling what it meant to have desire or goals for your life into narrow definitions of success and happiness in a system that doesn't come close to guaranteeing everyone the safety, stability, and support to envision their futures in the first place. That striving—as we'll see—pops up all around us, from the education system, to our sense of being "on track" (who is keeping time?), to America's history of ascribing worth, identity, and deservingness to work. It steals what we love and morphs it into outputs; gathers up all our little idiosyncrasies and secret dreams and mundanities that shape everything we are and attempts to smooth them out. What we want and what we're *supposed* to strive for—be it because of cultural expectations, fear of taking a wrong turn and it all going wrong, or what's structurally reinforced as good dreams, a good life—are like melted-down crayons, increasingly indistinguishable from one another as we search for where our ambitions end and expectations begin.

So many modern ideas of ambition are rooted in work-related self-development, self-improvement, and career mobility, but ambition isn't just about work. One study of the psychological characteristics of ambitious people said that "ambition as a person's desire for recognition and importance is realized in various spheres of human activity."[6] And there are deeper questions: desire for *what*? That's how I'd phrase it to a friend. I know I'm reaching, but what on earth am I reaching for?

Reading that also made me curious: if ambition can be realized across different spheres of life, can we be ambitious in relationships, friendships, or communities? Does that automatically render those connections transactional? Or can we be ambitious in terms of hobbies, even if we never plan to make them into a career or a calling? What would it look like if we spent our ambition on each other? When I sat down—on the phone, on Zoom, via email, and occasionally in person—with people to talk about how they'd lost their ambition, their relationship to striving, and what ambition meant for them, the above definitions were some of what I heard. As many times as ambition led someone to pursue what mattered to them, it exploited someone else. For as often as ambition was heralded as a means of individualistic striving, there were people pouring energy, time, and imagination into a kind of ambition that felt more collective. Even as we denounced ambition via quitting or questioning, it clung to us, the residue of a gold star sticker pried off the top of a page.

In these pages, we're going to complicate ambition further. First, this book unpacks the roots of where ambition even comes from—turns out that's more loaded than gold star stickers would have us believe. Moving through the impact of family and school systems on self-worth, the emphasis on timelines of achievement, and, of course, overwork, we're going to reckon with the stakes of ambition: what it grants us, but also what it steals; what it says about our worth; what it means when we don't define it for ourselves. From there, we'll explore a different definition: What does it take for ambition to be self-defined but also collective? How can we be ambitious about community, about fun, and about each other? What does it mean to truly be ambitious about *ourselves*, for that matter—not what we can earn, but about the kind of lives we want to live?

Because ambition is so loaded, so personal, this book doesn't seek to be a complete history or analysis of ambition—which would be a very *ambitious* book. It asks more questions than it answers, in part because reimagining anything means getting curious—including with ourselves—about what stirs us, drives us, and why. Throughout these pages, I've woven my personal story, discussing my chronic illness (which still evades a neat diagnosis) and mental health. I do not intend to be prescriptive: these are personal experiences that do not speak on behalf of larger communities. I'm still learning how ambition might have molded my relationship to these parts of myself, and there are no clean-cut conclusions. But my striving was interwoven around my understanding of and relationship to the self I was, the person I am, and the person I aspire to be.

In this book, you'll hear from people in a variety of life stages, identities, and circumstances and how ambition manifests for them: the pressures of endless striving and chronic never-enough-ness and how the stakes of that unfold in schools, in jobs, and at home. But we'll also explore their revised definitions: ambition about collective action, about play—from artistic swimming (in which swimmers perform a choreographed routine to music) to friendships. They generously discussed how grief changed their ambition, how care infrastructure is inherently ambitious, and what resources would make dreaming possible. Even their experiences, profound as they are, don't paint a full picture of everything ambition can be, of every way it functions. This book doesn't instruct *how* to be ambitious, or whether you should be at all. But my hope is that in complicating ambition, we move closer toward goals that feel more like us—to be more imaginative, more engaged, and more caring. That starts with the fundamental question: What is our ambition *for*?

1: So You're Calling Me a Striver, and Some Thoughts on Sin

Little did I know that by the time I sat down to think about how the definition of ambition shape-shifts depending on who holds it, *my* conception of ambition had already been glossed with everything I assumed it was. I could put names to it: "eager to please" in school, as if I was all good manners and nice smiles and no pulsating anxiety; "striver" in my early twenties, when it didn't feel cool to be outwardly enthusiastic about what I wanted; the more poetic "big dreamer," who would narrate visions for her life she couldn't back up with anything other than jittery inklings that she should be doing *something*, and just maybe, in all the striving, she'd find whatever she was searching for. Though the word *ambitious* itself didn't pop up until later, the points of ambition's stars seemed to touch everything.

Curious about ambition's influence, I wanted to better understand how ambition itself is shaped—where it came from and how the term itself and the phrases connected to it have evolved. That includes how ambition's historic and religious ties to Western society and Christianity give it a darker underbelly, more complex than the "persistent and generalized striving for success, attainment, and accomplishment" definition of it leads us to believe.[1] How it shapes us first means examining how ambition itself is shaped.

Back We Go

"Ambition has long attracted the interest of philosophers and laypeople because it is regarded as both a high virtue that can lead someone to significant personal and societal attainments as well as a vice that can inflict suffering on others in the pursuit of personal gains," wrote researchers from the Institute of Psychology at the University of Bern, Switzerland, in a study that sought to define understanding and measurement of ambition.[2] On the surface, blatant illustrations of ambition leading to suffering in pursuit of profit or personal gain are endless—take, for example, reports of workers who say they are enduring brutal conditions while billionaires who exploit their labor dabble in space travel, or how unmitigated political ambition has material impacts on people's lives. In her 2021 book *Ambition: For What*, Deborah L. Rhode wrote that "ambition is a dominant force in most civilizations, driving their greatest achievements and most horrific abuses."[3] Part of what renders it aspirational—a reclaiming of one's agency, passionate audacity, the force behind dreamers—is that it's thought of as making things happen, of creating and doing things we didn't know were possible. Understanding how the current conception of ambition came to be is important to better understanding our *own* ambition.

At least part of ambition's roots are in Roman politics: *ambitio* came from the Latin verb *ambire*,[4] and it referred to political candidates going around and soliciting votes. But we can also trace current understanding of ambition to not one, but three, separate Greek words, according to *Ambition, A History: From Virtue to Vice* by William Casey King: *philotimia*, "the love of honor"; *eritheia*, "rivalry or strife"; and *philodoxia*, "love of acclaim."[5] It made me think about ambition's dueling definitions today—how just as often as ambition is aspirational, it's seen as power hungry, encompassing everything from chasing our dreams to climbing over others on our way up to the skies those dreams are housed in. The multiplicity of how ambition was framed, even from the start, seems to mirror how much it touches now, a quality of both destruction and creativity, depending on who has it and how they use it.

Bundled into that, later, was ambition as sin. In the Geneva Bible, the margin notes make another facet of ambition clear, as King sums up: "ambition, therefore, is at the core of original sin," King wrote, citing Adam eating forbidden fruit "not so much to please his wife, as moued [*sic*] by ambition at her persuasion."[6] It was the "excessive desire to be and have more" that gave the world sin, based on this telling.[7]

When did ambition become a "good" quality? Ambition was justified as a virtuous Christian and national goal through settler colonialism, spreading the so-called word of God and seizing land and wealth. Then, "ambition became not only a necessary evil but a Christian good," wrote King. One review of King's work suggested that ambition was considered risky because, at least partly, it has no end goal. After all, its roots, relating to honor and acclaim, have negative associations.

According to this framing, it was ambition in service of "King, God, or country" that shifted the concept.[8] White supremacy as Christian colonization marked a transition.

As Jamila Osman wrote for *Teen Vogue*, "These colonizers did not care that land was considered sacred and communal. . . . Most believed that everything, including the earth, was meant to be bought and sold."[9] There is no full conversation on the allure of ambition that doesn't address the white supremacy, colonization, and imperialism inherent in how ambition has been defined and manifested historically in America and how it continues to appear.

Capitalism Is About Individualized Freedom

Other renderings of ambition's history draw a direct line from ambition as the selfish root of sin to ambition as the quality of aspirational, exploitative innovators via capitalism. Capitalism is an economic system in which the means of production are owned by private companies and dominated by the so-called free market, "in which both prices and production are dictated by private companies and corporations in competition with each other."[10] Capitalism generally presents the idea that rich, successful people are rich and successful because they are more productive than others. (Without fail, I think of a 2018 *Forbes* cover featuring Kylie Jenner—youngest of the Kardashian-Jenner sisters born into the familial wealth, familial businesses, and familial branding—with the headline "The 60 Richest Self-Made Women.") That's one reason—the emphasis on the virtue of productivity above all else—why capitalism is also a massive driver of social and economic inequality.

Now that we know ambition has been considered both a sin *and* something worth striving for, it's worth looking at how capitalism links the two. During our first conversation, Dawna I. Ballard, PhD, an associate professor in the Department of Communication Studies at the University of Texas, Austin, who studies chronemics, or time as it is bound to human communication, told me that if we're in the West, we're existing in a culture that teaches us our personal worth is based *literally* on what we do with our time—a living embodiment of "idle hands are the devil's workshop."

When I spoke to Ballard recently, she confirmed this comes from industrial capitalism. "Their time was what was being valued," she told me. "It wasn't the skill." Citing Max Weber's *The Protestant Ethic and the Spirit of Capitalism*, Ballard explained that Calvinism suggested there were certain chosen people of God who no one would know about until the Second Coming, but that they'd be doing "good works." (Another way to phrase this: in Christianity, predestination is the belief that God has chosen those who will be saved,[11] and in Calvinism, "faith had to be shown in objective results."[12]) "So, the idea is that even before capitalism came along, here was this religion that was, like, 'Hey, work hard,'" Ballard explained. "And then capitalism comes along, and they're, like, 'Trade your time for money.'" Now it's no longer religious, Ballard said, it's just part of the culture, and we're constrained by culture.

Around 1931, historian James Truslow Adams is credited with coining the term the *American dream*, which similarly was grounded in the idea that regardless of social class or resources, in America, everyone could rise based solely on their own abilities and hard work. Not only has the American

dream never been possible for everyone, but even when it has
been within reach of people who aren't white men, America's
policies have, historically, blocked or limited them by design.
Take, for example, the New Deal, which left farmworkers
and domestic workers, disproportionately people of color,
out of job protections.[13] But this fixation on meritocracy—
scaling a ladder of social mobility—has always promoted a
"socially corrosive ethic of competitive self-interest which
both legitimizes inequality and damages community by
requiring people to be in a permanent state of competition
with each other,"[14] ensuring that some striving is rewarded
and other striving is punished.

Lisa Baer-Tsarfati, who is a PhD candidate in the Department of History at the University of Guelph, studies
the relationship between ambition, authority, and gender in
early modern Scotland, Britain, and Europe more broadly.
Baer-Tsarfati argued, via a 2020 Twitter thread,[15] that, while
King suggests ambition lost the negative connotation after the
American War for Independence, the "shifting characteriza-
tion of ambition is tied more to the rise of capitalism" and the
concept of the self-made man. "Ambition was rebranded as
something admirable for men," Baer-Tsarfati stated on Twitter, but the negative associations were pushed even further
onto women. Women were an easy scapegoat: an ambitious
woman could still be sinful, while ambitious men maintained
the status quo. Even today, headline after headline details the
gender gap in ambition: the very definition of "good" ambition, slippery as it might be, relies on one kind of aspiration,
one kind of power, and one kind of person.

Part of this intersection of myths supports our basic concept of ambition, but these myths are just that: they skip the

profound disparities and structural discrimination inherent in meritocracy. Enter what Jhumpa Bhattacharya, vice president of Programs and Strategy at the Insight Center for Community Economic Development, called "toxic individualism," which is where the "pull yourself up by your bootstraps" mentality stems from. Would ambition exist without the undercurrent of pressure to do everything for ourselves, by ourselves or, more directly, to *make it happen*, as a million motivational tips across Pinterest quip?

Speaking of how pseudomotivational phrasing reinforces a certain kind of self-driven ambition, fun fact: while there is intense debate about the exact origin of the phrase, some reports date "pull yourself up by your bootstraps" to a fictional eighteenth-century tale, in which a nobleman, known for exaggerating about his grandiose achievements, purports to pull himself out of a swamp by his own hair. Other research suggests that the earliest published reference appeared in an 1834 newspaper article about a man who claimed he'd invented a perpetual motion machine. The article used the phrase to ridicule his claim, which suggests the idiom originally meant an endeavor that is outrageous and impossible.[16] Ironic, given it's been presented since as an admirable trait.

Capitalism is about *individualized* freedom, Bhattacharya said; it's about how you get yourself to the top. The most profound examples of this are structural ones. First, everything has been tied to work. "Some people are starting to realize: why have we put all our eggs in the work basket?" said Bhattacharya. "We tied health care to it. We've tied our basic needs to this notion of work in a very sexist and racist definition of work." Workers of color are more likely to be paid poverty-level wages than white workers,[17] and women and people of color are still disproportionately likely to be in jobs that pay low wages.[18] (Not coincidentally, these jobs are also among those flagged as "essential" throughout the COVID-19 pandemic.) Meanwhile, safety net programs have been villainized, and our ideas of "making it" follow the pattern of "we did it ourselves," Bhattacharya said. There is no fairy tale we love more than believing that we wrote our happy endings based on our self-reliance and stick-to-itiveness. Not unlike the origins of fairy tales themselves, though, the more accurate version is darker and more complex. Individual achievement is never going to thwart structural barriers. And ambition still unfolds within structures that reinforce that we're supposed to be able to work our way through any problem or challenge.

How Hustle Gets Packaged

My conversation with Bhattacharya made me think of the way American markets "hustle," like it's a lifestyle—complete with coffee mugs declaring "0% Luck; 100% Hustle" and posters proclaiming "good things come to those who work." But who has to hustle—and in what ways—also comes back to a conversation on who America does or doesn't see as deserving.

"The hustle is an idea, a discourse and a survival strategy often glorified as economic opportunity," wrote sociologist and author of *Thick: And Other Essays*, Tressie McMillan Cottom, PhD, for *Time* magazine in 2020.[19] "It is an ode to a type of capitalism that cannot secure the futures of anyone but the wealthiest." "What hustling looks like in 2020 depends on who you are," McMillan Cottom wrote, detailing how Black Americans have to hustle more—"the hustle itself is a site of racial inequality." According to Mc-Millan Cottom, if you're working class, hustling means piecing together multiple jobs; if you're middle class or upper class, it's piecing together "multiple revenue streams." Hustle might highlight the idea that we have to bust it to get ahead, but even "ahead" assumes something false: that everyone is racing from the same starting line.

Then there's a privileged offshoot, where hustle is framed as earning accomplishments that double as placeholders for meaning and security. Now, it's nearly impossible to talk about current versions of ambition without mentioning terms like *#girlboss* and *grind life* because, in a way, they have molded ambition too. Some research cites girl boss as neo-liberal feminism, which equates empowerment with "financial success, market competition, individualized work-life balance, and curated digital and physical presences driven by self-monetization,"[20] absent any focus on the collective good or dismantling oppressive power structures. One of the hearts of the girl boss critique is that it's *still* individual: *I can strive, I can excel, and thus, you can too!* We know that approach doesn't dismantle systems that, by design, are constructed for some to thrive and others to fail. (And still other systems are constructed so that someone *has* to fail or struggle for someone else to succeed.)

But, in a piece for *The Cut* titled "The Girlboss Is Dead. Long Live the Girlboss," Samhita Mukhopadhyay wrote that the spirit of the girl boss "did, for a moment, provide a template for young women as they move forward in their careers."[21] Mukhopadhyay explained that she knew, as the former executive editor of *Teen Vogue*, "hustle culture was the water in which many young women, especially women of color, swam."[22] In Mukhopadhyay's analysis, women she worked with "saw ambition and entrepreneurship as a way to change their material realities."[23] Without tangible resources or a safety net, the allure of striving one's way into the life one wants feels like a false premise, but this matters in terms of how we think about ambition, too—what its aim is, who packages it, what it promises.

Stefanie O'Connell Rodriguez, writer and creator of the newsletter *Too Ambitious*, told me that she hears in her work that people have grown up over the past decade absorbing offshoots of girl-boss culture, which she described as telling them: "You aren't ambitious enough. You weren't asking [for] enough. You weren't assertive enough." But then, as soon as they step up, the response from workplaces is that they are *too* ambitious. "The worst they can say is not no," she told me. "The worst they can do is gaslight you, demean you, make you question your skills and experience, make you feel like you don't belong." People are told to act in ways that are based on white, male norms of success, O'Connell Rodriguez said, "but if you express those qualities as a person of color, as a woman, or as somebody who's nonbinary, you're more likely to face personal, professional, and social penalties for doing so."

A few years into publishing my writing, I remember telling a colleague that I didn't care about being the *best* writer; I just wanted to write and learn. "Why wouldn't you want to be the greatest at something?" she asked. I resented, at the time, the implication that I was *unambitious* when I felt it was worth striving to be good. In the same conversation, I'd gone from batting out of my league with overeager ambition to not aiming high enough. By now, ambition has been sloganized—embroidered on sweatshirts, inscribed on bangles. Ambitiousness might be a quality, but the construct of ambition is also a product. As writer Pam Houston phrased it in an essay in *Double Bind: Women on Ambition*, "The harder I think about ambition as a thing, isolated from other things, the more it collapses in on itself."

Let's Talk About It

Eager to understand how ambition is talked about might shape how we experience it, I asked Rachel Elizabeth Weissler, a postdoctoral scholar in psychology, linguistics, and Black studies at the University of Oregon, about how some of this language pops up in workplaces and branding. "It's always about who is in power at the end of the day," Weissler told me. People in power often dictate how language gets used and even the meaning of it. "So, in these work spaces, I could see the glamorization of something like hustle culture—if we glamorize it and make it desirable, then we get more work to be done. And then we end up benefiting the institutions," Weissler explained. "Meanwhile, the people think that they're actually benefiting themselves because they now positively affiliated this term." All the self-described self-starters like myself, please stand!

Thinking about the language of the workplace specifically, Weissler pointed toward research by Kathrina Robotham, PhD,[24] who has looked at code-switching in the workplace. Robotham focused, Weissler said, on Black people and how they have to shift not just how they speak but also how they present themselves in order to be successful. "What is the workplace idolizing?" Weissler said, a question that could be asked of almost all systems, from government to school, when it comes to the language of success. "What are people striving towards? But very importantly, does striving towards those things actually get you the success that you want, depending on how you show up in those spaces?" she asked. What's found in the research is that no matter how much people code-switch, they're still not succeeding in those spaces. In addition, the valence changes, Weissler pointed out. "Going the extra mile looks different, especially for a person of color, than [it's] going to look for a white person in the space," she explained. Meanwhile, a phrase like *exceeds expectations* when applied to a worker can be very ambiguous: the goalposts can constantly shift depending on who sets the expectations and who is evaluating work performance.

We see it in schools, too. "We're teaching a very specific type of English, usually that was brought by a colonizer white person," Weissler said. Then you get a kid in a classroom who has a different accent or a different syntactic structure. "They might be told in the classroom that the way that they're speaking or answering questions is wrong, when in fact, it's not wrong," said Weissler. "It's just articulating what they're saying differently." In turn, those students don't speak up or ask questions to avoid being corrected or put down, putting them at a disproportionate disadvantage. We say language matters, and according to Weissler, it *really* does because "it influences how people think about themselves, how they think about the work they do, and how they think about the world around them." We can think of ambition in all these ways: What does an ambitious person sound like? What do they do? The meanings we create are composites and collections; crafting a self-defined ambition means examining the biases that already exist within it.

When someone is told "you're so ambitious!" as encouragement, it matters; when someone is told "you're so ambitious!" as a sneer, it sticks. Just like some striving is ambitious (scrappy, determined, persistent), a whole other version is uncouth (trying too hard, overbearing, pushy). Ambition is a constellation of influences, forces that take shape before we've had a chance to define it for ourselves— sometimes before we've had a chance to define *us* for ourselves.

2: Life's Good Behavior Chart

Attached to the email was a photo of notecards conflagrated in a "ceremonial burning."

By the end of Advanced Placement (AP) US History in high school, Bri, a now thirty-year-old who described herself as a queer, aspiring TV writer and current film educator, recalled being so exhausted that she and her classmates gathered at the end of the academic year to set fire to the notecards the class used to study—about three packs of index cards per person, she estimated. Nothing like a make-or-break test to fan the flames of one's ambition. Literally.

"I'm sure I got a literal gold star at some point," Bri told me. She also got a letter (for a letterman jacket) for achievement in speech and debate, was Student of the Week in her local paper, and won an award in middle school for "Optimist of the Month," something she thinks she was nominated for by teachers. "I remember being very confused because that was the year I was more depressed than I'd ever been," she recalled. "Apparently, I'd covered it up well!"

Growing up in a household where hard work was considered the "pinnacle of a respectable person," Bri told me, meant that she believed if she simply worked hard enough, she could achieve anything she wanted. She described being taught that laziness was a mortal sin. "Because I couldn't derive self-esteem or self-worth from my friendships or looks, I derived it from achievement," Bri explained. She received positive reinforcement from building her identity around being a great student, both in classrooms and at the kitchen table at home.

The gold star sticker, with its shimmery metallic foil, is a de facto symbol of achievement in schools, ubiquitous in education and beyond as a tiny, glittery marker of a job well done. Even a brief Google search turns up sheets of gold star stickers and instructions for how to use them effectively on behavior charts, alongside more grown-up uses: an executive coach wrote a post detailing how she *literally* began rewarding professionals with gold star stickers as a motivator that invoked memories of childhood. Coverage by the *Salt Lake Tribune* of a 2019 teacher walkout over low pay made note of a protest sign covered in gold star stickers.[1] The line "and you want to know why she doesn't kiss you on the forehead and give you a gold star on your homework at the end of the day" is from the 2006 movie *The Devil Wears Prada,* where, as writer Lindsay Lee Wallace wrote for Catapult, the protagonist is in a "precarious position that consumes people—including our heroine—nearly alive."[2] Gold stars offer up proof that we did it, and it was worth it.

When I think about gold stars, I think of how tokens of ambition start popping up earlier than we realize. In order to interrogate ambition from the beginning, I wanted to know how the first glimpses of ambition manifested during people's early years. Even though our childhood selves may not have used the word *ambition*, some of our earliest exposures to ambition—in our families and in school, two avenues we have for proving ourselves in childhood—have shaped not just how we think about ambition but also how we think about self-worth.

We're Here to Earn It

In my conversation with Bri, her use of the word *self-worth* jumped out. "From early age I tied my identity to my ambition because it was the only thing I was really getting any positive reinforcement from that seemed to be within my control," she explained. Bri came to associate achievement with social acceptance and validation, so the flip side—*not* excelling—felt like a loss. "I [felt like I'd] lose friends, the respect of my teachers and parents, my future," she told me. So she designed her life to essentially punish herself for anything that wasn't productive. This got so bad, Bri told me, that she made "cultivate two nonmonetizable hobbies" a resolution last year. "I had to make not being productive a productive activity so I could mark 'success,'" she explained.

The more distance Bri gains from her own time in school, the more she thinks about the kids she might have in the future. Whether she feels the school system worked for her is a complex question: she's an able-bodied, cisgender, white woman from a middle-class family, so the system was set up to work for her, she told me. Unquestionably, her education benefited her. But in retrospect, she wonders how much of her intensity and single-mindedness was undiagnosed

ADHD, because women are less likely to be diagnosed. She wonders how much of her self-esteem struggles can be attributed to only receiving validation through achievement and nothing else, because achievement being valued most highly is "very much a capitalism sickness, which is deeply rooted in patriarchy and white supremacy," she added. "I'm functioning exactly as I was raised to function, by parents and teachers and bosses." It wasn't just trying to earn gold stars, prizes, or Student of the Month—but, rather, earning feeling good about herself.

"Self-worth or self-esteem is contingent on satisfying some standards of worth or value," wrote researchers Jennifer Crocker, Shawna J. Lee, and Lora E. Park in a chapter titled "The Pursuit of Self-Esteem: Implications for Good and Evil." Contingencies of self-worth are areas of life in which people invest self-esteem.[3] What we stake self-worth on can vary: for some, it could be professional or academic success; for others, it could be being seen as attractive. While actually performing well in school might be a bonus, if our self-worth is contingent on seeing that gold star shimmering at the top of the test, we're also pursuing what performing well in school *says* about us. (And, of course, school is just one example: for some people, school might be a safe haven to explore, whereas their home could be the place where they must earn self-esteem because it is contingent on parental approval or being seen as a good sibling.)

When I emailed Dr. Lora Park, associate professor in the Department of Psychology at SUNY Buffalo, to ask about this, she explained that the pursuit of self-esteem reflects people's desire to protect, maintain, or boost self-worth in areas where they think they need to succeed to be considered a person who has worth and value. "In Western capitalistic cultures such as the U.S., people are encouraged to pursue the American Dream, which often involves being financially successful, having a good career, attaining status and approval from one's peers," she wrote me. But research suggests that extrinsic goal pursuits dependent on the validation of others—hello, gold star stickers—are associated with lower well-being.

When I think of pressure to earn goodness, I'm snapped back to third grade, when I wore navy skirts with shorts underneath so I could play on the monkey bars and participate in intense games of four-square and consistently sat in the wrong place at lunch thanks to a seating system based on putting a popsicle in a different envelope every week that I never riddled out and was too afraid to ask. I was a privileged child who had all her basic needs met and lucked out with parents who were of the "do your best and be a good friend" variety. When a teacher once suggested my parents would be disappointed in how I did on a spelling quiz, I didn't know how to tell her my parents would ask if I tried, and if I answered in the affirmative, they would remind me that I'm blessed to live in an era with spell-check and to try again.

But what I *was* attached to was the affirmation of being "good," and school gave me an outlet to earn that. I saw how hard my parents worked and knew I needed to work that hard if I ever wanted to take care of them someday or pay them back. (Something, to be clear, I was never asked to do.) I clung to the belief I could earn goodness like I was doing those monkey bars with greased palms. I studied hard, and I was a good student. I took care of my younger siblings, and I was a good daughter. I did these things, and somehow, I was a good person. Who doesn't want to earn *that*?

Not coincidentally, third grade was also the time I started getting sick. Teachers believed I was constantly asking to go to the bathroom to get out of doing work; classmates thought I was a baby. Like clockwork, we'd settle into pairs for timed multiplication tables, which my peers could rattle off like rhyme schemes. Meanwhile, the pressure of speed froze me and flooded my already upset stomach with anxiety. I bargained for extra bathroom passes like I was cutting deals on used cars. Once, I was given the choice to go to the bathroom and miss doing my times tables, therefore losing my "participation points" for the entire day, or not go. I went to the bathroom. I lost the participation points. The teacher asked me—making a statement and not expecting an answer—whether it was worth it.

And thus began a lifetime of thinking that discomfort in the name of earning goodness should, in fact, be worth it.

Remy, a thirty-three-year-old first-generation American, described herself as a Goody Two-shoes, a straight As, do-the-right-thing, perfectionist kid. From an early age, Remy told me, she had a desire to do life *right*. Her father grew up poor in a small city outside São Paulo, Brazil, and financially supported his family when his own father died early. Eventually, he went to college to study computer engineering. In Brazil, the best universities are public and free, Remy told me, but incredibly difficult to get into. There, he met Remy's mother at a cross-campus church organization. She was also ambitious, studying architecture. Remy's father's ambition—his hard work, his performance in school and at work, his dreaming—"lifted him and his family out of poverty; his ambition brought him to the love of his life, who shared a similar interest in intellectual achievement," Remy explained. When they moved to America, Remy's mother decided to give up her profession to raise their children. But she was also, in part, blocked from continuing her work because she'd have to recertify as an architect in the United States and also by the "pay your dues" nature of the field itself. Her mother is the oldest of three, and her entire family are architects: she has talked to Remy about her memories going to job sites with her own father—as well as watching her mother, Remy's grandmother, an equally brilliant architect, decide to leave the field to raise her children. "All of this to say, in addition to the general pressures on first-generation children to bear out their parents' bets, most of my immediate family lore continuously emphasizes ambition (plus intellect and achievement) as essential elements of who we are," Remy added. Plus, Remy's mother and grandmother couldn't put their careers first, so Remy felt a responsibility to do what they couldn't. "Add to this my people-pleasing nature and eagerness to live up to every expectation dropped on me, and it makes for a very difficult reality to shrug off."

Not only was this kind of ambition reinforced by familial history and academic performance, but church and school were somewhat interconnected for Remy. In her Pentecostal church and a Church of Christ school, she ended up conflating messages of being a good person—avoiding sin and hell—with achievement, which meant straight As and the National Honor Society. Obviously, no pressure. They describe one moment in particular when they graduated from their youth group and were preparing to leave for college.

The church invited a visiting prophet to prophesy about the achievements of Remy and other graduates. "As strange as the entire thing is, both my parents and I put a lot of stock in what they ended up 'prophesying,' giving me yet another set of standards that I felt I had to live up to, both spiritually and career-wise," she said. At the time, those were one and the same.

The early lessons stick around. Over the past few years, in rapid succession, Remy had a series of taxing jobs focused on social justice work. Ambition wasn't just about success but the right kind of success: it wasn't just about becoming chief design officer but also about changing systems that were broken for women, people of color, queer people, and disabled people. "I've had a lot of complicated feelings and guilt around the fact that I am literally all of these underrepresented identities: presenting as a woman in tech, bisexual, Latinx/child of immigrants, neurodiverse in several ways," they told me. But Remy added they also pass as the default in nearly every way. She felt it was her duty to use these privileges to fight for space for others who would come behind her.

The tension came to a head when Remy was building software that asylum officers used to process claims in the United States, right at the height of family separation, which she called the "most intense cruelty, enshrined into policy." It felt like "oh my God, if I fuck up, if I sleep, that's one person who is not going to get an asylum decision," Remy said. At the same time, "I did a terrible job of paying attention to my mental health and ended up falling into a really toxic cycle of working really hard all day, drinking really hard at night, and generally acting out in unhealthy ways because I wasn't paying attention to how I was internalizing what was going on." That ended up seriously harming a four-year relationship she had with someone. That's one of Remy's biggest regrets. "I ended up seriously hurting someone I deeply loved," they told me. Some amount of desire to make the world better is healthy—in fact, it's necessary. But what happens when that's the only reason you believe you're any good? "At my darkest points I have believed that I don't deserve to live, because I haven't been able to single-handedly break all the broken structures of the world. I don't want to define my self-belief like that anymore," Remy said.

In the background of all this, Remy had been part of several unionization efforts in different workplaces and started learning more about how capitalist frameworks were used to structure everyday society. For the first time, looking back, Remy said, she recognized that so many of the qualities they had positively associated with themselves since childhood—*I'm an ambitious person, I am a perfectionist, I care about the quality of my work and my craft, I really believe in what I do*—could be used as exploitation. It took carrying those qualities with her into adulthood, work, and relationships for achievement's shine to lose its luster.

There's a Western, American conceptualization that human beings are supposed to *grow* into good people and *prove* that they are good, Remy explained. We see this in how we talk to children and young people. We routinely ask, What do you want to be when you grow up? Worth is the *last* thing people achieve during their time on earth, when they've done enough to consider themselves self-actualized. Our accomplishments, tallied up, show a life well lived. "If you tell a child, 'prove yourself,' that's what they're going to spend their life trying to do," Remy said.

Wait. Is that what we're all spending our lives trying to do? Am I not the only one whose life has felt defined by my inability to answer the questions that crowd my thoughts and keep me awake at night?

A. Am I good even if I fail?
B. If I try *hard enough*, will that be good enough?
C. Is the best thing about me how hard I'm willing to try?

Where Does Our Self-Esteem Come From?

"People pursue self-esteem when they become concerned with the question, 'Am I wonderful and worthy, or am I worthless?'" write researchers Crocker, Lee, and Park on the pursuit of self-esteem and implications for good and evil.[4] In some cultural and religious systems of meaning, researchers point out, this isn't even a question. Everyone has value and worth, just because they are human.

But in other research, Crocker and Park note that "the pursuit of self-esteem is a particularly American phenomenon, born of the nation's founding ideologies."[5] By now, we've heard this before: the Protestant work ethic and Calvinist doctrine, which link worth to self-discipline and laud the intrinsic value of hard work; the emphasis on self-reliance, that we alone are responsible for our individual fate; and meritocracy, or the belief that all achievement comes from hard work and earning, not wealth, family connections, and privilege.[6] Add them together and it's not hard to trace the pattern: if our worth is based on achievement, of course we want to achieve as early and as much as possible.

For Harper, a twenty-eight-year-old, the importance of ambition has always been filtered through the lens of family—because it's never been an individual endeavor. As the child of immigrants, "my life is an extension of the actions and sacrifices my grandparents and parents made to get to the US," she told me. "Whatever I accomplish in my life is the result of my family immigrating, which then puts pressure on me to achieve things that made immigration worthwhile."

Harper's grandparents survived the Japanese occupation of Korea and a civil war, arriving in the United States with few possessions. Her parents were born outside the United States. They had managed to be upwardly mobile in a way Harper recognized as a child, and if she wanted to keep the level of stability her parents gave her, she had to be ambitious. "Ambition—which is a more concrete, material, achievement and status-oriented form of hope—is an intergenerational project for many people who for one reason or another carry their ancestors with them," she wrote to me via email. If she failed—at school, at work, or at the general idea of having a successful life—"that's not just my failure, but a setback for my entire family, who came to this country for the explicit purpose of improving our circumstances," she explained. From her earliest years, her understanding of ambition was shaped by cultural, familial, and structural context.

Growing up, she was put in a gifted and talented program. But Harper told me that among the qualities most people who came out of the program have—including a habit of forcing themselves to achieve more and more, even if they don't want to, and an identity based on excellence—is "deep-seated anxiety about falling behind or off your pedestal." Now, Harper's ambition comes from wanting to be happy and grow, and ambition seems like the way to do those things, since it is far from a given. "In a better world they would feel like natural parts of being alive," she said.

While Harper said she's always been ambitious, she thinks, in many cases, she would've been hesitant to describe herself as such. Ambition felt more acceptable in the context of her gifted and talented peers. Now, as an adult, she said she's seen as more arrogant and controlling because there's a sense that she "should" be more submissive as an Asian woman. "The ambitions I have and the way I pursue them are all complicated by the fact that I'm not white," she said. In some cases, ambition puts a target on her back. Because she is not only a woman but also an Asian woman, she is perceived as a threat, Harper told me. If she seeks to achieve something stereotypically associated with East Asians and succeeds, she bears the weight of success; if she fails, she carries not only individual failure but also "a belief others may have and that I may have internalized about how this failure represents a transgression against my racial identity." What complicates ambition is that though it might exist within us, how it manifests is informed by forces outside us.

At the same time, within her own family, Harper and her parents have had the same dreams for her life—to be happy, secure, and healthy—but vastly different versions of what that looks like. She became more determined to reach recognizable achievements quickly to reassure her family that even if her life wasn't going in the direction they'd planned for her, the future she was building was just as good.

When necessities like health care, housing, and a living wage aren't considered things we're entitled to, Harper said, it's hard to believe happiness, success, or security would ever come naturally. "Ambition has felt like a survival instinct or at minimum a key element in combating a sense of existential ennui," she said. "I have to prove things to others in order to get opportunities so I can get the stuff I need, and ambition is as much the pursuit of the proof-as-process as it is the pursuit of achievement-as-end." It's not just the abstract pursuit of self-worth that's a factor here. Our worth might be contingent on producing, but producing is also tied, in theory, to security.

Park told me that the more we want to feel good about ourselves by raising self-esteem in our areas of contingent self-worth, the more likely we are to experience "cumulative costs" to our well-being, health, relationships, and ability to make progress. Park mentioned that an alternative to pursuing self-esteem is encouraging people to be noncontingent or not having self-esteem based on anything. "The problem with this is that it's very difficult to do in a culture like the US, where we're socialized from a young age to tie our worth and value to our accomplishments, whether that be in academics, sports, looks, and so on," she told me. A second option is to engage in self-affirmation. The third option is to shift goals.

For example, Park told me, say you're writing a book, and you have a self-esteem-oriented goal: you want to be perceived as ambitious, or funny, or smart, or a good writer (words I coincidentally wouldn't hate if someone dropped them in a book review). That's OK some of the time, but when you get negative feedback or experience self-doubt, it can lead to anxiety, stress, perfectionism, and burnout. Early in life, we're expected to push through these stressors because of the elusive *worth it:* sacrificing my bathroom pass to do well on the test was supposed to be worth it; all-nighters in pursuit of that A-plus were supposed to be worth it. But by adulthood, we know those goalposts keep moving. As Bri pointed out, no one told her that doing "your work early" doesn't necessarily mean you get to relax later. "You'll just get more work, and it never ends," said Bri. Then if you've set yourself up as the person who completes things early and overachieves, anything less seems like you're slipping or slacking. Now as an adult, Bri knows that "exceeding expectations" doesn't guarantee anything. It doesn't mean she'll be paid fairly or find better work; it doesn't mean she'll eventually feel she's "earned" taking a break or even time off without worrying about leaving her coworkers in a crunch.

Which is why Park's other solution—adopting a goal larger than one's self—feels like the only actual antidote to the conveyor belt of achievement that keeps running no matter how hard we run or how fast we fall. "What is it that you care about, want to contribute to others, your community, the world?" Park asked. It's the fundamental question, and the one most of us aren't encouraged to ask until much later in life. Rather, early on, many of us are tasked with establishing worth for ourselves and stacking up whatever proof we can get hold of that we have it, at the mercy of what can be measured. That shuffles big questions across our desks:

How do I know I'm worthy?
What metrics are there to tell me?
How can I guarantee it?

Then, we're told to fill in those blanks.

3: Schoolhouse Rock (and a Hard Place)

Star and smiley face stickers, candy from the treasure box, McDonald's for learning times tables and earning advanced reading (AR) points: when I asked Charles, a sixteen-year-old high school junior, what signified success in school, they gave me a list. Sometimes the prize was an eraser shaped like a spaceship plucked from the Dollar Store's discount rack. Sometimes it was the promise that doing good work would lead to a good life.

Beyond the incentive element—whether intrinsic motivation is more meaningful than being in hot pursuit of a reward—prizes mirror measurements, tracking who earns what and when. A blog post from the National Museum of American History detailed how nineteenth-century school children earned "rewards of merit" that recognized focus, diligence, and attendance. The rewards or certificates were pieces of paper with both hand-drawn and printed illustrations of flowers and studious children holding books with the student's name written in by hand.[1] We have present-day versions, too: think perfect attendance awards, an ableist policy that negatively impacts chronically ill and disabled young people (the collegiate version of this looks like having a letter grade docked every time you miss a class—punishment rather than prizes leading to the same outcome); think students celebrated for pulling all-nighters fueled by Red Bull and camaraderie in the library at the expense of their well-being. A 1995 piece from the *Los Angeles Times* quotes a principal who was skeptical of cash for grades and suggested museum trips, an educational movie, or a trip to Magic Mountain, which I had to google to confirm is indeed part of Six Flags theme park.[2] Then, there's the iconic Pizza Hut example: the fast-food chain's Book It! program, where students reach reading goals set by their teachers and earn a personal pizza. (Now, the website notes,[3] goals are set based on students' reading ability: number of pages, number of books, and number of minutes are all accepted, and for students who aren't reading independently, teachers can set goals where adults read to them.) According to lore, when the program started, Pizza Hut gave out buttons with five spots for gold stars on them: a button shining with all five gold stickers could be exchanged for a pizza.[4]

More interesting than the incentive itself—personally, I am never one to turn down free pizza or a book—is the legacy of it: Book It! was in part born from Ronald Reagan's encouragement for American corporations to get more involved in education. A 1987 *Washington Post* article noted that critics said "corporate sponsors are motivated by profit and by the goal of cultivating an indoctrinated core of young, fledgling consumers."[5] This wasn't the first time "indoctrination" came up in conversations about academics. Bri, grappling with the privileges her education afforded her, noted that emphasis on

academic achievement shaped her "in the image of the perfect little capitalist." River, a thirty-one-year-old who talked
to me extensively about overwork, flagged that the pressure to
be ambitious starts earlier than entering the workforce: "We're
kind of indoctrinating these children to be good little worker
bees," he told me. In a lot of cases, what school prepared us for
was to work eight hours a day and cram life into after hours,
alongside whatever work we didn't complete during the day.
While programs like Book It! *did* likely encourage some kids
to read, these programs also measure: How much can you
achieve, and how quickly can you do so? How eager we are to
classify what people are capable of, usually according to standards not set by them, during an era of life where they are
required to ask permission before going to the bathroom. (A
concept I will clearly never stop fuming about.)

Charles described growing attached to the praise. He
doesn't need a bribe or incentive to do well, per se, but enjoys receiving "another little trophy to show that someone is
proud. . . . Now, instead of stickers and candy, teachers tell
us 'this [good grades] is the only way to get into college,'"
they added.

Measurements of what it means to achieve—achieve well,
achieve early—don't spring from nowhere. Rather, what it
means to be high achieving is reinforced and measured, so
the pressure is on to figure out what we're good at *early*.

The Ambitious, Awful History of Standardized Tests

"From the beginning, since grades have been introduced, we
have felt the constant pressure of: you're only as good as your
worst grade," Charles explained. It's not that ambition in

school is a bad thing, according to Charles. But the standard for "do your best" is too high. Charles is in Advanced Placement, and being one of only four Black students in the Honors/Advanced Placement courses piles on pressure of having to prove he isn't lesser than his white peers. Their peers feel the pressure of the churn, too. "Most of us are burnt out by senior year," Charles said.

In a 2019 piece for the *Atlantic*, Whitney Pirtle, sociologist and professor at the University of California Merced, wrote that there is a "modern-day form of segregation" occurring within schools through "academic tracking, which selects certain students for gifted and talented education (GATE) programs."[6] "Smart students" are put on accelerated tracks, with enrichment activities. "Other students are kept in grade-level classes, or tracked into remedial courses that are tasked with catching students up to academic baselines," Pirtle wrote. Pirtle's piece explains that less than 10 percent of students in GATE (Gifted and Talented Education) programs are Black, which is disproportionate to the number of enrolled Black students, and levels of disparities vary throughout the nation. This "racialized tracking," Pirtle said, is when "students of color get sorted out of educational opportunities and long-term socioeconomic success." Pirtle's piece also points to clear actions:

> Until we can develop better admissions tests, or pass legislation banning these tests altogether, or invest more resources in public schools to incorporate GATE-like curricula in all classes, those of us who are willing and able to do "whatever we can" for our children need to expand our idea of who "our" children really are.[7]

What the work of experts like Pirtle makes evident is that there is no such thing as a neutral system of sorting and categorizing people. One report—detailing how, from elementary school onward, Black and Latinx students are less likely to be enrolled in "gifted and talented" or advanced placement classes—cited resource inequities, educator bias and lack of access to diverse educators, and assessment or grading bias as key systemic obstacles.[8] The question isn't just whether or not someone is considered gifted and talented, it's what systems and structures define what that means and who profits or benefits. Wayne Au, PhD, wrote that the "assumptive objectivity of standardized testing was thus used to scientifically declare the poor, immigrants, women, and non-whites in the U.S. as mentally inferior, and to justify educational systems that mainly reproduced extant socio-economic inequalities."[9] What should've been about ensuring every student had access to classes, communities, and resources that met them where they were and helped them thrive instead enforced structural inequity. While gifted programs or standardized test scores might be one facet, the achievement-chasing approach to measuring and "sorting" students has defined the educations most of us in the United States have received in some way for the past twenty-plus years.

Via Zoom, Au pieced together the history for me: in the late 1800s and early 1900s, there was a shift in the United States—a shift that some would argue, Au said, was tied into the rise of child labor laws. This also coincided with the shift toward—you guessed it—factory capitalism, said Au, and schools were created to mirror factories. All this was happening within the rise of meritocracy with a hefty emphasis on competition, two of the foundations of standardized tests that most of us were told would make or break our futures.

In the United States, at the turn of the twentieth century, eugenicists and cognitive psychologists repurposed a French invention, the IQ test, to feed their own racist, classist, sexist beliefs about categorizing society, first using the IQ test on World War I army recruits. Not long after, they started marketing their intelligence tests to be used in public schools. School administrators believed they needed ways to sort the mass numbers of students entering the public school system. "Even now, really, the outcomes of our tests are not so far off the blatantly white supremacist tests from one hundred years ago," Au explained. It reinforced the idea that some young people weren't "smart" and would be good laborers; others were "smart" and should go to college. That fed the idea of meritocracy, too. "You can see how ambition ends up being about self-advancement as an individual," Au told me. The whole system of testing, and the whole idea of merit within the context of capitalism, relies on climbing over people on the way up the ladder, even when we don't know where the ladder is going or why we're climbing. We might throw graduation caps and age out of the school system, but the lessons linger.

Kelly, a forty-one-year-old with a doctorate in religious studies, said that her own mother didn't attend college and was always of the belief that college lends itself to mobility. To her working-class parents, that's the way you did it: you went to college, you got a better job. "And so, in kindergarten, she's telling me that I always kind of have [to have] good grades if I wanted to go to college," Kelly explained. That was the constant refrain through high school. "It was just very much, like, 'You have to make As, you have to do well, you have to go to college.' And there was very little room for failure." If someone grew up working class like Kelly did, she said, good grades paved the path to scholarships, and scholarships were the way to college. That was coded into her wiring. "It meant that any overachieving that I was already doing then was turned up to eleven," she explained. "Because the idea is if you just work hard enough, you get the life that you want." But that's something she's trying to do differently with her own children. She talked about her second grader's homework—writing an essay every two weeks. Kelly is a writer and point-blank said the assignments were making even *her* hate writing, and she doesn't remember second grade being quite so challenging. Kelly emphasizes to her children that grades don't define them as people. "Well, they're also getting messages from school that it does," she said. "We definitely [live] in a system that trains us to think that grades determine who we are."

Now, generations of adults who grew up hearing grades would define their lives are the parents, caregivers, neighbors, teachers, and friends of young people who are receiving the current version of that messaging: a good life can be yours, and grades are the price of entry. But we know how many people that talking point fails; how many people that purposely leaves behind. The golden thread of meritocracy tying the education system together—the good grades to good jobs to good lives pipeline—is the same one that renders housing, health care, and a livable planet as rewards we earn. In other words, our striving is supposed to keep us safe.

In writer Taylor Harris's acclaimed memoir *This Boy We Made*, she wrote that she wants to tell her fourth-grade self she's doing a good job. "The straight A's, the ambition, will help her earn a full scholarship to college, where she'll find her people and the love of her life," Harris wrote. "But I also want to warn her, to take her hand and tell her she can't fill the void by collecting achievements, gathering them like gems, clutching them to her chest. They will vaporize. They're not meaningless, no, just aren't made to fill us." All that glittered wasn't supposed to be our foundation; it's a confetti pile we jump in with both feet, only to hit the floor hard.

When I spoke to Harris by phone to ask about this passage in her book, she told me that when she hears the word *ambition* it could certainly have a happy or positive meaning to people. "But I think I still sort of recoil when I hear [it], because I hear ambition, and then the next thing that comes with it is this fear of failure right on its heels," she said. Her parents did go to college but didn't quite finish, Harris told me, and while her mother did complete her education later in life, she hadn't when Harris was growing up. Both her parents encouraged her and her sisters to pursue education, to go further in their careers than they did. They never explicitly told Harris that her success—or the success of her siblings—would fill a void for them, but that's how it felt, "like my sisters and I could close it, fill them up enough with our achievements and our accomplishments," she said. She recalled the physical proof of accomplishment, too: going to Cheryl's Cookies in the mall and getting six free cookies for As. "I love the idea of honoring our parents and their sacrifices by being able to go to school, the school that I wanted to at that time, or get graduate degrees," Harris added. It's more that she had this idea "that it would fill us up or that it would solve things, that you just get to this one finish line." At the finish line, everything is OK; you've made everything OK. "But I just feel [like] there's always more," Harris explained.

Now, Harris sees glimmers of her academic experience reflected in her children. She constantly reminds herself that there's not one meaning of success, and their paths may not look the same as hers. "Then, to be to be honest, I kind of zoom out and be, like, yeah, it was great that I got a scholarship to college. I got to choose where I wanted to go. And I was miserable in high school," Harris told me. "I was getting straight A's and was a captain of the tennis team, and I was surrounded by white people who didn't really see me, and I had no friends and I was lonely, and I was depressed." As her book came out, Harris's therapist asked her what success looked like. She thinks about the question often. Whereas her impulse is to ask, "Did you not get an A on that? Did you not get at least a B?" she works not to react that way. "I always thought my kids would go to college and beyond, and I started to pull back on that—not to discourage them," she explained, "but just reimagining what is a good or worthwhile life."

With Student Loans, We're Owned

If anything, as one grows up and moves through the school system, the stakes of achievement get higher. When debt, a future career and livelihood, and future well-being all supposedly hinge on what happens in school, achieving at all costs doesn't seem to be an option. It's a requirement. Adults I spoke to were swift to call out that series of broken promises. College costs are skyrocketing while wages stagnate.[10] With student debt totaling around $1.5 trillion at the time of writing, millennials hold roughly 31.94 percent of the total debt, whereas Gen X holds the most at 38.40 percent.[11] The current student debt crisis exacerbates the racial wealth gap, and Black students borrow and owe more than their white classmates.[12] While all the tests were supposed to be the great equalizer, the "college experience" and its aftershocks stem from a similar place: a system that never fully addressed the fact that achievement on its own isn't enough.

Ria, a first-generation American, has a part-time customer service job and is also a senior in high school, focusing on the ACT, extracurriculars, and internships to be competitive for college, while advocating for education reforms, including removing police from her school's campus. When I talked to Ria, I was struck by how such a young person could feel great nostalgia for a time in her life when she was even younger. "There is not a single day I have had in at least five or six years where I could just simply feel like I had no responsibilities—like nothing to do at all," she recounted to me. A child looking back on her life yearning for when she had time to be, well, a child is perhaps the most profound indictment of making "overperforming" a standard. "I think it feels very overwhelming, as a youth, to consider the future that you have ahead of you knowing that there is no time to rest," Ria added. Those are the terms of achievement as they've been outlined.

Achievement crystalized into a number for me the moment I paid to retake the ACT with money from my job at a dance studio, which I secretly thought held far more promise for my future than my dismal test scores ever could. My teenage self would be thrilled to know I have forgotten my exact score—and a rummage through old email accounts proved futile—but what I did not forget was how the emphasis on performing well felt like a doomsday scenario.

By that point, I'd developed a steady routine: I'd come home from the dance studio and then spend the night replaying the laundry list of things I'd been told linked to a test score, including financial aid for college, whether I got to go to college at all, what would happen if I didn't go to college, and the abstract, all-consuming vision of my "future" I was supposed to be living for. Then I'd wake up at an ungodly hour to dose myself with Imodium and Pepto Bismol, praying that my faulty GI system and anxiety so electric it could've jump-started a car wouldn't flare up and cause me to exit the test in the middle and have to start all over.

Please let me make it, I'd offer to up to the testing gods and all the gods beyond them and pray for someone else to map the stars that were supposed to lead me onward. I didn't care about perfect scores; I cared about *good enough* scores—a side effect of believing that the worst thing you could do was fail, and all good achievement existed to protect you from that reality.

Measuring and sorting are counterpoints to reimagining; all this earning carries the weight of our childhood selves' aspirations in its pockets. My takeaway wasn't pressure to achieve; it was pressure to *not fail.* I carried that with me to college, where I left after a year despite a great GPA. Ironically, I received some traditional academic validation, but was too depressed to understand why it felt so empty.

When I emailed Au about ambition, his first thought was grit: "We have to talk about grit," he told me. Ah, grit— ambition's cousin, the gospel according to success stories, underdogs winning the day, and meritocracy itself. When one believes in measuring merit, they're focusing on the individual, Au explained, at the absence of all the structural issues surrounding them. The irony of the individual focus is that decades and decades of research, according to Au, point out that the strongest correlation with tests has to do with life outside school, including whether a kid has housing, food, and access to health care. Instead, it becomes about individuals persevering at all costs, even if the cost is themselves. "It's all totally tied together, because grit, resilience, meritocracy—all the same thing, just with different labels around it," Au said.

When I look back on my own education, what floods my mind isn't the red 100 percents written on a college literature final or the smiley face sticker I was proud of in elementary school. It's how I was described: "You persevered through that test," a teacher told me as she handed me a math test with a D at the top. But I hadn't; I'd sat and finished it because leaving the room wasn't a choice. "You're so committed," a college professor told me as I sat, with a high fever, through an exam he'd refused to reschedule. In retrospect, not only had I figured out a way to exploit the system—I'd be an average student and achieve in *enthusiasm*—I'd reinforced parts of my personality that would later rub me down like an overused eraser.

For all intents and purposes, the system was designed for a student like me. But in addition to profound inequities embedded in how students are measured, there's a significant gap that young people fall into after they are systemically weeded out, including before college. "It's pretty terrible to see what happens with students who aren't perceived to be ambitious or smart or gifted," said Kolbe, a thirty-two-year-old English teacher in Texas, who is also a doctoral student studying school improvement. "I think even the idea of labeling students as gifted and then, like, general education is problematic because what really makes someone gifted?" By the time young people reach high school and it's been decided whether they are on a "successful" track or not, "if their spirit is broken, it's kind of hard to rebuild that and it's hard to get them ready to go to college or trade school or something else," Kolbe added. For example, Kolbe explained she has students who want to start their own construction businesses—aspirations not reflected anywhere in the school curriculum. "And people who look down on construction workers aren't going to view that as an ambitious career choice." Just as bad as being expected to live up to the gifted kid label is no one bothering to believe you're worthy of those labels—of having your own ambitions, your own dreams.

Who Gets to Decide Their Dreams?

Calling me right after her work commute, A'ja, a twenty-seven-year-old, proudly shared she had an A in one college class and a B in another. A'ja had just begun work on her bachelor's degree in business administration after recently finishing her associate's degree, while working a full-time job and single parenting her eleven-year-old son. A'ja would consider herself an ambitious person, she told me. But when she was younger, no one thought she was ambitious or hard

working, let alone high achieving. A'ja's mother didn't finish high school, so her main goal was to complete her high
school education. College never seemed like an option, a
feeling that escalated when she became pregnant in high
school. Her twin sister, A'ja explained, received offers to go
on college tours. Meanwhile, A'ja was overlooked because
she was pregnant. No one bothered to ask about her college
interest. "I wasn't the smartest or the best. I didn't really get
good grades." That was enough for most of the adults in her
life to decide they wouldn't discuss her future at all.

Later, the same theme—that she was asking for too
much—came up in work. A'ja was working minimum-wage
jobs to support herself and her child and yearning for what she
described as "growth in my intellectual self." She began earning administrative certifications and then opted to pursue her
associate's degree. "I had someone tell me how stupid I was to
leave a full-time job making minimum wage to go to school
full-time and work part-time," A'ja explained. While working
on her associate's degree, A'ja and her son experienced housing instability that eventually led to becoming unhoused. She
couldn't afford a home on her minimum-wage income. They
stayed with family for a while, but the distance and commute
proved a strain in getting herself and her son to school every day. She eventually found a shelter, which enabled her to
maintain a routine, her life, and her other ambitions—to finish school and ensure her son's individual education plan was
in place. "At the time, I did not think of being homeless, parenting, or doing school as ambitious, but looking back, I guess
you could say that," A'ja said. "I was just determined to make
a better life for me and my son."

For A'ja, it wasn't until she found Generation Hope—a nonprofit devoted to the success of student parents in higher education through national advocacy, technical assistance, and two-generation support for teen parents and their families—that she had the resources to put her own dreams into action. The deciding factor in opting to pursue a four-year degree was her Generation Hope coaches telling her not to stop. A'ja's goals are an ongoing journey, but each step gets her closer.

Part of her ambition stemmed from a desire to live a happy, safe life with her child and to continue learning. How do you measure that? Around 37 percent of college students today are twenty-five or older, around 46 percent are first-generation students, and a majority work while going through school, according to a report by the Lumina Foundation.[13] (Also, it's worth noting that some reports point out student parents achieve higher college GPAs than their child-less peers.[14]) Students are also parents, caregivers, workers, and human beings, and when school is supposed to be one's dominant identity, the *only* thing one is focused on, people are pushed out, left to piecemeal their own solutions and abandoned to the belief that it's up to them to "overcome." "The disparities across the board in K through 12, and that sorting and decision-making about which students are going somewhere and which students aren't, and which students are worthy of resources and support, starts so early, even in preschool," explained Nicole Lynn Lewis, founder of Generation Hope and author of the book *Pregnant Girl.* "By the time you get to high school, so much of that has been built into your educational experience."

Generation Hope frequently does college readiness work-shops where facilitators talk to current teen parents in high school or young parents who are working and got their GEDs about college possibilities. When a young person be-comes pregnant, Lewis said, people often stop talking about expectations altogether. But many times, even before a preg-nancy, no one was talking to them about their expectations or their potential to begin with.

When Lewis started Generation Hope, people who heard about it pressed the organization to narrow the scope for students—to only support certain majors, like those that seemed "practical," or only partner with certain schools or credential programs in specific trades. That, to Lewis, missed the point. "I think a lot of it is the freedom to choose is a privilege," she told me. "The freedom to look out at your life and say: Who do I want to be? What makes me happy? What are my passions?" That's supposed to be one of the endeav-ors of college, but it's set up in such a way that students who *don't* have the resources to choose are pushed to the fringes, and systems describe for them what a "successful" future looks like, just as adults who discouraged A'ja from continu-ing higher education did. To use another example, that's why Generation Hope uses the word *scholars* to refer to students they work with. "Because we want them to know that they can be ambitious, they can be driven, they can be studious, all of these things that I think people have not associated with them because they're teen parents," Lewis added.

Lewis underscores to the scholars that they are worthy and incredible, with or without the degree. She described a scholar who earned her associate's degree and, during her first year at a four-year college, met someone and decided she wanted to be a stay-at-home mom. "First of all, you earned an associate's degree, which is a huge accomplishment," Lewis said. "But second of all, if that's what makes you happy, that's what makes us happy." Recently, Lewis had a call with a funder who is potentially interested in funding a universal basic income initiative for Generation Hope, and to her, that follows the same lines: it's about giving people resources and community to decide their futures. "My own experience as a teen mom has helped me in my own knee-jerk reaction to define ambition and success for my own kids," Lewis told me. "Because I took a very different road to finding my path than my mom and dad would have liked." That's why it is critical that every young person is given the resources, investment, and time to define success or fulfillment for themselves on their own terms.

Think of what our world loses when we decide whether or not a student is worthy of investment, resources, belief, ambition. The measurements that stifle how we think about ourselves in relation to the world—what we can do, how we can help, what we can imagine. I wonder, still, what I missed being curious about or trying because I was so afraid of getting it wrong. The stories we tell our children are ones of dreams coming true rather than failing—maybe so they will dare to imagine a world better than the one they have inherited. But as long as they're earning worthiness through gold stars and good scores, they are fighting to be ambitious in a world that truly only wants their *earning*, not their dreams.

4: Parental Guidance Suggested

As the only child of divorced parents—and raised primarily by a single mom—my mother was expected to be perfect. Perhaps because of that, she made sure I grew up knowing I didn't have to be. By the end of third grade, the era of infamous timed multiplication tables, I had two formative experiences. First, I discovered the school library and, with the diligence of a fact-checker, proceeded to check out every book about cats, building a steady body of research. Second, right before school was out for the summer, I made my case. I told my mother that the other third grade teacher's cat was having kittens and explained to her, based on my extensive research, why I needed to adopt a kitten and how I would take care of it. (Childhood habits die hard: reading all the books and adopting all the cats remain two great ambitions in my life.)

I had a mom who thought this was hilarious and mildly impressive. There was no "if you bring up your math grade" or "if you ace your spelling test." There was just a little girl standing in front of her parent, asking—via a research presentation—to let her love a cat. When I think of my mom and parenting, that's the memory in the forefront of my mind because it demonstrates what I know now was an invaluable gift and an intense amount of work on her part: her willingness to support her kid's wildest desires, no matter how weird they might be, with gentle caveats like, "You'll have to clean its litter box."

This was her approach to nearly everything. Oh, the downpour flooded the backyard and you all want to try wakeboarding with a cheap plastic sled? Go for it, and notify me if someone hits their head. You want to quit playing cello after a few recreational lessons because the instructor terrifies you? Seems logical. I am the eldest daughter of parents who would've sacrificed anything for my siblings and me; who traversed the ends of the earth and back again for, at various points, the right medical care, the activities we wanted to pursue, and what we needed to thrive, even when it was inconvenient or blew through their budgets. Even as a kid, I realized the privilege in that, though I couldn't have articulated it: Parents who let you define ambition for yourself and sought to uplift you rather than control you? Adults who—even when traumatic events happened—gave you a soft place to land, a safe space to discover yourself? I lucked out.

Now I'm at the age where having kids is an actual, eventual consideration (she types with terror and hope). I'm sending baby gifts and cherishing watching friends become parents; I'm talking to my parents about their experiences raising us, not just my own experiences with their raising. And I know that as lucky as I might be, my luck is, in part, a product of their hard, ambitious, often impossible work: parenting. Which meant I wanted to know about the labor of parents—the love, too—and the personal and professional dreams that bloom in both domains. Looking at parenting—and, for the purposes of this chapter, particularly motherhood—relates to and affects how we think about ambition, even for those of us who aren't, or aren't planning to be, parents. In some ways, motherhood and ambition are set up to be in competition with each other. Being a parent and working or having a personal goal is a given for fathers, a "bonus" for mothers, and a set of impossible standards about what it means to be a "great" parent. Complicating that are stereotypes of what it means to be a stay-at-home parent and a working parent and America's institutional failure to support parents, which makes it nearly impossible for parents to take care of themselves without sacrificing something else. The standards that coil around the ideals of work, parenting, and identity—expectations given, resources rarely provided—shape what we think of as ambitious, too.

Parenting is work. Parenting also strikes me as inherently ambitious—ambitious for someone else, ambitious in raising another human being. Parents described intersecting versions of ambition. First, their own ambitions, limited by societal perception of what it means to be ambitious, in which caretaking is rarely included; ambition narrowed by lack of resources, like affordable childcare, universal basic income and living wages, and paid leave, which makes parenting more sustainable instead of self-sacrificing. Second, the benchmarks of "ambitious parenting," the kind that often set both parent and child up to fail. Think handbooks on how to hack your family's schedule, the optimal habits to build successful adults from scratch, and the endless lists of hobbies, activities, grades, and family bonding you're supposed to embark on, alongside homemade lunches with sandwiches cut into star shapes, organically sourced clothing, and educational toys—all done while remaining endlessly chipper and enlightened the whole time. ("Parents are drowning—the cost and unreasonable schedules take so much of the joy and humanity out of parenting," Mary Ellen, who we'll hear more from shortly, told me.) Third, the omnipresent "have it all" mentality in which, somehow, nothing is supposed to give—not the professional goals, not the personal goals, not the time or wages, not the childcare needs, not the personal needs. Just endlessly holding it together, all the time.

The benchmarks of ambitious parenting start with the construction of the family itself. As with everything, parenting and ambition—whose ambition has value, which ambition comes first—are shaped by the larger social structure they spin in, including the individualism of the American family and lack of support for people raising children. In the book *Work Won't Love You Back*, labor journalist Sarah Jaffe wrote that "the family itself was and is a social, economic, and political institution," describing how the family developed alongside institutions of capitalism and the state.[1] In fact, according to historian Stephanie Coontz, writing for the *American Prospect*, the "male-breadwinner family is arguably the least traditional family form in all of world history."[2] This nuclear family surged following World War II, with some research arguing that governments promoted the breadwinner-homemaker model as a means of pushing women back out of the workforce to create jobs for men returning from war.[3] It's impossible to name every kind of family or household this construction leaves out—single parents, divorced parents, anyone raising children who isn't a parent, multigenerational families, families in which there aren't children being raised at all—but as Sophie Lewis wrote for *Dissent*, the myth of the nuclear family is harmful to women and children and has especially "lethal consequences for Black and brown, im/migrant, Indigenous, poor, and working-class queer, trans, feminized, sex-working, and gender nonconforming people."[4] This is still steeped in nearly every policy America has related to work and family. Whose work counts as work? Whose ambition, in the home or beyond it, gets to be considered ambitious? Who gets support?

Caring Is Work

In the United States, there's a deep history of care work— including parents who stay home with their children—being systemically devalued or not being considered labor at all. A 2020 report by Jocelyn Frye from the Center for American Progress stated that during the earliest years of the United States, "Black women's labor was exploited to serve and care for white slaveholders while different waves of immigration saw Hispanic and Asian women confined to jobs as laborers, domestic workers, and farm workers, as well as service occupations," and Native women endured mistreatment and lack of economic resources or opportunities as their communities were invaded.[5] In a piece published by the Economic Policy Institute, Nina Banks, PhD, associate professor of economics at Bucknell University, explained that in the 1970s, large numbers of white, married women entered the paid labor force—leading to what Banks called the "marketization of services" usually performed within the household.[6] "Revealingly, although whites have devalued Black women as mothers to their own children, Black women have been the most likely of all women to be employed in the low-wage women's jobs that involve cooking, cleaning, and caregiving even though this work is associated with mothering more broadly," Banks wrote.[7]

America has built an entire way of life, including work, school, caregiving, and basic societal function, around the unpaid or underpaid labor of parents. As the writer Meg Conley detailed for *Harper's Bazaar* in her piece "What the Conversation Around the 'Great Resignation' Leaves Out," people who left the workforce often cited unpaid care work as the reason for quitting—the so-called childcare worker shortage often framed childcare as something happening in the abstract, like someone, somewhere must be caring for kids while parents worked. But, as Conley noted, most childcare workers aren't even paid enough to pay for their *own* children's childcare.[8] "Care work may build capitalism's heaven, but it's never going to inherit it," Conley wrote, pointing out that universal basic income would provide security for those who care and those who need care, universal paid leave would let parents care for their babies, and universal childcare would let parents do work outside care work.

"Two crucial lenses to view care work through are capitalism, the system in which trade and industry are privatized and controlled by owners for profit, and colonization, the action of taking control of the land and Indigenous people of an area," wrote Angela Garbes in *Essential Labor: Mothering as Social Change*.[9] Over the phone, Garbes explained that American capitalism relies just as much on domestic labor and care work as it does on "professional work," and if we had to pay people commensurately who do the work that makes all other work possible—parents, caregivers, teachers, childcare workers, eldercare workers, and so on, the list is plentiful—less profit would be made. Then, Garbes told me, colonization persists, continuing to give people permission to think of people of color, mainly Indigenous and Black people, as less worthy. The reason people are fine with employing those who "take care of that which we say is most precious, our children and our future," at less than a living wage is "because they are comfortable thinking that women of color are less human," Garbes continued. "In America specifically, that's a legacy of slavery." Garbes noted that the home has always been a workplace for Black women. The protection and encouragement of "work-life balance"—or, in some instances, "work-family balance"—often comes at the expense of someone else's labor, paid or otherwise. Caregiving makes other kinds of ambition, including professional ambition, possible.

Two ideas are at odds, Garbes told me: the idealization of motherhood in America and the lack of support once you become a mother. "We don't take care of you afterwards," she said. "We want to venerate this idea [of motherhood]. We want you to buy into that. But we don't want to hear about the realities of it." Because it's so culturally ingrained in this country, people internalize that something is wrong with them, rather than realizing and acknowledging they exist in a system that sets them up to fail and thwarts happiness or success at every turn. In her own life, Garbes told me, she's always felt fairly unbothered by the standards of marriage and motherhood largely because, growing up, she knew she wasn't going to meet any standard. "I was never going to be the standard of what a good girl was, [what] a nice young woman was, and part of that is because I'm not

white," she said. For women of color and marginalized people, there's a certain freedom in not having to pay attention
to the parenting advice dished out like it applies to everyone,
Garbes said.

In her own parenting, Garbes explained she wants her
children to have "the things that I feel I had to really work
towards, and came late to, which is that I'm enough [as I
am]. . . . The things that people of color have to learn in order
to insist on our full humanity," she continued, "I just want
my girls to have that." That foundation itself is the parenting
goal, if there is one. Garbes told me she actually felt naive
because she didn't have goals going into parenting, and now,
the "goal" is as simple and as profound as wanting the things
that were hard for Garbes to not be hard for her children.

For some, their experiences with how they were parented
directly inform how they try to parent now. "Even at a young
age, I was looking at my mom as a single mother and saying, 'What are the barriers that she has to make me—her
children—successful?'" Ashlee, a thirty-year-old from California, told me. "So, the generational, social, economic, upward mobility for us, and the opportunities that she could
provide us as someone who is a woman of color, who's disabled, [a] single mom, who's previously incarcerated, living in
concentrated poverty." Ashlee looked at the way her mother
displayed motherhood and immediately saw the racial and
gender disparities she experienced from the time she was as
young as six.

In between transferring from community college and
starting her four-year degree, Ashlee got pregnant and was
made to feel utterly invisible on campus as a low-income,
first-generation student of color who was also a parent. It was

a constant battle in instances big and small, from a professor refusing to let her miss a final to go pick up her sick child ("Now I have to choose between whether I'm a good mom or a good student," she told me), to attendance policies. Eventually, she organized a collective of student parents—about sixty, more than she realized were on campus—to change policies. Now Ashlee does similar work, leading an organization with a community health worker model to ensure families most impacted are leading changes in increasing educational attainment, reducing poverty, increasing higher wage jobs, and improving neighborhood conditions in her city. Ashlee's family has experienced generational poverty and food insecurity, and she described how her own mother spent most of her time as a homeworker, meaning she was a stay-at-home mom, because of racial and gender disparities that prevented her from accessing work with a livable wage. "I'm really proud of the work that my mom did," Ashlee told me. "I think she did a great job. And she was really ambitious."

Work-Family Balance: A Faulty Expectation

The lack of resources, policies, and accessible help for parents seeps out of the home and into work, in part because workers who are parents are expected to behave as though they are not. In a study on how society views parents fitting into parenting roles, researchers found that when parents experienced high levels of "parental identity threat"—when something that happened at work made them question whether they were a good parent, like working late and missing a piano recital—they found parents experienced higher levels of shame and lower levels of productivity.[10]

In fact, a lot of the ideal worker myth—which we'll explore more later—comes from ideology and gender roles associated with the Protestant work ethic, at least according to some research, which outlined how the ideal worker "was a hard-working man who left the house each day to work, while his wife stayed home to tend to household and child caregiving duties."[11] For Mary Ellen, a thirty-three-year-old single parent of a three-year-old and a five-year-old, fear of the future looks like overwork—and the anxiety that drives the hustle-at-all-costs overwork is hard to shake because it's not really that illogical. "As a single income woman with kids, if I lose my income, I risk losing my house and my ability to parent," she said. She grew up in poverty, raised partially by a single mother who had Mary Ellen at age nineteen and didn't get to finish her education. Mary Ellen didn't experience high expectations from her parents: they were proud of her at times, she said, but never checked her grades. At school, she recalled some counselors, teachers, and other students having negative or low expectations of her—something she pointed out is the experience of many Black children, including her, and one that she internalized.

On top of that, there's the punitive nature of how America treats people living in poverty. For one thing, as a 2020 report from the Center for the Study of Social Policy states, modern work requirements are attached to lots of public assistance benefits, like the Supplemental Nutrition Assistance Program (SNAP), including[12] "policies designed to withhold assistance from families in order to force them into the wage labor force."[13] These work requirements are fundamentally racist[14]—and so is America's economy, dating back to the "coerced and exploited . . . labor of Black families, going back to slavery."[15] (The report states work requirements also discount the labor of caregiving, instead pushing people into low-paid jobs. It frames people as deserving versus undeserving.) Getting help becomes a punishment. Taking care of a family becomes impossible. And "work harder" gets presented as the solution that never actually is one.

Mary Ellen pointed out how America makes living in poverty undignified—like, for example, limitations on what someone can buy at the grocery with food stamps. After going to a technical school and then becoming the first in her family to attend a four-year college, Mary Ellen eventually got a job in corporate communications, where she's built a career she enjoys, makes good money, and owns her home. But she maintains that the narrative of hard work and ambition being enough to override one's circumstances isn't true. She's had luck. She's had advocates in her life. She pointed out that though capitalism appears to reward hard work, hustle, and grinding because it generates wealth for some, going "above and beyond," "doing it all," and being praised for working hard doesn't always indicate that drive is *good*. All it indicates is that drive or ambition is *useful*, Mary Ellen told me.

Within that, "there's the capitalism piece, where you're doing things that make people money [in order] to get praised," she said. "There's the patriarchy piece, where you're doing things that make men's [lives] easier, so that gets praised," she said, like handling child rearing. "You're conforming to a gender standard, so that gets praised—I get praised for being a good mom, being an active, engaged mom, all the things, and that's great," she continues. "But also, nobody ever stops and says, 'Wow, she's doing a lot of shit; should she be doing all these things?'"

That's the core question: Should *anyone* be?

During the pandemic, the expectation certainly seems that parents—especially mothers—should be doing it all and not blinking as the mass death, illness, school and childcare closures, and impossible work schedules swirl around them, with "Baby Shark" playing in the background. Sans policies to support families of all configurations, 2020 catapulted women into what has been called the "women's recession"— the point where female unemployment hit double digits for the first time since 1948.[16] This means it is, literally, the first female recession since experts began counting. "By the time I was parenting a toddler and a newborn in lockdown, my idea of ambition had been permanently altered," wrote Amil Niazi in a masterful 2022 essay for The Cut. "I had to keep working to keep everyone fed and alive, and I realized I didn't want or need more than that."[17]

As the pandemic continues, parents are still making impossible "choices"—in quotes because capitalism renders them not choices at all. The assumption that every household is a two-parent household or has grandparents to help with childcare skims over the reality of what it takes to figure it out alone. It shouldn't take ambition to get by. Data from the Bureau of Labor Statistics in May–December of 2021, analyzed by the Brookings Institution, found that mothers spent the hourly equivalent of a full-time job caring for children over the course of that year *while* working a paid position at the same time.[18] Meanwhile, 2022 data from the Pew Research Center, polling working parents with children under age twelve, found 43 percent of fathers and 58 percent of mothers had difficulties related to childcare responsibilities.[19]

And because parenting—including much of the material on parenting and work—is so gendered, transgender and nonbinary parents aren't represented in headlines on working mothers exiting the workforce at skyrocketing rates, or how the number of stay-at-home dads has almost doubled since 1989, according to some estimates.[20] In one review of fifty-one studies by the Williams Institute, between one-quarter and one-half of transgender people report being parents, and those trans parents reported having social service needs, such as childcare, networking with fellow parents, and family planning support.[21] Regarding the pandemic and parental labor, specifically, one report by Derek P. Siegel, a PhD candidate in the Department of Sociology, at the University of Massachusetts Amherst, emphasized how COVID-19 exacerbated social, economic, and legal challenges faced by trans parents, including unemployment, financial dependence, and increased isolation. "COVID-19 has left some trans parents in a state of limbo, concerned about what the future holds for them and their families," wrote Siegel.[22] Even in terms of how we think about parenting and work, lack of resources and support impacts what ambition, work, care, and time look like for families. Caring for another generation of human beings feels inherently ambitious, but without resources and support needed to thrive, where does that leave families?

Parents I spoke to reiterated versions of the same concept: frustration with the scarcity of support provided to make it possible to be ambitious in other contexts *and* to just get by. Mary Ellen wants her children to see her as a whole person—career ambitions and all—so they see their versions of wholeness as possible. When she stayed home with her children when they were younger, she realized how much she missed working outside her home: she loved the mental work of planning, writing, and playing with language. Her dream is for more flexibility and breathing room. She doesn't struggle with the notion of "doing it all" alone because she believes raising kids should be a community effort. "I do often feel judged as a divorced mother," she pointed out. If she loses her job, she loses her income; if she loses her income, she could lose her house; if she loses her house, she could lose her kids. "I think my ex is an all right person, but I don't think that if I was homeless, I'd get to see my children," she said. "Life shouldn't be that precarious." She thinks about it all the time.

Ashlee also pointed out how more resources would help parents at work and their families as a whole. For example, she lives in a county where there's such a crisis of access to childcare that people are on waiting lists even before they have a child and where parents can pay up to $3,000 a month for one child to be in childcare. "I believe that we need high-quality, early childhood education that is affordable and accessible," she told me. "Access to childcare—being able to have my kid in a place that's safe, or he's learning and growing—allows me to perform better at work." Ashlee considers herself lucky to have a job she loves, one in which she can center her ambition of creating equity in her community. But she does notice the biases embedded in her working life—like attending a networking event and someone asking her where her child is, when there are dads in the room, too.

Being ambitious in one's own work and in the home offers up one set of idealized standards. But being ambitious on behalf of your children? That's supposed to be a whole other category.

The After-School Hustle

By the time Mary Ellen's and my conversation shifted to talking about her children, it was clear that one priority she had—reminding them that she cared more about them making their best effort than she did their grades—wasn't enough. Being ambitious for her children meant wanting a radically different world than the one they were already growing up in. That meant, in short, wanting them to be free. "I would love for my children—for all children—to not be confined by what is useful to capital." She wanted more for them than what was useful and profitable because "that really flattens your life."

"We're not raising people. We're raising profit centers. And that's gross," she explained. She listed all the information she was flooded with on the importance of STEM programming, some from schools, reinforced by business and political leaders. Among her kindergartener's school options was an elementary school centered around STEM education. What was highlighted wasn't the ingenuity of STEM: the way it could build a better world, the creativity involved, or the curiosity required. Instead, the selling point—literally—was that STEM careers were well paying and dignified, a means of avoiding low-wage work. She looks at the parents whose child is in private school and taking piano lessons and wonders if she's failing her kids. "I can't afford it as a single mom," she noted. What she *can* do is review her son's homework at night, encourage his interests, and remember that she grew up far less resourced than her son and she's OK. If he wanted to play piano, she'd make it happen, she said. "But I don't have the energy or drive to *push* him proactively into all the things."

The media latches onto the multipack of these stories: There's the dreams-paid-off version, where the sacrifices of the patient parent led to a prodigy child turning into a superstar. There's the extreme versions, like "Operation Varsity Blues," better known as the college admissions scandal in which wealthy parents, including celebrities, were charged with bribing their kids' way into elite Ivy League schools—sometimes going as far as to have their child's face Photoshopped onto the image of a student athlete to score athletic scholarships.[23] The reality show *Dance Moms* literally ranked children via a pyramid, but the mothers—for whom the show was named—were portrayed as even more ambitious than their daughters. There is an entire industry of "kid influencers" on YouTube, TikTok, and Instagram, where children are either minicelebrities in accounts run by parents or are the children of influencers and built into the parents' overall brands; in either case, the adults' ambition drives the profit the kid makes, despite child labor laws and social media guidelines that attempt to limit people under thirteen from having accounts.[24]

But what jumped out at me was how many parents weren't ambitious on behalf of children because of some undying quest for fame or recapturing of youth—those stories are out there, to be sure. There was also a kind of ambition in simply wanting life to turn out OK for your kid. "I'm, like, 'Oh, these people are doing this for their kids. I wish I could do that,'" Syeedah, a twenty-three-year-old finishing a graduate degree in school counseling while working two part-time jobs and parenting her daughter, told me. "And it does make me feel kind of like I am a bad mom, you know?" She said that the internet—Facebook and Instagram—get in her head sometimes.

Syeedah's daughter does martial arts two days a week, and typically her grandmother takes her, because Syeedah is in class at that time. Anything her daughter's school allows her to sign up for, Syeedah permits, because it's free and happening somewhere her daughter has to be anyway—that's how she wound up playing tennis. Syeedah is currently budgeting to sign her daughter up for swim lessons in the summer. But even just being involved as a parent comes with barriers. At one point, she joined the PTA but could only attend a few meetings because sessions were held on a day and time that overlapped with her work schedule when she was working retail.

The pressure is two sided: pressure to be an ambitious parent—to have her child in multiple activities and to attend them all—and then, because she is a young mother, Syeedah feels there is no standard for her, which adds pressure in a different way. "Because people don't expect teen parents, or just people with kids in general, to be able to achieve anything," she told me. She had to learn plenty of times to ask for help, and it still doesn't come easy. "We want to succeed," she said of teen parents. (Syeedah had her daughter at sixteen.) "We are doing our best to make sure we can get there. We don't want people to feel sorry for us. And we're not trying to make excuses, but we genuinely need help."

The version of ambitious parenting Syeedah was describing—to be the most involved parent, to be the one at every swim meet or afterschool meeting—came up as an exhausting offshoot of ambition that took more than it gives.

Social media has enabled people to build entire brands, careers, and identities around performing as a good parent. Motherhood, presented as a lifestyle with family outfits that manage to always pick up a subtle color in the wallpaper or a slate of overscheduling that never reveals when someone has time to cook dinner, is positioned as the individual, aspirational workaround to the grind of parenting.

Kelly, who spoke to me about the pressure of her own academic experiences as a child, told me it felt weird to see other parents having "wild ambitions for eight-year-olds." At one point, Kelly and her family lived in a suburban neighborhood where extracurricular activity schedules were coordinated with the precision of an academic calendar, which she described as the most competitive parenting environment she'd ever been in. Parents had private coaches for their third-grade baseball players. Kids were in multiple types of music lessons and competing in karate. Every day had an activity and, along with it, the objective that the child would excel at *at least* one of them.

Meanwhile, Kelly explained that one of her kids loves to dance, but no one, including Kelly's child, has expectations that she'll become a world-famous tap dancer, but a lot of parents in that community thought Kelly's approach—low key and casual about activities—was *weird*. Doubling up on that was the pressure on parents—mothers, in particular—to be perfect and always *on*, not just in their own lives but also in the lives they are attempting to craft for their children. She recalled one moment when a group of parents were talking about spring break plans, and Kelly mentioned she'd be working. "No lie, there [was] an audible gasp that I wasn't doing some sort of enrichment activity or family time," she said. But Kelly had been on the receiving end of those pressures—and expectations that matched them—as a child. "I had parents that expected that I always had the grade, that I always did well in school. There was not a lot of room for air," she told me. With her kids, Kelly said she wants them to do their best but without parental pressure. And it isn't just parents putting pressure on kids. It's also the pressure on parents to show *they* have done their best, via their kids, which should be a condemnation of a society in which "doing your best" is never quite good enough, and parents are held responsible for anything less.

That was a refrain from parents: the desire for their children to be better off than they were, much like what their own parents had wanted for them. But today's parents articulate a different version of what "better" means: parents I spoke to described wanting more opportunities for their children to find hobbies they enjoy, to see their worth beyond work, to have more financial security and a greater sense of stability. But better also includes a degree of removal, which includes wanting their children to not have to work quite so hard to get by and to not have to prove their ambition over and over and over again.

How many times will parents have to defend having work, passions, and dreams outside their children until it's universally acknowledged that they can be great parents *because* of their own dreams and goals, not in spite of them, because fulfillment doesn't only take one form? Or, given how many parents are working, how resources like universal childcare or universal basic income might give families more flexibility, creativity, and breathing room? What responsibility do all of us have to children—not as parents, but as a society? There is abundant research on the harms of ambitious parents pushing their own dreams onto children, but less discussion over what happens when we dump a broken society onto parents and children, then wonder why they aren't thriving.

It was Harper, who talked to me about ambition's impact on her childhood, who pointed out how parenthood is ambitious—something she thinks about often, because she doesn't want children. It's ambitious, she said, to want to raise children. Having ambitions and dreams that don't include children paint people—women especially—as selfish or self-centered, but having children is rarely presented as an ambitious pursuit. In particular, she told me, she thinks about some women facing major challenges in their journey through parenthood, including being forced out of the workforce and into their homes—or being penalized at work via lack of advancement and low pay—while being expected to handle the mental load and invisible labor of a home. Meanwhile, Harper said she even feels penalized for opting out of having children. "I feel like we can't talk about ambition as it relates to women without talking about how parenthood impacts those who pursue it as well as those of us who don't," she added.

"To be a good parent in a world that is so difficult is ambitious," Harper added. "To heal yourself enough to break cycles of intergenerational trauma and dysfunction is ambitious. To take on the spiritual, emotional, and economic challenges that come with raising a child is ambitious." Parenting doesn't happen in a vacuum, and neither does ambition. Rather, expanding a definition of ambition demands communities, resources, and support—what we should be striving to pass on.

5: "Just" a Hobby

The first time I ever loved an activity—maybe the first time I felt passion—was standing at a ballet barre, trying to point my flat feet hard enough to make them look like bananas. Trying to make this hobby-turned-passion I loved so much into a job was the first time I ever remember hating myself. But I *worshipped* ballet. From the *jeté*, my relationship to hobbies was ambitious, an outlet not so much for exploration and enthusiasm as a chance for hard work to pay off, and I loved every second. Maybe because I still have a bag of old pointe shoes sitting in my closet, stained with blood from my blistered toes, I have wondered where "following our passions" could lead us—if not toward finding an ambitious hobby, maybe toward discovering a new piece of ourselves.

That's what I thought about as I climbed over some boxes in my parents' garage in search of an old Walmart tennis racket with neon-yellow grip tape unraveling from the handle, put on running shorts that were still slightly damp because I forgot to move my laundry to the dryer, and walked to the nearest tennis court, determined to do something that had no sense of purpose, meaning, or plan other than the fact that I was here and doing it. That June day, so sweltering I could practically see the weeds in the asphalt cracks wilting, was the culmination of two years of procrastination on trying out a new hobby—a hobby I did not have to practice, would never be good at, and existed solely as a pleasant way to fill time.

As a kid, following my passion through activities I did outside school felt freeing. In adulthood, random efforts to pursue activities for fun backfired: bless the patient instructor who gently informed me I might "not be suited to string instruments" during a fleeting spurt of adult guitar lessons. I've quit the Nike running app so many times, the app has quit me. I opted out of adult ballet class when I realized the instructor wouldn't let me come in sweatpants. In most hobby scenarios, never once did I think, "Hmm, sounds like fun!"—the way I'd respond to a friend who wanted to go get coffee and pastries. (I am always ambitious about this invitation.)

From my earliest encounters with hobbies, I associated doing something with *practicing* something, which I further conflated with being *good* at something, and therefore hobbies consistently dovetailed into more work—granted, work I enjoyed. Writing went from a hobby to a career, all because I started pursuing my passion outside my day job. Now, writing is a job I do on the side of a day job, and on the side of writing, I read, bake, play tennis (cheering when I manage to hit the ball), and vanish into the abyss of Instagram cat videos—on the side is a very big thing for me.

Especially in my late teens and early twenties, all anyone could talk about was monetizing passion projects. If we were spending time on them anyway, why wouldn't we want to get paid for that? Some people I knew burnt out immediately—realizing that once the hobby became com-modified, it didn't feel fulfilling anymore—and others thrived, excited to have produced supplemental income for something they would've been doing anyway. Others, like me, existed in the middle: eager to make their passionate hobby into a job but stumbling when making the leap.

Now, the script has flipped: *everything* has become a job. Not only do we need spaces to show up as our full selves beyond work, but at some point, hobbies became a buffer between Our Work Selves and Our Fun Selves, the barrier guarding us against overwork. In this way, having a hobby we loved that wasn't also work we loved felt like rejecting the idea that work should get all of us, the best of us. Monetiz-ing our leisure activities makes it harder to separate what we do from who we are. But hobbies, by definition, are exten-sions of ourselves, because we're choosing to do them.

More complicated than whether to monetize a hobby or not—or even whether to be *ambitious* about a hobby—is whether hobbies are an opportunity to blessedly *not* be am-bitious. A hobby can be a passive use of free time, an oppor-tunity to explore safely and freely, a chance to profit off our talent, or a means of following passion whether we're paid for it or not. But hobbies don't automatically save us from striving, and maybe that's not inherently a bad thing. After all, we're striving to fill our time—usually with meaning.

Hobbies, AKA Fancy Leisure

Hobbies developed as a "category of socially valued leisure activity" around the nineteenth century, according to *Hob-bies: Leisure and the Culture of Work in America* by Steven M.

Gelber.[1] Back in the 1880s, a hobby was considered a negative obsession.[2] For example, Gelber's book cites the example of an "eccentric amateur scientist" who believed he'd one day be famous and was said to be "riding his hobby to the death."[3] Obsessive, preoccupied behavior was condoned at work but not in the hobby space. Then, Gelber notes that the labor movements of the Industrial Revolution eventually created the five-day workweek, and with it, time that could be used for leisure—which led "guardians of public morals to fear that time spent not working would be time spent getting into trouble," wrote Gelber.[4] It is not an overstatement to say we are having a conversation on how hobbies get commodified all because of Satan's love of free time.

Enter what sociologist Robert Stebbins calls "serious leisure." Casual leisure is defined by being "intrinsically rewarding," a "short-lived, pleasurable activity requiring little or no special training to enjoy it."[5] (My endless pursuit of baking every chocolate chip cookie recipe that scrolls across Instagram would fall into this category, though working a hand mixer without flinging batter everywhere certainly feels like "special training" to me.) Serious leisure, on the other hand, includes the need to put in effort to gain the skill, a unique social world, and an attractive personal or social identity.[6] A lot of hobbies fall into this category, even if they are considered leisure, because we're still earning new knowledge or a new skill, and it is still technically an "achievement-generated pleasure," as Gelber phrased it. As he pointed out, the most common forms of *passive* leisure don't actually make you feel accomplished: there is no pride in watching TV, reading popular fiction (beg to differ), or chatting over coffee with a friend versus "serious leisure," like volunteering or producing an outcome via a hobby. Like when I make contact with the tennis ball! Or don't accidentally smack a nearby house's home alarm system with it.

What this tells us is that even leisure isn't inherently separate from ambition, achievement, or striving. For the past one hundred years, "society's most powerful defenders of the status quo"—business, government, and education, according to Gelber—have promoted productive leisure.[7] American hobbies have a "symbiotic relationship" to capitalism, Gelber wrote, because this kind of leisure cloaks celebration of the work ethic in pleasure. This is one of the reasons why advice to "get a hobby" to combat overwork or poor working conditions doesn't hold up. First, hobbies and activities require free time and money to do them. Second, pleasurable time spent out of work or school doesn't absolve employers from their responsibility to provide better working conditions or cancel out the wrong-headed belief that we have to earn relief. Finally, hobbies aren't inherently the equivalent of doing nothing: we aspire to get something from them, whether it's pleasure, a fun chance to disconnect, or even earn twenty dollars for doing something we would've done anyway. That's the tricky part.

Follow Your Passion—to a Point

When I asked Erin A. Cech, PhD, associate professor of sociology at the University of Michigan and author of *The Trouble with Passion*, about the Great Monetization Question, she cited a specific example. In her research, students she interviewed at Stanford were more likely than students she interviewed at other schools to look at something they were passionate about and think: *How can I make this the way I participate in the paid labor force?* First, Cech said, that's the culture of Stanford, but wealthier students also have access to social networks and more capital. In other words, it's one thing to want to make our hobby of baking cookies into a business—to follow a passion deep into the folds of jam filling and frosting. It's a very different thing to have parents whose lawyers can advise on business proceedings and offer seed money—a term I had to google. That ups the stakes of the monetization game. Yes, we want to follow our passions, but do we all have the capacity and resources to spend printing labels, invoicing, and being our own customer service?

I was curious about Cech's work on the "passion principle," a term she coined referring to the belief that self-expressive, fulfilling work should be the central guiding principle for making work decisions. Often, "pursue your passion" is the first thing we hear before being told that maybe we should monetize our hobbies. "Part of it is, there's just not a whole lot of time to do anything," Cech told me. It's not just you: it truly feels like there isn't enough time to do things simply because we want to do them. Because time is money, we have to have a good reason for how we spend time—and typically, pleasure isn't considered productive. In *The Trouble with Passion,* Cech wrote that, amid the rise of neoliberal political and economic policies of the 1980s, the expectations for self-expression and individualism turned up in the 1980s and 1990s. That created an excellent opportunity for economic advancement to saddle up alongside a "calling," part of the Protestant ethic,[8] the idea that we have a moral duty to our work.[9] Work wasn't going to be something we *do;* it's going to be something we *are.*

Cech's book is grounded in interviews that follow students from college into careers, asking a big question: *What's the dark side to "following your passion" straight into the workforce?* (In the introduction, Cech notes the irony of the work she does: she wrote about her "passion for sociology" when applying to graduate schools.) Even colleges, Cech said, are molding more to the idea that students will have hobbies that excite them infinitely more than whatever classes they're taking, leading to an "individualistic cobbling together" of majors outside traditional departments. In her research, Cech found fewer points of variability in who opted to pursue their passion by gender, race, class, and immigration status than she anticipated. She fully expected the passion principle to primarily apply to rich, white students. That was technically true: white workers, Cech found, were slightly more likely than African American or Asian workers to emphasize passion. But she found that for *all* groups, passion was the preferred way to think about career decision-making, even more so than finding a good salary or job security. If we have to work, we want to not hate the work. Turning hobbies into work is like a two-for-one. The assumption is we'll get more time for ourselves, and in reality, we often get more time on the job. We care about it, so we're willing to put more work into it. And because the work feels personal, the stakes feel high. The aspiration is even in the language:

"Don't settle; do what you love."
"Follow your heart, not a paycheck."
"Life is too short not to do something meaningful."
"Doing what you love is worth the sacrifice."

Read out of context—aside from the line that includes "paycheck"—the above lines don't sound like they're about work or even ambition. Rather, they read like striving toward a higher ideal, a better self.

Tiffany and Chris, both in their twenties, launched a small business shortly after they were both laid off from jobs in tech during the pandemic. Tiffany paints, and Chris is a photographer. Figuring out how to generate extra income from their art seemed like the right next step. Since then, they've both been working other jobs while running a virtual art shop, where they're breaking even and not paying themselves yet. "It doesn't seem possible to keep a hobby kind of leisurely or enjoyable if you do want to survive on it," Chris told me, "because survival takes a particular amount of money, honestly."

At their former place of employment, they were offered a slate of activities designed around relaxation, in the hopes that—I'm sure you didn't see this coming—employees would be more productive. There were yoga classes and meditation workshops galore, but slowing down on work was not an option.

Hobbies shouldn't have to exist to counterbalance work or to cope with it. There's a difference between doing something just for fun, or doing something because you need a reprieve from the thing you're required to do. "I don't consider it leisure to have to do meditation because your work is stressing you out so intensely that you are having to do these leisurely activities in order to cope with day-to-day life," Tiffany said.

Chris told me he thinks a hobby *can* be leisure but not always. For example, his photography can be done in a leisurely way, like when he has a day off and takes pictures for himself, but it also requires focus and education, which makes it feel distinct from leisure. Tiffany said she didn't have hobbies for most of her life and originally set out to "paint weird things and not think of it like a hobby." Slowly, it became what she'd zone out to in the evenings while listening to an audiobook, as well as a source of income. "If one side of capitalism is you can work for this giant corporation and sell your soul to them forty hours a week, sitting at this desk, looking at the screen, or you can—on the flip side of that—be an entrepreneur and hustle really hard and do this thing and die doing it . . ." Tiffany trailed off. "I don't want to exist in either of those spaces." Existing in the middle ground, somewhere between making a hobby a job and working a job around what they love to do, has been the best-case scenario they could find.

The Quest for Significance

Think of it like a series of jumps: if we aren't pursuing what we love through work, we might pursue it through a hobby or activity. And because it's a thing we love, it might be a thing we want to be good at. It becomes an outlet for passion, even without compensation. "We propose that ambition leads to extremism through passion," wrote researchers in a study assessing the role of obsessive passion in the relationship between ambition and extremism.[10] When you think "extremism," your mind may not immediately flash to ambition, let alone hobbies, but stick with me.

Extremism can be defined as a motivational imbalance, Molly Ellenberg, one of the study's researchers, told me. On top of having our basic needs, we have self-actualization needs—including feeling we have purpose, dignity, and like we're respected. What happens with extremism is that one need—the quest for significance—outweighs all the other needs. While research has found this is a personality trait, Ellenberg added, cultural and community environments impact the outward presentation of it. "Depending on if you're in an individualistic culture, [or a] collectivistic culture, what does it mean to succeed?" Ellenberg prompted. "Does it mean to honor your family, to get married, have children? Does it mean to get a college degree? What does it mean within your environment?" The United States is so individualistic, Ellenberg said, that having personal goals are what other people respect and what we learn to respect in ourselves. This could manifest in our jobs for some of us, but as we know, passions exist outside work, too. There are plenty of people who are ambitious but aren't necessarily extreme in their craving for significance, Ellenberg explained. If they are ambitious and *aren't* extreme, that need for significance in a given area isn't outweighing their needs to belong, have a robust circle of family and friends, or to relax.

In the literature, that's also a difference between what's called obsessive passion and harmonious passion. In our conversation, Ellenberg cited the now infamously meme-able clip from the docuseries *The Last Dance*, where Michael Jordan said, "It became personal with me." He admits he's at his best when he interprets any random interactions, any threats to his game, as threats to his identity—his passion and his identity are the same, Ellenberg said. That's obsessive. We can be great at something; we can be passionate about something. But that sole passion also shouldn't represent all that we are.

The study gave Serena Williams as an example of harmonious passion, of someone who has control over a beloved activity, who aligns her identity, her passion, and her profession. Williams, the research outlined, speaks openly about being a fashion designer and mother, in addition to being a tennis player. She's the greatest athlete in the world, but that isn't all she is. Experiencing or embodying harmonious passion can happen for others as well: when we feel harmonious passion, an activity is a significant part of who we are and our lives, *but* we're also able to have other interests, relationships, and other sources of meaning.[11] As some research puts it, we control the passion rather than the passion controlling us.[12]

In theory, our hobbies should be outlets for harmonious passion. But dependence on any single activity—or meeting any single goal—to define our identities can be harmful. All his life, Ken, who is in his forties and from the South, was looking for "the next goal, the next mountain." In high school, it was getting accepted into college; in college, it was being offered a job; in work, it was earning a promotion or raise. Then, around age thirty-five, he decided to go to medical school, which came with a built-in series of mountains: getting accepted in the first place, passing the boards, landing a residency, and, finally, becoming a board-certified attending doctor. Achieving the last step— the last mountain—didn't feel like running across a celebratory finish line. It felt like a loss. "To [have] forty-four years looking for that next goal, to all of a sudden, that's it . . ." he told me. "I think probably that hit me fairly hard."

The depression that followed finishing residency dovetailed with the loss of Ken's hobby—extreme races, including Ironman Triathlons. "My motivation was to win, was to come in first," he said. He was able to go out after work, bike one hundred miles, have dinner, and do it all over again the next day, training because he liked the end result. That was his hobby, technically; it wasn't a profession. But it was also his ambition. When Ken became depressed, he stopped racing. People asked him why he didn't race anymore, and he'd say he had a chronic illness flareup, which was technically true. "But what really [happened] was, I got so depressed, I couldn't get on the bike," he shared.

The flipside of pursing your passion is what happens when the passion begins pursuing *you*, gobbling up chunks of self-esteem, identity, and free time, like pixels on a game of Pac-Man. The rush I got when I got my first piece published is the same rush I felt when I landed a double pirouette: *let's do that again*. I even found myself doing it with my half-hearted tennis attempt: Today I hit the ball seven times in a row without catching the net. Wonder how many I can do later this week?

That "what's next" sensation after an objectively big moment or accomplishment feels like it's knocking the wind out of us right as we start to cheer, nudging us toward the sensation that we are only as good, only as fulfilled, as the last big thing we did—so we best find another one. It wasn't just career transitions, like retirement or moving into a new role. People described finishing everything from home renovations to marathons as being split-seconds of exhilaration, followed by the crush of realizing the goal was missing and had taken a piece of them along with it. "What's next" can be an invigorator; it keeps us going. It can also end up as a reminder that pauses aren't built in, even to savor what we love, what we're proud of.

Rather than chasing goals now, Ken is working on reorienting, enjoying what he's doing and being more mindful: getting a patient to the right specialist, keeping someone from dying (which sounds, um, like a big goal to me), and getting better at a given procedure. That's translated to his hobbies, too. "I've gotten to where I can exercise a little bit more now and just kind of [be] in the moment a little bit more, rather than having to make [it] competitive," he told me. Now, he mountain bikes—something way outside his comfort zone. He's OK at it, he said, but he's never going to be at a pro level. "I can just go fast down the side of a mountain and just enjoy the fact that I'm going fast down the side of the mountain," he added. The mountain metaphor has carried all the way through, but the relief of descent seems different than the yearning of the climb. And of course, he noted, it helps when he actually stays on the bike going down.

Someone's Leisure Is Someone Else's Labor

Meanwhile, I was fixated on the idea of harmonious passion. To me, tennis felt like a safe hobby to try because I am not passionate about it. I'm never going to monetize it because, I mean, I routinely whiff the ball and have to chase after it like a golden retriever. I wasn't seeking passion or practice, just pleasure.

But as Mikey, a twenty-four-year-old pursuing a doctorate in public health, pointed out, sometimes people monetize a hobby to leave a toxic job, and for others, monetizing hobbies is the only way they can justify doing them at all. I immediately wanted to know more because that's how my writing hobby became part of a career: I process via writing.

I learn what I think or feel by writing. And eventually, it got to the point where writing needed to pick up some slack in the income department, or I needed to spend less time drafting pieces in my phone's Notes app between tasks for a collection of part-time jobs I was working while trying to find a full-time one. Perhaps because I've never only been a writer, I feel like an imposter in both directions: writing gets far too much time, attention, and extremism energy to be a hobby, but it's also not the employment that gives me health insurance. I'm lucky to get to do it, *and* it has made additional work—work I am choosing that erodes my free time.

"There's been a lot of sort of self-improvement-adjacent conversations happening right now [because of the] pandemic," Mikey told me. "People picking up hobbies, people working out at home . . . just this idea that as we are being traumatized by this pandemic, and being distanced from each other; we're supposed to be working to improve ourselves or emerge from this horrible, disabling, traumatizing event with new skills and a better body." And beyond that, the world didn't stop. All those walks people took to safely be outside? Someone is responsible for maintaining parks and public spaces. The takeout that was a saving grace, a way to break up the slog of the week? Someone was preparing that food and someone else was delivering it. The hobbies that kept people going, like adult coloring books? Someone was making them. The lines between what is labor and what is leisure have never been as distinct as perhaps we'd like. Precious few leisure activities exist without being work for someone else.

In addition, research points out, there is no activity that can *only* be leisure. Any activity is always going to be an obligation or work for someone. Painting, singing, playing a sport, fixing up houses, gardening, reading, dancing—nearly any activity we can imagine is technically work or labor in some way. Even the ones that are fun.

Plus, not everyone prioritizes leisure the same way. For example, researchers point out that for many women, home is a primary place of work, too, so it shouldn't be surprising that work and leisure activities are often intertwined.[13] In addition, researchers note, if we're going about our days feeling generally good about our lives and how we spend our time working, playing, being with loved ones, and relaxing, we're not likely to categorize our activities as hobbies or leisure at all. We're just living. "On the other hand, individuals who feel they lack the balance or have either few play opportunities or perhaps too much time on their hands, may be acutely aware of leisure's meanings," they wrote.[14] Time outside of work feels fleeting, especially when we factor in the activities that are technically nonwork but are absolutely work, like grocery shopping, cleaning, and ironing our pants. Even "free time" isn't free of responsibility. It leads to a split: every activity needs to be steeped in personal meaning for us to spend our free time on it, and any free time we do get needs to be spent doing *something* meaningful. That means, even subconsciously, we're seeking something from a hobby, whether it's money, pleasure, a momentary release, a chance for connection.

Mikey told me about a friend who likes to make pins and buttons. She also has a job she works eighty hours a week. "If she's not charging people for the buttons, she can't reasonably decide to take half a day off of work every so often to do that thing that gives her pleasure," Mikey said, "because she's fucking exhausted otherwise, and she's working otherwise." She also can't justify making time to do the activity she enjoys if she doesn't have income to compensate for hours she'd otherwise spend working.

On Mikey's part, she puts most of her longer writing on Patreon. Writing for Mikey takes a lot of creativity, a lot of mental resources, and a lot of physical resources. Mikey is a disabled person who has ADHD, she told me, and she cannot do as much over the course of a given day as she used to. If she's crafting a piece someone suggested she write, that's the activity she's doing for the next three days—not responding to emails that have paid opportunities. "Somebody pointed this out to me, and it's absolutely right," Mikey shared. "A lot of disabled people, a lot of chronically ill people, do work that is considered to be hobby-ish, that is considered to not be formal work." This is in spite of it making consumers and artists happy.

When that work gets relegated to the hobby space, there's a notion that it is inherently less ambitious, less significant, and less financially and culturally valuable. "But it's all labor," Mikey added. "You're spending energy regardless." And it's a legitimate source of survival. "We need to complicate our understanding of what a hobby is," Mikey told me. "We need to complicate what it takes to do a hobby, to sustain a hobby." Namely, leisure—and leisure activities—take time and money. They aren't givens. They aren't universally applied because neither is our time.

How We Spend It

Maybe it would help us unload the heft of ambition from work if we could be ambitious about our hobbies. But the more I thought about it, the more it seemed like, really, hobbies were actually a way to be ambitious about our *time*—how we choose to spend it in ways that feel most attuned to us. Whacking the tennis ball around a cracked neighborhood court didn't make me smarter, more athletic, or more aware of tennis rules, but it *did*, somehow, give me an outlet to feel more like me. It felt like me because I chose it, and I chose the low level of emotional investment I put into it.

But, as I attempted to bounce the tennis ball on the side of my racket, frustrated I couldn't master something I'd done about twice as a seven-year-old, I realized this might be a form of ambition, too. I wasn't practicing the sport, but I was practicing different ways of structuring my time, one in which the most significant result was that I'd showed up to play at all.

Nichole Marie Shippen, author of *Decolonizing Time: Work, Leisure, and Freedom,* pointed out that the depoliticization of time frames has made time an individual's possession, rather than a collective and social resource.[15] In other words, we've put the onus of achieving a work-life balance on individuals, rather than making it a wider societal issue. In this paradigm, how we spend our time is inherently all about our choices, and hobbies are elevated to be a saving grace from the cyclic churn of work and less a source of pleasure and meaning.

"Political-economic conditions that make the good life possible include the guarantee of leisure," Shippen wrote.[16] In Shippen's assessment, so-called discretionary time should be considered a central aspect of freedom. The value of leisure time doesn't inherently mean doing nothing, and it's not even necessarily about doing *less*—even as most of us would love to slash our to-do lists down by an item or two. Instead, if we had more free time, we could actually do more, and it could be more meaningful: more chances to reflect, to take meaningful action, to forge friendships. Without opportunities to maintain healthy relationships, build community, be creative, volunteer, and care—which, as Shippen noted, take "immeasurable amounts of time"—we lose opportunities to build meaningful lives. How we spend our time is also, at its most precious, how we create meaning. Thinking back to harmonious passion, other research details how harmonious passion positively contributes to psychological well-being,[17] defined as happiness, life satisfaction, and self-growth. That gives us the opportunity to ask: What are we curious about trying? What feels like *us?* What does freedom—in our passions, in our time—feel like? We need every chance to find it.

6: A Ticking Time Bomb

The stopwatch seemed to descend from on high, positioned somewhere between the frozen potatoes and my subconscious, as someone I'd known in middle school flagged me down in the grocery store to ask what I'd been up to these days. Had I finally graduated college? Did I have a real job? Was I married? Oh, well, I still had time—as if I wasn't stalled in a conversation with someone who knew an old me, clinging to my on-sale thin crust and suddenly aware I was behind in my own success story. Not long after, a 7 a.m. email from an egg-freezing service reminded me that I "didn't have as much time as I thought," as if that was news to me. The fertility marketing didn't feel much different than the "do your work early" mentality drilled into me throughout adulthood. The more we do early, the more time we have in the end.

If only.

Perhaps my worst habit was that I tried to run a race in pursuit of not a finish line but of not being "behind." I watched how others' steps built a ladder, one foot in front of the other, the correct next step moving into the next chapter,

as I racked up a collection of false starts, unfinished business, and loose ends. Then there were the lists: the thirty
under thirties and twenty under twenties; the supersavers
with a million dollars in a Roth IRA by age twenty-five and
nary a footnote that most of it came from their parents; the
instructions on the right age to have the kid, the right age to
make a career change, the right age to start thinking about
retirement, which is always about a decade prior to whenever you started thinking about it. Even Elizabeth S. Avent,
MA, a doctoral candidate in gerontology at the University
of Southern California, mentioned the infamous lists. "Now
they have forty under forty lists," she said, which doesn't
make it any better. "Now you have these people thinking,
'Oh, well, I have to be successful by the time I'm forty.'"

That's impossible for a lot of reasons, but among them is
the fact that we're still learning about ourselves in our twenties, thirties, forties, and beyond. We're learning about what
we want, and where we bring our ambition, throughout our
lives. In our first conversation, Avent mentioned that America assumes everyone lives on the same type of timeline,
namely, one that involves a primary and secondary education followed by college, then a career with a salary and a
job title, then marriage, then children and owning a home.
Interwoven with economic precarity and what someone can
pursue with the resources they have are deeply personal decisions, like how or whether to attend college or whether to
have kids. Much of the do-it-all-by-thirty mentality, Avent
told me when I called to discuss the idea of "being behind,"
comes from the belief that one needs to achieve their ambitions *before* starting a family. (As if everyone can. As if
everyone does. As if "family" must mean parenting in all

cases.) "We do need to abandon the timelines, and every decade of your life is important, not just the first three," Avent pointed out.

On the microlevel, I pictured my own lists: what's next after I move through the to-dos taped to my desk for so long it's a kaleidoscope of coffee rings. What's next after I publish this book or after this moment—the one I am most likely to blow right past and the only one I am guaranteed. The only thing better than getting a gold star is getting one *early*, like ambition has an expiration date. If I was *really* ambitious, I would've had all this—a good job, stable housing, a care plan for my parents and grandparents, my five-year plan, my morning routine—settled by now.

Ambition and time are like two hands on a watch: one moves the other. First things first: there is no behind. But to capitalism's great benefit, being ambitious is positioned as being ahead, which means we're always running. Some research outlines the four c's of industrial time: *commodification*, how the "time is money" assumption dominates daily life; *compression*, where speed becomes an economic value; *colonization*, when Western conventions of time are pushed as the norm; and *control*, which upholds the others.[1] Reporting from *Quartz* detailed how the Industrial Revolution changed the nature of work, which changed the nature of time: productivity was measured by how much work could be "wrung out of a worker over a period of time," and time became currency.[2] In part because of how time is structured—"optimize your time," "make the most of your time," "earn your free time"—the timelines, milestones, and chapters of life we pass through aren't objective or value-neutral. We're constantly supposed to be looking over our shoulders, back at what we could have done, produced, or achieved, or forward to the future, as if there's no ambition in standing firmly grounded in the only moment we're actually guaranteed: this one. Which leads to big questions about ambition: Do we grow out of it? Is it a "use it or lose it" situation? And what happens when our best-laid plans don't fit the timeline of success—when our ambitions *change?*

How Behind Are You on Growing Up?

None of us are growing up as fast as we used to, headlines say—apparently no matter how old we are or how long we've actually been adults. The twenty- and thirty-somethings are behind the so-called adult milestones, as are their elders. Retired people haven't saved enough for retirement, and young people aren't working hard enough to be able to retire. Whatever we're doing now is supposed to be something that sets us up for success later and later and later after that—as if the future isn't something that could fly away or fracture at any moment.

Renée, a forty-one-year-old woman living and working on the West Coast, initially messaged me to say she finally feels like she's in a comfortable place professionally and personally but she's about ten years behind. The behindness is by design: thanks to dire gaps in resources and privilege, most systems in America are set up for people to feel perpetually that way. Renée was a first-generation college student who spent a combined six years at community college and then at a large, well-known state school in California. She felt "old" as an undergraduate and more so when she graduated and realized the degree alone wasn't enough to get her a job: she needed work experience and internships no one had ever spoken to her about. She started an internship at twenty-five, which she only landed because she happened to be listening to the radio station when they made a call for interns, and she was working a part-time waitressing job across the street from the station. Postinternship, she still couldn't find work, so she spent two years in South America teaching English, but "coming back from South America felt like starting all over again," she told me. She walked right into the Great Recession and a dismal job market. Even with her years of waitressing experience, she couldn't get a job at Chili's. "I was unemployed, about to turn thirty, living with my mom, not in a serious relationship, [and] just feeling like crap," she told me. "It would keep me awake at night." It wasn't as simple as hitting none of the milestones; the milestones were no longer there.

Because Renée's parents didn't go to college, she and her sisters had to figure out the system on their own. Her plan was to eventually be a political science professor, but after six years in undergrad, Renée needed to make money. Graduating with her degree felt like a safe bet for getting a job, but by now, we all know how this story ends. Right in the middle of a financial crash, housing bust, and recession, millennials came of age, and according to a report from the think tank New America, in 2007—prior to the economic downturn—over 50 percent of four-year college graduates had a job offer when they graduated; less than 20 percent did in 2009.[3] (Now, according to an analysis of Bureau of Labor Statistics data by Pew Research Center, 2020 college graduates saw a larger decrease in "paid labor force participation" than people who graduated in the midst of the Great

Recession.[4]) In general, millennials earn roughly 20 percent less than the previous generation did, the report states, with stagnant wages,[5] higher costs of living,[6] and student debt that lingers whether someone finished a degree or not. The disparities within those numbers are stark: the Black-white wealth gap widened, where Black households held one-tenth the net worth of white households in the immediate years postrecession.[7] Rising inequality and declining mobility were a perfect storm.[8]

Right as we're supposed to be making so-called adult decisions, the impact of systemic issues becomes especially pronounced as people emerge into adulthood without the basic resources needed to build a stable future. By now, it's not news to most of us that, contrary to outdated jokes on avocado toast siphoning retirement funds, the milestones associated with adulthood have always been dependent on economic standing.[9] The pressure to do everything comparatively early in life doesn't change the fact that a lot of people aren't running out of time; time is being structurally stripped away from them.

Renée told me she thinks a lot about her choice not to have children, mostly because "my whole adulthood has been about surviving economically and barely surviving, and trying not to end up back at my mom's house or couch surfing at my friends' houses." She saw how her younger sister struggled as a single mother, *and* how her older sister struggled as a married mother, a particularly damning testament to the state of America. The only reason she can feel financially stable at all, Renée said, is because she doesn't have kids—and she feels really sad about that. Rather than giving people the structural support and resources needed to make life decisions like whether or not to have children, it's easier to personalize that ambition, to suggest that if people *really* wanted to have kids or buy a home or change careers, they would have found a way to make it happen—a talking point that underscores the utter failure of individual achievement being positioned as the ultimate solution to everything.

Who Are Timelines For?

A lot of the way milestones or timelines are packaged is somewhere between a coming-of-age Netflix movie plot, a marketing scheme, and a capitalist reminder that there's something good waiting for us on the other side of all that hustle, and if we want to stay "on track," we best pick up the pace. Many of what are considered milestones are actually "normative age-graded influences"—events that happen throughout our lives that happen to be correlated with chronological age and can be shaped by biological or environmental aspects that tend to correlate with age.[10] (For example, getting a driver's license at sixteen.) There are also history-graded influences that relate to development across historical cohorts (think war or a pandemic) or nonnormative influences (think individualized flukes, like winning the lottery).[11] In lifespan theory, researchers wrote, these influences create the context in which we "act, react, organize [our] own development, and contribute to the development of others."[12] Organizing life according to set benchmarks—college graduation in one's early twenties, dream job by twenty-five, and owning a home by thirty-five—shouldn't imply that we all pass through these stages nor that we've failed if we don't. They are just patterns.

And the emphasis on those patterns doesn't take into account the nuances that shape us and our worlds, nor do those "norms" account for what is the norm for whom. The conformity to certain timeline ideals are interwoven with privilege, assumptions of heteronormativity and able-bodiedness, and a dismissal of aging. For example, some research specifically addresses how capitalism and heteronormativity also produce chrononormativity "or the use of time to organize individual human bodies toward maximum productivity" and how "queerness, in contrast, produces temporalities outside of these norms," leading to new possibilities for future community, including what markers of life we celebrate.[13] (Why should we only celebrate the occasions that are predetermined? Making our own occasions is ambitious.) Other work notes that "queer uses of time and space develop, at least in part, in opposition to the institutions of family, heterosexuality, and reproduction."[14] That connects to what writer Gabrielle Kassel detailed in a story for Healthline on "second queer adolescence," writing that "the concept of 'developmental milestones' is rooted in compulsory heterosexuality."[15] For example, many queer people don't get to experience some of what are considered milestones—first relationships, first time feeling comfortable dressing as yourself, first time identifying with media you consume, to cite examples from Kassel's piece—until after they come out. Far from the limited view that the time for finding ourselves ends in our twenties—do it then or forever hold your peace—often, we're growing into ourselves along the way. The most meaningful milestones are often ones that are self-defined and unfolding on our own timelines.

Victor, a twenty-eight-year-old who grew up in a Texas town of about two thousand people, told me that the dominant timeline in his community was marriage by age twenty-two. "Then there was me, who stayed there but didn't give in to the white picket fence, with the two and a half kids, and golden retriever," he said. That experience was great for his friends, he emphasized. It was truly what most of them aspired to. He just didn't. During the pandemic, Victor had COVID and began thinking about the last five years, ten years, how he'd spent his time. The very next day, he started calling people. "I was, like, I've known that I was gay since I was eight years old and I'm done doing what I feel like [is] expected of me, what I felt like wouldn't disappoint anybody," Victor continued. Not long after, he moved to New York with his best friend, began a new job, and developed a new community. It's been a revelation. Paths don't just go from point A to point B; you might have to go to point Q, then back to B, he told me.

The linear coming-of-age story has always left something to be desired—whether we think of that as moving on a certain timeline or clinging to specific milestones as if they are a life raft drifting toward happiness. But if those "milestones" don't feel compatible with our lives, they can do the opposite. Cass, thirty-three, told me that, for them, the timelines behind those milestones have varied or been different from the norm. They told me about getting married and having kids— parts of life Cass never saw for themself until they met their current partner. Changes to their ambition corresponded with other life events: Cass noted that, from an early age, they had to work twice as hard to get half the credit. After being the first in their family to attend college, Cass landed a dream job in TV news until the work environment, and environment of America as a whole, forced them out of their workplace, making them feel as a Black, Latinx, queer person they didn't belong in the newsroom. Up until recently, Cass was working at Starbucks and enrolled in a software development bootcamp, hoping to eventually start a new career.

But Cass's mom still assumed they'd be first to hit the "adult" milestones simply because they were the oldest. "But I'm also the only one who's gay and/or trans," Cass told me, "which throws more wrenches into what those timelines are supposed to look like." (Cass's mom dropped those assumptions immediately after she became a grandparent—Cass's sister had a child—and has been supportive of Cass since they came out, Cass clarified.) "There's still the societal expectation that cis, hetero couples meet, date for a couple of years, then get engaged, and then have kids after getting married," Cass told me. When Cass came out as nonbinary trans, some of those standards shifted. "I'm not sure society has standards for me—and I am more than OK with that," Cass added. They said they were lucky to receive support during their transition process, but they still feel pressure to follow society's "rules." One example they shared is having a baby: they've never wanted to give birth, but part of them thinks they "should"—the "should" is the heteronormative standard popping up to dictate what happens next, they explained. "Now in my adult life I've started to break the tie between standards and timelines," Cass told me. "I've started to be OK with not knowing what comes next."

Ambition for them has been defined as getting through the day, Cass told me. They think their gender identity made them reshape their ideas of timelines and ambition—for example, it's difficult to find trans-friendly employers, which impacts job trajectories. Cass has been focused on themself over the past couple years, and now they're looking to mix being ambitious about their work *and* about themself personally. That means thinking of the future in different ways, too. "Even though I'm actively figuring out how to propose, my partner and I are in no rush to get married," Cass added. "I have to remind myself that the only standards or rules I have to follow are those my partner and I come up with."

While the so-called norms of timelines might be oriented toward maximum productivity and achievement, there are countless ways time is shaped. Researchers who have studied the life course through the lens of ableism have written that it "is a social, historical, and cultural product."[16] Normative life courses—how different life stages are passed through or achieved—are built on notions of ableist time, the research details.[17] Typically, productivity and, by extension, work are time centered—both in everyday scheduling, such as multitasking designed to milk every ounce of energy, production, and optimizing out of each minute, and in how we move through time in a larger sense. In contrast, crip time—which, according to this research, "challenges ableist normativity and recognizes diverse bodies and minds by redefining time"—creates a different understanding of time.[18] First, researchers detail, is extra time needed to perform a task—this "extra time does not only depend on a person's slower pace but just as much on ableist barriers." Second, there's society's understanding of extra time as *wasted* time, which ties back into ableist notions of productivity. Third, crip time can be used as a tool for "understanding flexible temporalities for different people and not one fixed normal temporality."[19] Just as our free time is political, so is how time itself is shaped. (To use a personal anecdote, I internalized the belief of "on time" so much, I often skipped over asking for extensions when my own health made getting out of bed hard. Why did I think the solution was for me to work more in the minutes I could be upright, rather than to ask for more time?)

Despite everything we know about how time is shaped and experienced, society tries its damnedest to reinforce an incentive structure around hitting certain markers on certain timelines, including markers that aren't milestones at all but are supposed to be choices. In her article for Vox, Anne Helen Petersen described how American society is "structurally antagonistic toward single and solo-living people," including the tax code, written to benefit "people in 1950s middle-class marriages who own their homes" and other public safety net programs. She explained that "pensions, health insurance benefits, IRAs: all of them are organized to best accommodate the needs of married (or widowed) family units."[20] Marriage has long been an economic survival strategy for women; it was more than a personal choice. And when personal decisions moonlight as a crucial security scheme, the stakes of choosing something else balloon.

Similarly, homeownership is considered a tool for building wealth and financial well-being in the United States, one of countless reasons it's harmful that racism and ableism are features, not bugs, of the housing system. Then, throw in how ageism, embedded in both ends of the workforce, incentivizes picking a track and sticking to it as the closest thing one might get to job security. When trying to secure work in her field, Renée found her opportunities shifting because of her ethnicity and, later, her age. One example she shared came when she applied for a community manager job, only to have the hiring manager send her a job listing from an entirely different organization for a Latino Outreach Coordinator job. She was getting pigeonholed, "which is really, really quite depressing at times." Because of the emphasis on tidy career trajectories—no breaks, pauses, or course changes—and the emphasis on youth, the job application process and interview cycle became more exhausting every time. "I feel like I spent so much of my career feeling like no one would take me seriously because I was a younger woman," Renée told me. She named a "very small window" in her midthirties where people heeded her expertise, then the stopwatch started: she hit forty, and the pressure to "keep up and stay relevant" reared its head. Encouragement to "move on your own timeline!" is fine, but the incentive structure in America is that productivity equals worth, time equals productivity, and the only thing better than keeping up is getting ahead.

Despite knowing timelines of ambition are largely a marketing scheme, I was mystified by how people set life plans and seemingly stuck to them. A few years after I graduated college, I moved to New York, something I'd steadily planned and tried to save for. I'd intended to be there at least two years, one of the first times in my adult life I became the kind of person who, with marvelous predictability, knows what she'll be doing this time next year. I lined up an hourly job and studied Google Maps. Within a year, my starry-eyed plan combusted: after being sexually harassed multiple times in a community I was part of, I found myself perpetually looking over my shoulder as I walked home.

Anxiety that someone was following me replaced the pride I'd felt in learning my way around. Meanwhile, my reliance on over-the-counter medicine to get me from one bathroom to the next was hitting a peak, and I felt the strength seep from my body. I remember slumping against the brick wall of Joe's Pizza because I was too tired to stand and too brain fogged to give my order—one slice of pepperoni, one slice of caprese whenever they had it—thinking that I had a job interview the following day and that I needed to move back home. *Shouldn't I have grown up by now?* I remember thinking. *Shouldn't I be ambitious enough to follow through with any plan?*

My sense of time—because I'd tied all my plans to it— vanished. I cobbled together part-time jobs and applied for anything, watching everyone around me, well, grow up. Every thump of my own heartbeat felt like the ticking of a clock as I braced for how this slew of setbacks would inevitably crash into other dreams and cause a failure pileup. I sent registry gifts for wedding showers, baby showers, the shower for the friend who graduated law school and wondered when I could sign my name on the dotted line of finding a path and sticking to it, wondered why everyone was hurtling ahead in a race I hadn't realized we were running.

On Failures and Fresh Starts

Just as there are milestones of young adulthood that are treated as givens, later adulthood comes with a similar, less-discussed slate of to-dos: the underlying development tasks of this stage of life are "to settle for a few key choices and pursue long-range plans and goals within it." That research outlines exactly what this "settling down" period is designed to do: it's considered a time for people to "realize the hopes of their youth."[21] Which sounds like we're all supposed to take a ticket and get in line for a midlife crisis.

But even that framing of midlife is about achieving what we picked off the dream tree when we were young. Inspirational in one way, because how many social media posts have we read about someone achieving a lifelong dream or growing into the person their child self longed to be? In that framing, this is what we root for. There's affirmation that it was *worth it* in the end.

But so many of us are striving for our endings in the midst of our middles. There's one oft-cited poll of two thousand participants that floats around the internet outlining the exact age our ambition starts waning: thirty-three is the age we peak, allegedly; make your plans accordingly.[22] And, of course, there are obvious reasons one might stop striving quite so hard at work, including parenting or caregiving responsibilities entering the picture, changes to financial or living situation, or plain old renegotiation of what matters. But given so much of the ahead versus behind approach to ambition exists on a success-failure binary, it feels like there's more complexity than ambition dissipating in a poof of birthday candle smoke. What if ambition *changes*, a betrayal of the best-laid ten-year-plans and of the society that prizes them so highly?

Kelly, forty-one, who'd talked about the pressure of grades growing up, felt she was behind in her career—not that it would matter if she *was* because people's careers take different trajectories. She's written books. She's been an editor. She's an academic. And last year, following the grief of losing her father and undergoing surgery herself, her life was flipped upside down. "It's one of these things where I think that folks in their thirties and forties kind of want to hope that they figured their lives out," she told me. "They've done the things that they're going to do, that they're settled in a career, they have a sense of where their life is going right, or they have some sort of plan." That hasn't been Kelly's experience. She has a game she plays where she imagines what her twenty-one-year-old self would think of her today. She wonders if her younger self would be disappointed. "At one moment, I might have been super ambitious about being the superstar and now I'm just, like, I would like to be able to pay bills," she explained.

It feels weird to Kelly to be almost forty-two and figuring out the next thing—but she knows it happens all the time. "The idea here is that we're just supposed to succeed, right?" Kelly said. But failure is also instructive. "When we fail at something, we can actually learn something here about our-selves, about what we want." Or even failure as a redirec-tion. "The kind of message I got is that failure meant that you were a failure," Kelly said. We have to separate those things. Just because you fail at something doesn't mean *you* are a failure, she noted, "the same way that just because you succeed doesn't mean you're a success." Kelly makes it a point to talk about failures—and not in the "oh, it turned out OK in the end" way but in the "here's how I failed, here's what changed" way that doesn't minimize the struggles of life, love, careers, or paths not unfolding the way you expected them to. She doesn't have an answer to what's coming next, and through being open about failure or changing course, she's learning to feel OK about that.

Because so much of our sense of time is shaped by how we fill it, clinging to the next thing isn't just an aspiration but also a safety net. In a story for the *New York Times*, journalist A. C. Shilton explored the arrival fallacy, the belief that once we "make it"—we hit our goal or destination—we'll experience everlasting happiness. Even on a microscale, at eighteen, I told myself if I had a full-time job by twenty-five, I'd be happy. When I began writing, I told myself if I could publish one piece, I'd be fulfilled. Joke's on me!

"The problem is that achievement doesn't equal happiness—at least not over the long term," Shilton wrote, noting this isn't a message most of us are familiar with.[23] "In fact, it's almost antithetical to the American dream, which tells us that hard work and achievement deliver a happy life." And of course, the happy life is always the part that comes *afterward,* later, once we've grown into it, once we've earned our worth. The limits of my ambition threw up a roadblock: because so much energy was focused on getting to the *after,* I somehow stopped being able to imagine what *after* consisted of, what it would feel like and who I'd be once I got there.

During our conversation, Renée shared that about three months after she started her current job running a media relations program for a large union, her sister died by suicide. Ten days after her sister's death, she was working on high-profile press conferences and with elected officials on political campaigns. Working through grief was gutting, and so was the fact that, had it been ten years earlier, Renée said, she would have taken some time off. But since she's in her forties, she felt that she couldn't afford to leave the job market. She always felt behind "until I didn't feel behind, but then I just didn't want it anymore."

She also thinks often about her dad, who died suddenly of a heart attack at sixty, only a year and a half after he retired. He worked constantly as a telephone cable tech to build up his retirement, putting off traveling or enjoying his life because he assumed he was going to get to do that later. "It was, like, wow, my dad worked and saved up this retirement that he never got to enjoy." Renée described her dad saving up so much joy for *after* the ambitious parts of life and ultimately getting so little of it.

Renée found herself thinking, *what is this for?* "I'm spending so much time on something that in my twenties I thought oh, this is it. This is the goal. This will make me happy," she continued. "This will make me whole." It didn't. What she's describing is the arrival fallacy, which promises that we're *one away*—one all-nighter, one promotion, one more great thing—from all the work being worth it, from getting to slow down. She wants to be able to earn a living and support herself and *enjoy* herself now. But she doesn't think of a great career or even a single amazing accomplishment as the be-all, end-all goal. Ambition changed shape.

It isn't that ambition vanishes when we reach a certain accomplishment—or a certain age. "The ambitions probably change," Avent confirmed. As she pointed out, older people are more likely to retire, if they can. They're less likely to contribute economically "to the shape of capitalism" or to "making anyone else money." (Some reports estimate that the number of workers aged seventy-five and older is expected to grow by 96.5 percent in the United States by 2030,[24] and nearly half of all families in the United States have zero retirement savings.[25] The hypothetical "arriving" has never been further out of reach for so many.) She noted that older adults are changing careers and going back to school, in part because lack of a social safety net impacts them and some can't afford to retire, or because they've decided to pursue a different line of work or something they enjoy.

In a report on ageism, a researcher detailed how America's obsession with youth is the undercurrent to the country's bias against elderly people and fear of aging. The report states that "a growing sense of individualism and an increasing concern with staying young, older people have had to face an escalating level of disregard, disrespect, and marginalization."[26] (Another report on ageism said: "Ironically, most people consider living a long life to be an achievement and they strive to live as long as they can."[27] We strive for it, but the infrastructure doesn't support it.) But the more I asked, the more I heard about how aging created opportunities to discover a new version of ambition.

Janice, seventy-one, grew up pursuing a career she was passionate about: in high school, she wrote a column for her local newspaper, with a rate of ten cents per inch—her first check was for $1.40, she recalled. Later, she graduated from college with a degree in journalism and became an associate editor for a monthly magazine focused on the union of a pipeline company, where she traveled to report on different posts. "I was really quite shy," she told me. But "I found I was always challenging myself and doing things that I was afraid to do." Later, she freelanced while raising her sons, including Brandon, now a forty-year-old writer whose career also includes being an independent filmmaker, bookseller, and puppeteer.

The pair shared a passion for writing and had a plan. After Brandon finished his MFA in New York and moved to

Chicago, it'd be around the time Janice was going to retire. She wanted to go back to school for creative writing. Janice was already taking classes in memoir, working on personal essays about her kids, her divorce, her parents, and her late brother. They always had vague plans to write something together, Brandon told me. "It was always that big thing—that we'll be there one day," he added.

But life had other ideas on what "one day" meant. Brandon ventured home from New York to help Janice when her health took a negative turn—and he ended up staying, working as a full-time caregiver for Janice, who was diagnosed with Parkinson's disease. It was a significant shift for both of them: Brandon had never even cared for houseplants before, he joked; Janice described initial denial that she needed care at all. Then, there was their plan: Brandon's novel, Janice's memoir. "We'd learned by now that you don't always get to do those things that you plan on one day, so we got to make one day today," Brandon told me.

Now, they sit across from each other with the same Google document open, working on a new dream, a new ambition: Brandon and Janice are writing a memoir focusing on caregiving and receiving care, without forgetting who they are. The manuscript includes essays from each of them, as well as pieces that they are writing together, weaving their styles.

"Ambition to me is opening the door and letting in opportunity and being able to accept it even if you're afraid," Janice added, explaining that writing with Brandon is a true challenge because they craft differently. But she also said that Brandon is the best editor she's ever had. In light of the pandemic, the project has taken on new urgency because, as

Brandon pointed out, there are going to be more people who need care in the next decade, and we need resources for how to talk about the subject and how to share information with one another.

In addition to the importance of the project itself, Brandon described how both he and Janice needed to find a sense of purpose again—one that was different than what they'd known before; one that was responsive to their lives *now*, not just a future plan. If everything always feels just a little too late—too late to bother, too behind to try—maybe it could be an incentive to work harder to catch up. But getting ahead is a myth when it comes to the paths we take. Ahead of *who*? Why are we trying to outrun ourselves, as if the future is the only time that counts?

I recalled something Dawna Ballard told me, thinking about how capitalism and the Protestant work ethic shape how we spend our time. Why did it matter so much how we spent time? I'd asked, knowing that time was all we had. "Because it's our tie to life and to other people," she told me. "It's our signature of what's left here of us." Not timelines we meet. Time: how we're able to spend it.

7: Nine to … Forever

The first time Britney, twenty-two, and I spoke, she was chronicling her introduction to the paid workforce via text. She'd been hired into a full-time administrative support role at a New York City hospital right as the pandemic surged. That meant her routine included walking past morgue trucks lining the streets outside, and the sounds of her workday followed her home and into bed, where her mind replayed the desperate and tired voices on the other end of the phone, the overhead speaker bellowing out stroke codes, and code blue after code blue. Beginning her professional life in the midst of a crisis—one in which everyone around her was losing their jobs—meant overwork was her baseline.

Sometimes, it felt that everyone else was functioning as usual and Britney was "the weakest link" for not keeping up, she said. She recounted how trauma was compounding around her while being overworked: Black and brown workers were in the most vulnerable jobs throughout the pandemic, and Britney, a Black woman, was watching patients die from COVID at the same time protests were unfolding in the streets, following the murder of George Floyd by police. Meanwhile, work was supposed to go on anyway. Britney was trying to survive.

Eventually, unrelenting stress took a toll on Britney's health. It destroyed the lining of her stomach to the extent that she wound up in a different hospital—as a patient. In a weird way, she said she's glad she entered her working life when she did because now, everything is laid bare: "Where company priorities lie, where your personal limits stand, where governing bodies move and stay stagnant," she explained. For example, she knows that, had she not learned these lessons now, she would've saved her paid time off (PTO) for a someday vacation and muddled through if it got pushed back or unapproved. A coworker of hers had a month's worth of PTO accumulated by the time he resigned. He hadn't taken a single day in three or four years. "I saw a potential future in front of me, and I didn't want that," she said.

The pressure from overwork can result in everything from insomnia and heightened anxiety to depression and even heart attacks,[1] yet overwork is held up not just as a necessity but as an inherently ambitious quality, a requirement for the ambitious. Which is why I called Britney again, around six months after she resigned.

She was still living in New York, where she'd initially moved because she's disabled and needed access to public transportation. She's pursuing her master's in urban studies and working a part-time internship. After she departed her hospital job, she felt half relief at escaping and half guilt for leaving her colleagues behind. As we talked, she mentioned she had to mail a crocheted blanket to her sister—a hobby she picked up when her medical issues landed her in the hospital. Her dad suggested she could make a business out of it. "I was, like, please never say that again," she laughed. I think often about how she told me that overwork, to her, meant removing the ever-thinning line between your own needs and your job's needs: skipping meals, crying on breaks, and becoming ill from the stress and strain of working. No employer will ever list these "side effects" to overwork in a job description, but they get accepted as the status quo. This presumption of overwork being necessary and inevitable is a sometimes fatal, systemic flaw in the workplace in general.

"My relationship to work and ambition has definitely been formed by overwork," Britney told me. Because she was a young essential worker, she was ambitious in the sense of feeling fortunate to have a job when so many people were being laid off, not thinking she deserved a break because it was so early in her working life, and zeroing in on surviving the day-to-day, rather than thinking about longer-term purpose or meaning. She did not have that luxury. She thinks about how wanting to be fulfilled with how you spend the bulk of your waking hours—working—should be a good thing, but that lifting self-worth out of work is critical to restructuring it. She's dropped the societal expectations to achieve, she told me, because walking away with her life intact was all she could ask for. "We have to organize for us, for our lives, for our livelihoods, because our workplaces are sure as hell organizing for their best interests," she said. Especially during such an intense period of overwork, Britney realized that, yes, a lot of ambition comes from within. But "the more and more that I'm in the working world, it seems like ambition is formed a lot from these pressures that work is putting on us."

The prevalence of overwork is not because too many caffeinated strivers logged on at once, eager to impress their boss by mentioning that they worked on a Saturday. Overwork is a systemic crisis, and ambition is implicated because we're expected to work our way through the overwork crisis, too. A global study from the World Health Organization (WHO) found that in 2016, 488 million people were exposed to long working hours, which they defined as fifty-five hours or more per week.[2] Propped up by the fact that the "U.S. government guarantees very few benefits for workers, chaining them to their jobs," according to reporting by *Vice*,[3] a 2019 report published by the People's Policy Project in collaboration with the Gravel Institute stated that over the course of one year, the average American works more hours than the average worker in any other peer nation.[4]

Working to the point of burnout, feel like your brain is crispy and your soul is torched? The rejoinder is that it must feel good and satisfying to pour your heart into something. Working a job that's abusive, has unfair or inflexible scheduling, offers no time off, and underpays you, or working a job you just don't like? The rebuttal is either work harder or find a better job. Working a job that you like but feeling exhausted? The response is to work harder and get ahead, cementing yourself as indispensable so you can, eventually, rest. Notice how the solution in all cases is, in fact, more work.

I didn't notice I was taking that literally until it was nearly too late. The allure of overwork was twofold: first, it made me feel safe—ironic, given how precarious it was. Second, it felt like the only thing I had the illusion of control over. I'd tell you that I overwork because I need to keep my health insurance through my day job and still want to write—and that I'm lucky to get to do both. I overwork because I don't worry about retiring—that seems inconceivable to me—but I worry about how I'll take care of my parents. But that isn't the whole story. I also overwork in pursuit of meaning. Despite my years-long attempt to unravel what I do from who I am, I feel hypocrisy gurgle in my stomach whenever someone asks me how I prioritize life beyond work. The flush of shame overtakes me when I have to tell a young person asking for advice about not working on weekends but wanting to write that I have yet to manage it, though I know people who do. This mentality had me question, over and over, how much I was *really* willing to decenter my ambition—because I was certainly willing to overwork to protect its presence. Here I am, sitting with how overwork harms people, while knowing good and well that if it wasn't for overwork, I wouldn't get to write this book. My inability to square that conundrum has made the meaning of my ambition crumble, tumbling into the abyss below me as I climb toward the all-consuming "making it."

There Is No Good Overwork

There is no good overwork; there's only justification for it. And, uncomfortable as it is, ambition can be one. "Doing your best" is one thing. "Do *the* best at all costs" is something else entirely. But there's a difference in my form of overwork and the overwork that dominates much of the labor force, a distinction that doesn't get enough airtime amid conversations about checking email on vacation but is critical to how we address this.

A workaholic and someone who has to work a lot of hours might both technically overwork, but that is mostly where the similarities stop. (The term *workaholic* is said to have been coined in 1971 by a psychologist who was also a minister, meaning "the compulsion or the uncontrollable need to work incessantly."[5]) Research by Malissa A. Clark, PhD, emphasizes that a workaholic tends to work because of internal pressure, works to perform above and beyond what's expected of the work (beyond job requirements or personal economic needs), and has persistent thoughts about work even while not at work.[6] This research tells us that workaholism is actually *not* significantly related to work performance, and there were strong negative relationships with workaholism and work-life conflict, or incompatibility between work and everything outside it. (Even the phrase *work-life balance* implies an equal split between the two, when you think about it.)

Overworking isn't equally applied. In a report from the Center for Law and Social Policy, it's outlined that "women and people of color are disproportionately likely to have jobs paying low wages," and workers paid low wages also typically have less access to medical leave, paid family leave, or fair scheduling.[7] Not knowing what you're going to make month to month or week to week makes it harder to do virtually everything else, including planning key life logistics like childcare or transportation. In addition, gig workers often lack crucial labor protections and access to benefits like time off.[8] Overwork is both a demand—how else are workers supposed to survive?—and presented as the solution.

Those who have spent their lives working hard know for a fact that overwork and ambition tie into the realities of a workforce that benefits from people overworking. Martha, sixty-three, initially described her relationship with ambition as "zippo, none, nada, complete burnout," elaborating that she has been "ambitious out of necessity." At one point, Martha went back to college at thirty-five, taking a full course load while balancing two jobs—she worked at her university in the dairy and animal science department as a research associate, then cleaned banks in the mornings and at night. Her daughter would sit in the bank's kitchen space, doing homework, while Martha cleaned. "We actually did a lot of homework together during those four years," she told me. Later, when working at another university and making $24,000 a year, Martha got a raise and asked her employer to take it back—it put her over the income threshold to receive childcare assistance by twenty-four cents. Twenty-four additional cents meant that her childcare assistance was taken away, leaving her to manage $400 out of pocket per week. "That happens a lot and people go into poverty very quickly that way," she told me. "When I think of an ambitious person, I don't think of myself," Martha added. "I [think of] some aspiring twenty- or thirty-year-old who's moving up the ladder."

The job she has now is the best she's ever had, but it doesn't pay her enough to live on. She prices clothes at a store that's similar to a local version of Goodwill, where profit goes toward community services including fuel assistance, housing, and food. She downsized her life, moving to New England to be closer to family. "I didn't want to do a big job anymore," she told me. Her children are both grown, which helps, but when you're making $15 an hour and your employer wants to take $200 out of your monthly paycheck for health insurance, "Do the math," Martha said.

She cited the now-infamous adage—find a job you love and you'll never work a day in your life—and said, "Frankly, that's bullshit." She believes people want to have a job that doesn't make them cry on their way to work and lets them go on vacation. That happens for some people. "But I think that expectation of that is really hard when it doesn't work out." As is the case for countless scenarios where well-being seems to hinge in the balance of how hard one can work, Martha summed it up: "I think I seem like an ambitious person; I consider it more adrenaline . . . and fear."

Worked Up: Overwork as a Standard

America has a long history of running on overwork. The Industrial Revolution, where economic systems moved away from agriculture and handmade goods to industrial manufacturing, fundamentally changed the nature of work. In the 1800s, some estimates put the average workweek around seventy hours or more—measurements that are complicated by the fact that what constitutes work and who is considered a worker aren't totally clear.[9] Before workers fought for the eight-hour workday, which remains a theoretical standard, the struggles for the ten-hour work day carried on, with the first enforceable law written in 1874.[10]

It wasn't some sudden concern for well-being or goodwill from people profiting off the labor of others that got the eight-hour work day. It was workers fighting for improved conditions over decades. And still, efforts to stop overwork weren't extended to everyone. As labor journalist and author of *Fight Like Hell: The Untold History of American Labor,* Kim Kelly wrote for *Teen Vogue*: "Following Emancipation, Black people were a major part of the labor movement but were still limited in their job prospects due to racism and the violence of white supremacy." White Americans "frequently clashed with Black workers—who remained excluded from union membership until well into the 20th century—and immigrant workers, particularly those who were Chinese."[11]

Some reports suggest that back in 1908, a mill in New England put a five-day workweek into place to accommodate Jewish workers who observed the Sabbath.[12] Without the federal government doing much to ensure limited work hours, workers continued striking and fighting. In 1902, the United Mine Workers of America went on strike for an eight-hour workday and won.[13] Around 1912, the eight-hour workday was part of Teddy Roosevelt's presidential campaign platform, along with a minimum wage for women and a social security system.[14] In the 1920s, Henry Ford put a five-day workweek in place at Ford Motor Company—at least in part to increase worker productivity.[15] Then in 1938, the Fair Labor Standards Act was passed, limiting workweeks to forty-four hours, banning child labor, and setting an hourly minimum wage.[16] By 1940, Congress revised the Fair Labor Standards Act to limit workweeks to forty hours a week.[17]

So that brings us to now: eight-hour workdays, five-day workweeks for all! Except that wasn't the case then and isn't so now. The point is, how work is structured didn't fall from the sky and suddenly materialize in factories and office buildings with flickery lighting and Slack channels. Workers have consistently fought for work to dominate less of their lives throughout history. "Working hard" being seen as a virtue has been a persistent fixture of overwork, too, creating the fertile ground for ambition to sink its roots into the work we do *and* how that work relates to sense of self. Some research connects that back to the Protestant work ethic, or the idea that "constant labor and diligent work" are the tickets to attaining grace and salvation.[18]

Then, there's unpaid work: time spent job hunting and applying and performing unseen labor like commuting and the compounding stress of toggling between multiple work schedules, parenting or caregiving, and school, or otherwise coordinating how you're going to get yourself into a place where you can work. Sometimes, just enduring a hostile work environment becomes a job in and of itself. River, a thirty-one-year-old who worked in tech, told me about a breakdown in winter 2020 "that really I can only describe as a complete inability to go forward in the same way I had been." Working in customer service for an online management software platform, River had been, for years, "scraping by on not enough sleep, not enough food, not enough time with my partner or family, and critically, not enough money, and the pandemic only intensified all of that."

For a while, his job was bearable, River said, with nice coworkers, a casual atmosphere, and plenty of activities for bonding. Then, there appeared to be a mass exodus. People were burning out and leaving, seeking new jobs or getting better offers. The commute—ninety minutes each way, because River lives in a city where only the outer reaches were affordable—was becoming unbearable. One week before River's performance review, where he'd planned to make a case for a salary increase, his whole department was reorganized, reducing a team of six people to just River and one junior team member. The assumption was whatever work didn't get finished during the workday would mean workers came in early or stayed late with no paid overtime. River and the junior team member "worked ourselves to the bone," he said, trying to keep up with customer queries and calls. He'd go to the restroom and cry, get water to prevent going hoarse, and then hop back on Zoom. When the pandemic hit and employees were sent home, River was relieved not to have to commute and get a few more hours of sleep. "I was butter scraped over too much bread," he said. "I was just the thinnest version of myself that could possibly keep stringing things along."

On top of that, management became openly hostile, according to River. "As soon as I came out as trans, my manager got so cold towards me," River said. As soon as his pronouns changed, River's boss stopped using pronouns for him altogether. Suddenly, River was always "in trouble" for something, he said. The pandemic and increased workload took a toxic work environment and dumped it into a pressure cooker. "I stopped showering regularly. I stopped cooking. I was eating basically nothing that couldn't be microwaved from frozen. I was barely scraping by at work," he told me. His therapist suggested he request FMLA (Family and Medical Leave) time to take a break from an obviously worsening work situation, but he felt guilty abandoning his only coworker. "I remember telling my manager shortly before I needed to take medical leave that I felt like I was broken as a human being," River said. "And her response was, 'How can I get you to focus 110 percent on work today?'" More work: that was the answer to overwork and what felt like abuse at work.

Not long after, his workplace handed him a new slate of responsibilities, with no additional resources to tackle the additional work. At that point, River, who is autistic, had "an absolutely shredding autistic meltdown, and wound up in my closet heaving sobs and flapping my hands and hyperventilating," he told me. When his employer implemented a Performance Improvement Plan, describing how River needed to be more positive on Slack, more responsive after hours, and essentially do *more*, he told them he felt stretched too thin to keep up. The decision to leave the job was necessary but terrifying. They hadn't paid River enough for him to have significant savings, and he didn't have a backup plan. "I really felt like I was just hopping out of the frying pan and hoping I didn't land in the flames," he added.

"Overwork—in America, and at least a couple other countries—is really the only way of proving you have ambition," Nat Baldino, a policy analyst on the Education, Labor, and Worker Justice team at the Center for Law and Social Policy, told me. In their own career, Baldino started out as a doctoral student in gender studies, where they were a full-time graduate student working full-time as a professor (without being allowed to call themselves a professor) and, at the same time, working at a coffee shop. He'd worked in service or blue-collar jobs since he was fifteen or sixteen and started noting how *trapped* everyone he worked with was. "No matter how hard I was working, it still wasn't enough to make ends meet," Baldino said. They were severely overworked, with workers expected to be two to three employees instead of a single person, they said. That's what made them want to unionize their workplace. But before they were set to turn in their union election cards, the pandemic hit, and lots of staff, including Baldino and other members of the bargaining unit, were laid off.

Baldino told me in one of our first conversations that work-places are a microcosm of our society. "The structures that we exist in replicate the structures of society," Baldino said. "Of course, if we're a country founded on white supremacy, and that means we only want some people to be able to be desig-nated as valuable, then we're going to create a work structure that reinforces that." Work does not stay at work—sometimes literally but also in how it reinforces and replicates oppressive structures that depend on isolation, focus on individual ac-complishment, and the idea that you can "pay your dues" into a better life. The historical point here, Baldino said, is that this is by design: US labor is racist and gendered and built on America's history of slavery. Even groundbreaking legislation like the New Deal illustrates this. The New Deal, which in-cluded the Social Security Act, the National Industrial Re-covery Act, and the Fair Labor Standards Act, left domestic workers and farmworkers, many of whom were Black work-ers, out of Social Security and minimum wage laws, continu-ing the same exploitative patterns of low wages, no benefits, and no job security seen today.[19] The country was founded on racial capitalism and labor, and modern workplaces still repli-cate that. Ambition functions as a characteristic necessary to "make it to the top."

Ideal Workers and Less Than Ideal Work

One term I kept seeing, the *ideal worker*, felt relevant, mostly because the current definition doesn't seem far off from the history of overworking that's been structurally in place for centuries. Some research refers to the "ideal worker" archetype as one that stipulates workers should "be

completely devoted to their jobs,"[20] or a worker "who is totally committed to, and always available for" work.[21] Ideal
workers don't oversleep and are never too sick to pull out
all the stops to help a team member. They do not resent
unpaid hours on the weekends because they are passionate
about the work. They do not have children or partners or
family members or pets or priorities beyond those notable
in a performance review.

You might have seen the ideal worker pop up in job de-
scriptions, too: there's at least one viral example of a doctorate being required for a position paying sixteen to eighteen
dollars per hour.[22] "Multi-tasking is a LIFESAVER!" in-
structed a job posting for a childcare worker in Indiana,
which also indicated applicants must be "100% flexible."
"Beating self-set deadlines" popped up on a social media strategist listing in Washington. "Team player/flexible/
adaptable to frequent change" *and* "positive energy, vibrant,
professional, and unflappable" appeared in a job description
for an assistant position in Chicago, two lists that sound
more like you just took a personality quiz than applied
for a job.

Largely, work treats life the same way we treat our neighbor who wants to describe their bout of food poisoning—
we'd really rather not know much about that. When people
started working remotely in droves in 2020, the ideal worker
stepped out of cubicles and into homes. There was an in-
flux of articles on making homes look professional: artfully
arranged bookshelves in the background, no dogs barking
or toddlers waving, no evidence one was working from bed
even if it was more comfortable or there was no room for a
desk, no signs of life. (Raise your hand if your boss said at

least once that increased workloads shouldn't matter since everyone was at home with "nothing else to do.")

The ideal worker myth is still all over overwork. Ideal workers are *ambitious,* and it's evident how many people that definition leaves out by default. Disabled or chronically ill people, who can't perform the ungodly work hours associated with striving, are at an automatic disadvantage. Black workers receive more scrutiny from bosses than white peers, leading to worse performance reviews and lower wages[23]— and the whole swath of metrics on which "professionalism" is based is rooted in racism and classism. Part-time or contract work is another crack in the ideal worker armor, because these workers do not have the ability or opportunity to be constantly available or to put the job ahead of themselves so "employers stigmatize and penalize workers who work part-time."[24] There are a million unspoken rules of jobs and hiring, like knowing how to network, how to explain gaps in a résumé or being laid off, and how to market yourself, which we're supposed to learn through osmosis or through a mentor that not everyone has. Think about panic-purchasing a pantsuit you couldn't afford for your first "real" job interview. Or about assessments like "strong handshake" or "high energy." Wait, you mean you took those benefit package days off to chaperone your child's school trip or for your own health? Hah, someone *really* devoted would've used those days to catch up on work.

Sadé Dozan, thirty-four, was the director of a development department, where she was working forty to fifty hours a week. She worked up until the day she gave birth to her daughter, after negotiating her paid leave up to four months. The workplace culture was very much to "prioritize work over all," according to Sadé. "I think society has just taught us that if you have a good career and you're really good at your job, then you'll be successful," she explained. She *wants* to do good, and that means showing up and saying yes to everything. But once she was back from leave, she remembers being on the elevator and thinking: *I don't know if I can do this anymore.*

She took a reduced title, moving from director to grant writer in an attempt to balance caring for her daughter, since her husband was working too, and her mother supported them with childcare when she could. Then, as Sadé dropped her daughter off with her mother, Sadé's mom had a heart attack while holding the baby in her arms. That scene is burned in Sadé's brain. It also—unbeknownst to her at the time—would entirely shift her career trajectory.

At the hospital, where Sadé's mom was in an induced coma, she said her supervisor called and explained they knew her mother was in the hospital but pointed out a report was due and asked if she could finish it. "What am I supposed to say? No?" Sadé asked. She needed the money. The next day, she clarified that her mother had actually had a heart attack and asked if there was any way she could take leave. But according to Sadé, her employer didn't allow her additional leave—Sadé noted they legally didn't have to—because she had expended it all with her child's birth. As if life, and the need for leave, only happens in moments scrounged from out-of-office messages and planned absences from work with documentation to prove one *needs* to be off. No matter what, work is the part we're supposed to handle first.

Now, Sadé works for Caring Across Generations, a national campaign of family caregivers, care workers, people with disabilities, and aging adults working to make care more accessible, affordable, and equitable. In her current role, needing time to care isn't a mark against her; it's part of her work. "We run into this cycle of telling ourselves that hustle culture, overwork, making it work is just the norm, and it's not and it shouldn't be," Sadé said. She has a couple of co-occurring conditions—rheumatoid arthritis and severe general anxiety disorder—and there are days when her knees or arms hurt so much that she can't pick her daughter up or run around playing the way she normally would, and work is really hard. She doesn't know how many work years she has left. "And what I think about is her having to take care of me at fifty-two," she explained of her toddler daughter. "Is she gonna be right out of college trying to navigate the workforce and also provide care for me?"

In this way, overwork is wired into systems. While naming what would help—an extension of the tax credit and not having to pay for a care worker out of her own pocket—Sadé also mentions flexible leave policies as critical. In her prior job, she was hustling to supplement her income in order to build a buffer of savings in case she couldn't take leave twice in a year. "The nightmare that I think a lot of parents and caregivers face is being one check short, right?" she added. "And I think part of the reason why I work the way I work [is] so that I'm not ever one check short and even still, it could happen to me."

The fact that success at work is, by design, supposed to only encourage those who can make work the centerpiece of their life plays out in other ways, too. While Britney didn't strive to be at the top of her classes in school, she was very ambitious academically—in part because of her personality and in part because of her disability, she told me. She spent most of her school years learning by listening, and because of that, she put tons of energy into schoolwork and measured her own success by academic success for a long time. Later, in work, Britney didn't want anyone to find reasons to fault her. "I already felt like I kind of had a fault with my disability, and it's, like, hey, you already took a chance on me to hire me," she told me. "I don't want to give you another reason to not like me or to not like my work." She described feeling that whatever experience an employer had with her, they'd project onto other disabled applicants in the future, especially if the workplace hadn't had disabled workers on staff previously. "I just felt a lot of pressure of being like: you have to be the best in all the different ways—interactions with customers, interactions with management, clocking in," she continued. "Everything needs to be right, because if you mess it up, you might mess it up for a lot of other people." It'd be inaccurate to call this a systemic failure. Work as goodness, overwork as ideal, and disparities in who gets "good jobs" to begin with are largely functioning exactly the way the systems were designed.

It was Jessica, who works full-time in communications and digital strategy, who pointed out that even the structure of advancing at work, scaling up or being ambitious, follows this trajectory. Especially in the corporate space, Jessica said, it's a trap that "people are always being pushed to go after the next title, go after the next level of achievement." It pushes people onto a leadership or supervisory track—even if they aren't actually a great fit for managing people. Jessica said her own unhealthy relationship with work started when she entered a workplace that was understaffed. Initially, she was enjoying the work and "raising my hand to do a lot of things." The tipping point occurred during the start of the pandemic, when she ended up serving as the acting head of her department. "And that was really just when things started to snowball," she told me. She wouldn't leave her work phone out of sight, in case something happened. She argued with herself about whether she could spare ten minutes to make a sandwich for lunch; she wasn't eating regularly. After a year acting as department head, she learned she wasn't being considered to hold the position permanently and decided that she needed to channel her ambition toward what she found to be personally fulfilling. "And the bottom line was, I just couldn't sacrifice my well-being in pursuit of success, not to the extent that I had been," Jessica said. "So it just forced me to just kind of think about things beyond professional success."

Can't Stand Together on a Ladder

Because the whole conception of professional success is so limiting, reaching up from wherever you are becomes a given. Why would a student aim for a B if an A is possible? If we're not striving, does that mean we're settling? It calls to mind something Baldino, our labor expert, brought up with regard to the language of overwork, an example most of us have heard at some point: climbing the ladder. We think of the workforce and careers as being ladders in which we climb over people; there's someone we need to be ahead of in order to get wherever we're going. That framing, he explained, underscores how individualistic and isolating overwork really is. "People can't really stand next to each other on a ladder,"

Baldino said, and that's on purpose. We're supposed to stop for nothing.

That persisted even throughout the pandemic. Sawyer, a thirty-year-old, worked for a satellite television provider. He'd start at 7:10 a.m. and routinely would be out until 10 p.m., performing in-home service. People constantly wanted to shake hands at the door and laughed off precautions even as Sawyer entered their homes, which he described as "not being taken seriously when we're trying to protect ourselves and our family that we have to go back home to. On top of that, we're working sixty-, seventy-hour weeks," he added. "You just can't find time to spend with your family and enjoy that time. You're just trying to rest up until it starts again in the next couple of days." The company, whose motto is "keep up the good work," was overbooked on customer work orders, so it started doing forced overtime: if an employee didn't show up, they'd either have to take their limited PTO, or it was labeled a "no call, no show"—which led to disciplinary action.

Especially because it was blue-collar work, Sawyer said, there was zero focus on addressing mental health concerns, which he believed came from overworking. "The whole grind mind-set thing is not what humans were built to do," he told me. "Everyone's seen CEO pay or executive pay go through the roof while regular wages have stayed stagnant," he added. None of the issues—from understaffing to overwork's impact on mental health—were addressed by management, even when they should be. "They should be the ones that are seeing their employees dealing with these issues and trying to address them," he said. "But it's always just, 'Keep working. Keep it up. You're doing great. We're so proud of you.'" And as Sawyer pointed out, it's hard to step away from that. Most people can't take time off to go search for a job that'd be better for them. It keeps people stuck—because there's never enough time and never enough work to buy back your time.

Part of what ambitious overwork is supposed to provide us is the chance to make meaning through work. If we work long enough and hard enough and enthusiastically enough, we'll feel fulfilled, the mentality goes. Despite how untrue this is, that mentality persists and, it turns out, is another way individualism is the horse ambition rides in on. For as long as I've been working, my approach was to say yes to everything, like that would protect me—including not daring to question a boss when he asked me to cart a printer around in the backseat of my car, because who doesn't have spontaneous printing needs, really? Of course, I didn't recognize burnout even as it singed me. That would require noticing I was fanning the flames with the thing I thought would bring relief: work.

"Burnout is defined by work," Dr. Jessi Gold, director of Wellness, Engagement and Outreach in the Department of Psychiatry at Washington University School of Medicine, told me. What that means, Gold said, is that burnout by definition occurs in the workplace. It's associated with emotional exhaustion, depersonalization, and, ironically, reduced sense of personal accomplishment, which Gold described as not meeting your goals and not feeling personally good about it. We're actually most likely to notice the last one—reduced personal accomplishment—Gold said, because it's easy to blow off everything else with "work is supposed to make me tired" or "I just had a bad day." But because there's so much value placed on getting things done through work, it's not until work-created burnout starts interfering with work that some of us flag it as a problem. Then it comes full circle.

"If one finds self-fulfillment in one's occupation, then expectations to live up to ideal worker norms may seem less self-estranging," wrote Cech in *The Trouble with Passion*. Cech's work noted that the "neoliberal norms of self-sufficiency [has] led to an increased emphasis on life trajectories driven by personal choice rather than collective or communal priorities."[25] If our meaning as well as our capacity to live is situated in work, we'll go out of our way to ensure we're living up to our "full potential"—which is, in turn, characterized by what we produce, not who we are. The emphasis on work as our most significant outlet for meaning makes those one and the same.

Overwork is not an individual problem. In fact, the state of overwork is *so* not an individual problem that Baldino paused midconversation to tell me that when, during my interview with them, I said the word *individualism* in reference to the misguided belief that "working too much" is everyone's personal choice. Baldino talked about isolation and collectivity, and they were right. That distinction matters. Work isn't just individualized; it's isolated. And that's what makes overwork an accepted norm.

Baldino told me one of the things individual ambition and overwork can rob us of is our ability to imagine. When people are in the grind, when they are so overworked and underpaid, "it becomes an isolating tactic—[it] keeps us from being able to imagine otherwise, to be able to imagine that something else is possible," they said. "When we think about ambition and individualism, and we play the opposites game,

I think that the opposite of ambition might actually not be rest, but might be collectivity," he said, "and imagination of the ability to take a breath and think of how things can be different."

Someone asked me recently to describe myself outside of work—a question that, a few years ago, would've launched one thousand identity crisis ships. But what came to mind were the parts of my life I squished in around all the gold stars I was striving for: the phone calls I missed because I was on a deadline; the relationships I'd let fall by the wayside because I was overwhelmed; the fact that my writing became less curious and more output driven. And if work is all about self-expression, I'd like to imagine myself beyond work. Maybe, I thought, that means a new kind of ambition. But first, that means sometimes the old one has to shatter.

8: When Gold Stars Shatter

"It fills a void."

"It proves that I'm worthy."

"It is how I get through."

That's how people described their ambition to me. I'd tell you that ambition is my coping strategy, the quality that didn't make me shiny but, rather, the one that got me through. When stressed, I grabbed for more work—more deadlines, more tasks pulled off my colleague's plate onto my own, more blocks of time crossed off for meetings I couldn't remember the purpose of—as a means of "putting my anxiety to good use," I'd joke, because I didn't know what else to say. The fact that my mind was in a seemingly ever-present state of fight-or-flight—and, frankly, felt most inclined to try to fight *itself*—wasn't a hindrance to my ambition; it was an asset. The more anxious I became, the more ambitious I was.

In retrospect, this pattern of hyperambition was a signal that I wasn't doing well, but ambition helped me hide my struggles. "I think I might be depressed?" I half asked the nurse at the doctor's office after a particularly bad couple weeks of searing stomach pain. The colonoscopy and upper scope offered more questions than answers. I was begging for Zofran (a medication that prevents nausea and vomiting) just to be able to leave the house. Every time my GI tract flared, my patchwork solution was to do as much work as possible from the bathroom, which is so decidedly unglamorous, it doesn't even have the valor of "she's so committed to her work." No one would compliment my dedication or passion for that one. They would silently wish I'd quit talking about bathrooms and send up a prayer that I consistently wash my hands.

But again, it was technically working. So what was the problem here?

Are you still able to work? the nurse asked.

Yes.

And still getting dressed.

My shirt is ironed. I show up on time. I smile when I'm supposed to smile; email when I am supposed to email.

So you still have goals; you're clearly ambitious, she said, answering her own half question. She was writing something down before I even answered, and I didn't realize until later that it was the first time I'd heard "ambitious" in a doctor's office being used as a compliment.

This isn't a unique story. Most of us have been on the receiving end of a well-intentioned pep talk, a quip about how capable we are, or the assumption that we're just fine when we aren't. And within much of the framing that floats around how-tos or Instagram infographics, "cope" is doing a lot of work here: how to cope with overwork, how to cope with failure, how to cope with perfectionism.

"Perfectionism is kind of like ambition gone wrong, in a sense," said Anishka Jean, a first-year doctoral student at

West Virginia University, whose research interests involve understanding risk factors that maintain anxiety disorders, including perfectionism. She thinks of ambition as an inverted U-curve: too little ambition isn't necessarily good because it's important to stay motivated for things we care about; too much ambition could potentially be harmful and lead to practices that perpetuate perfectionism. I have a hard time figuring out the difference between striving that's healthy, I told her, and full-on perfectionism. If there is a line, I keep stumbling over it. In her opinion, if it's about wanting to challenge yourself and be the best you can be, striving or ambition can operate in a "healthy, adaptive way. If it starts to become harmful to your own well-being—if it's impacting your self-worth, or your value as a person, or if it's preventing you from wanting to try things because you're afraid that you're not going to be good enough, I would say that's where the line crosses into the harmful territory," she added. That "harmful territory" is where I've set up camp, leaving my metaphorical lunch bag open to be slashed apart by a hungry family of bears.

But what made me curious is that while clearly the impacts of overstriving are personal, I wondered how they are shaped by all that exists beyond us. Over the past fifty years, researchers on perfectionism wrote, communal interest and civic responsibility were swapped for self-interest and competition in a "supposedly free and open marketplace."[1] That means that not only are there more ways we can be measured (and more we can be ambitious about), but outperforming others is a measurement of value, of worth. From the 1980s onward, researchers explained, neoliberal government—including Ronald Reagan and Margaret Thatcher, they note in an article about the research—emphasized "competitive individualism,"[2] which feeds the idea of a self that can be perfected. To be clear, perfectionism and ambition aren't inherently the same thing, but because of the overlap of individual achievement, they connect to each other. And sometimes, when we're striving, we exist in an environment where it feels almost impossible to know when to stop.

Beyond Burnout

Mikey phrased it best: "We hold ambition and constantly striving higher as something that you need to do to have a good life," she explained. "I think it's a justification and also a way to placate us when we're struggling with the ways that society keeps us apart, keeps us isolated, keeps us struggling, and keeps us feeling dissatisfied." And the things that do bring fulfillment, including connection, love, and bonding, are really hard to do and to have in the way our world is currently structured, she added. I nodded in agreement.

Society has to keep us going somehow, Mikey continued, "and the way to do that is by promoting this idea that more money, more accolades . . . more travel . . . more blah, blah, blah—these are the things that are going to give us the fulfillment." Because that's what we're looking for. We pursue this through ambition because we want to be fulfilled. It is, of course, somewhere between a lie and a warped marketing strategy about what a "good life" means to begin with. "I got plenty of writing awards when I was younger; still hated myself. I graduated undergrad with plenty of accolades; still hated myself. I got into grad school—Ivy League first round, top ten public health programs—still hated myself," Mikey told me. "And now I'm taking a break from school, reevaluating all the things that I have believed in for most of my life, and now I'm hating myself less."

I want to plaster everything you just said on a billboard, I told her. When I look at myself, it's a lot of: Where is your own ambition coming from? And the answer is: self-loathing and trying to earn a self that I could tolerate. Writing it down now, it feels a bit like I stumbled out of the confessional and into a crowded room, handing over a secret everyone would've been more comfortable I keep to myself. But that was perhaps the worst slow-burn realization: that self-loathing could actually be *productive*. I internalized the belief that the more anxious I was, the faster I'd work. The worse I felt about myself, the harder I'd strive to make my work good. I strove, really, as a means of separating from myself.

The worst of it is that I couldn't define, exactly, what I loathed—it wasn't like I had a bad habit that bugged me. I came to despise the fact that I wasn't a better listener, a better friend, and a better *person*. I panicked over the fact that my past is paint-splattered with mistakes I should've known better than to make. I hated that I easily got my feelings hurt, desired the reassurance of loved ones, and was needy where I should've been independent. Whatever the flaw, I should've been better, and I resented that I couldn't quite figure out how to be. So I was proving myself to everyone, but I was also trying to prove myself to *me*. It's striking how, to me, "be better" felt so much like "be more."

People look at Mikey and wonder how she's done everything she has in a relatively few years on Earth. Her life has been lived at light speed. Mikey was basically raised by her older sister and said the two have always "pushed through things." She experienced a traumatic event in high school and should've taken a break before college but didn't. She was applying for PhD programs her senior year of undergrad. Now she's the youngest person in her PhD cohort, and one of two who didn't go in with a master's. She got married at twenty-one. Mikey is also a fat liberationist who does speaking engagements and writes, focusing on analyses of science, public health, and culture through the lens of fatness and Blackness.

If she were a different person, maybe doing all this—and doing it all so early—would give her some pride, she said. But she has no sense of how to slow down. She's been anxious about being poor, about not being able to support her family, her entire life. "I've been worried about bills and credit cards and things like that since I was like four, for as long as I could remember," she told me. "I have never not worried about poverty and never not worried about things that a lot of people just never have to think about."

A 2017 piece in *The Atlantic* by Tanya Paperny stated that despite there being virtually no empirical research on links between trauma and overwork, a number of researchers and clinicians "believe the connection between trauma and overwork is likely. Some believe coping with trauma is at the very heart of a work addiction."[3] If work equals worth, then it makes sense that achievement feels like it equals stability or safety.

In a piece for Bustle, Eve Ettinger expertly detailed whether burnout could be a trauma response, writing that they asked sources whether there was any overlap between complex PTSD symptoms and their own experiences with burnout. "If their burnout was a response to trauma, perhaps they would have approached their recoveries differently,"

Ettinger wrote, explaining that mental health benefits at work are unlikely to fix the issue, since it dumps responsibility of healing burnout on the individual.[4] When I called Ettinger, a writer and educator, to ask about the piece, they added that burnout isn't caused by trauma, but the way we are experiencing burnout is a trauma response.

The span between the quote-unquote middle class and the 1 percent has never been this intense, Ettinger said, and it's life or death: the stakes are high, work is tied to health care, and work isn't able to sustain us. "Of course your body is going to go into that primal fight-or-flight, adrenaline spike response," they explained. "We are physiologically incapable of living this way." When we think of burnout, the association is typically white and privileged, and Ettinger said that it's only recently that burnout has started to impact the leisure class, and so it's become a conversation. Because the casual use of burnout has been so reinforced, Ettinger added, it's a distraction technique: self-care and finding the right therapist might be personally important, but as Ettinger stated, "it becomes an individual solution, which essentially divides us from each other." Instead, Ettinger said we need to organize; we need to start treating our elected officials as if they are accountable to us—because they are supposed to be. The solutions lie in tackling the source.

When I asked Gold whether she thought overwork could be a trauma response, she said "for sure." "For the most part, people aren't talking about grief or trauma in the workplace," she explained. "And so, it's sort of like the only thing that matters in the workplace is work, which has its own problems." The workplace creates an opportunity to put our heads down and attempt to hustle through our grief. In this case, the trauma response is avoidance, Gold said. There's so much going on in your body feelings-wise or physically, and your mind decides to take a break, Gold explained, hence the heightened focus on something like work. "You're attempting to protect yourself in so many ways by avoiding emotions and focusing solely on productivity and work. A lot of it is unconscious and prevents you from processing the trauma, but by doing so, you can keep going. Often, it can feel like if you think about or deal with trauma you will simply fall apart, so you basically are protecting yourself by working," she added. This can backfire, Gold said, because one can only push things down for so long before something triggers them, or enough happens that they emerge anyway—like attempting to push a beach ball underwater, she explained. And sometimes, when we avoid processing what we were avoiding initially, Gold told me, when we finally do, it can feel bigger and more life-interfering.

My entire subconscious ideology had been informed by earning my way to goodness and safety via pushing *through*, something I expected of no one but myself. Traumatic event in childhood? I practically puffed up with pride when a neighbor told me I was composed, I was brave. Sick and met the deadline anyway? I relished being "so committed." Grief, sadness, loneliness—I could turn them into something good if I funneled those feelings into a project. And you know, it always felt good. Until it didn't anymore.

Breaking Points

For Mikey, the pressure was vivid and all-encompassing and started early. And thinking of that, she flagged that the language of ambition as resilience almost presents ambition as a reward—because you're ambitious now you'll endure. When she was a kid going to school, experiencing sexual harassment because of the way her body developed, Mikey said people would tell her, "'You're smarter than them. You have bigger dreams. You're going to be fine.' And it's, like, what does any of that have to do with the fact that I'm not safe at home? I'm not safe at school," she continued. "What does that compensate for? Nothing."

Mikey told me that she's been passively and actively suicidal for nearly every year of her life since she was eleven, and if she doesn't feel she's doing well professionally and academically, there's an increased chance she's going to feel suicidal or predisposed to self-harm as punishment. Only in the past year, she said, has that relationship had less of an impact on her—and that's only because she reached a "breaking point."

In 2020, Mikey's brother-in-law was diagnosed with a brain infection. He was in his last semester of his undergraduate degree and was in the midst of applying to law schools. By 2021, it became evident time was running out. Mikey got ordained online and officiated the marriage of her brother-in-law and her sister a month before he died at age thirty-one. He'd died, Mikey said, without having done the stuff he'd truly wanted, like going back to Haiti, where he'd been born and raised until he was ten, or going on a trip with his wife. Instead, he'd pursued being a lawyer and not just because he wanted to help immigrant people with citizenship problems, Mikey clarified. He did. But he also wanted to never struggle again.

As they planned the funeral, Mikey and her sister both got COVID and were sick and sitting on the floor of the bedroom they'd grown up in together. "And I was just, like, I don't want to waste any more of my life doing things that I'm not happy about doing," Mikey recounted. "And she was, like, 'me either.'" Mikey emailed her school and told them she was taking leave. In a way, it was a rejection of the ambition-as-making-it-through she'd known her entire life.

That, coupled with her relationship with her husband, proved healing. Mikey had never had anyone say anything nice to her unless it corresponded with doing something for them—either the "visual clout" of being next to her as a marginalized person, she said, or literal tasks and accomplishments. But her husband believes she deserves a good life, not because of ambition but outside of it, regardless. "Even if I'm not being the gold star that I've gotten used to being throughout my life," she told me. "I don't have to be the gold star because he makes me feel that way."

The line feels narrow: work, achievement, and the very act of dreaming have been described as healing for some people, that their work or motivation to achieve something actually saved them in some way. Sometimes those lines crisscross, and the striving and effort that got us where we are becomes the very threat dragging us backward or down to the floor. Sam, a thirty-nine-year-old chef who lives in the South, called me on the way to the airport for extensive work travel and described herself as an overachiever—someone who wants to do it all, do it well, and do it on her terms. She grew up with the expectation of being a doctor or a lawyer and at one point even went back to business school after dropping out of medical school. "I say this a lot about the kids of immigrants—our parents didn't come halfway around the world to show off their B game. They came for their A game. They came for everything," Sam told me. Her dad, at eighty-one, worked full-time until the end of 2021. "That always led to, like, I don't want to let them down. And part of that meant that I was ascribing my worth to their expectations, which did not align with what I wanted for my life," she added.

After launching a pop-up food tent in 2016, Sam was, for all accounts, completely successful. But slowly things started to compound. Sam had not come to terms with trauma from her college years, and when her culinary career took off, she said, "It just gave me something else to jump into without processing." It was her ambition. It was also her way to hang on.

Then the pandemic zapped her entire calendar, scrubbing away routine fourteen-hour workdays and calls at 3 a.m. because that was the only time to squeeze them in. "I was to the point where I could just stare at a wall and I would get stressed out," explained Sam. She had family members ill from COVID. Her uncle died overseas from the Delta variant within eight hours. A close family friend died shortly after from progressive dementia; her friend's husband died within months of that. It was a cascade of loss. Unlike before, when Sam's ambition kept her creating projects, making connections, and establishing the next best chapter of her life, this crisis was different. She couldn't use ambition to cope. At least, not in the way she had before. "It didn't help them in their moment of need," she said. "What helped them was peace."

Instead of avoiding processing by leaping into the next project, Sam got ambitious about, well, peace. She started therapy and began coming to terms with her trauma. She mourned the all-hands-on-deck, everyone's-emergency-contact, always-hustling version of herself that she knew was not coming back. "So I mourned for a couple days. I mourned my youth. I mourned my innocence. I mourned everything," she told me.

That change in identity—changing as circumstances change, rather than clinging to a fixed goal that no longer feels true—can feel like racing a ghost of yourself. My ghost self, my former self, was faster and sharper and willing to do anything; she said yes to everything and pleased everyone; she's who I see in the mirror sometimes when I say *no, I can't*, or *no, I won't*, or when I wonder what happened to the girl who would prove herself a million times over to an audience of no one, and smile while she was doing it. I mourned her and didn't know how to stop striving to be her, all at once. But I noticed that ambition was not making me feel safe for as long, like my stamina was depleting faster. Before, the fuel of pouring myself into something would have me floating for days, tickled that I'd published a piece, kept up my routine of trying to learn to run every day (emphasis on *trying*), or giddy with anticipation of the next big idea to work toward. The stakes of everything felt higher, while I ran round and round, wondering why it felt like striving was making me exhausted instead of inspired.

Into Pieces

Unbeknownst to me, my gut was churning—literally—with that question. The sicker I got, the more disruptive to my daily life my gut became, and no one knew why. (Spoiler: they still don't, and arguing with health insurance is my third-favorite hobby behind baking coffee cake every week-end.) My body wasn't holding a charge, which meant my brain felt it needed to hang onto *everything*. Details that mattered to no one but me. All perceived slights. A worst-case scenario for every occasion. With the same zeal with which I had studied yet flunked math, practiced ballet, and worked as a young adult, my mind started attaching to details with the attention of a forensic scientist. I fixated on terrible things I was convinced I'd said on the phone, even while there was no evidence I'd said those things or thought them. I replayed failures, missteps, or mistakes I'd made when I was younger, as if I could snap back in time and solve them if I just analyzed the postgame footage enough. I tried to slow my mind down, to "trust my gut"—but my gut was telling me that everything was wrong. Whereas before, I would've worked through it—literally—it seeped into my work, too. *Did I trust myself enough to say something, to stand up for myself, let alone to pitch a piece or talk in a meeting? Did I overreact? Am I really sure? Have I ever been sure, in my whole life, of anything?* I kept getting a vibe of "no."

I was supposed to have hit peak ambition. My first book was coming out. I had, by the sheer luck of something holy, managed to hang on to employment through the pandemic. I couldn't take this for granted; I couldn't stop now. I patched myself together with yeses: sure, I could do that; yes, I'll write that piece; yeah, I totally have time to help. The more I held myself together with work, the less time I had to crumble.

Simultaneously, I was attempting to proceed with a harassment case that had derailed my life plans as I would've recounted them on single-spaced lines of a résumé or a

Twitter bio and—whether I knew it or not at the time—how I thought of my own self-worth. I was down a bullet point of accomplishment and with that came a gap in my once-upon-a-time five-year plan, my sense of safety, and, worst of all, how I thought about myself. Recounting one set of memories I didn't actually want to recall seemed to unearth all the others my brain had promised I'd forget if I could outwork them. I hadn't known how much I was running from until they all caught me. But so much started coming back in flashes not even ambition could dim them.

I bumbled over legal terminology I didn't understand and couldn't pronounce, feeling like I was a college freshman tripping through words like *atrabilious* when asked to read aloud. Even as I worked on writing projects, I was scouring my email inbox and my memory, cross-checking my life like I was out to prove something had happened, while center stage in my day-to-day, I pretended nothing had. The worse my physical and mental health got, the harder I worked. I couldn't explain what was bothering me to friends, but I could change the subject. I couldn't fix every mistake I'd ever made, but I could outdo myself at my job. I didn't think I could repair habits like absentmindedly pulling my hair out while rereading the same sentence four times looking for mistakes, but I could set a new goal.

All the scouring for what I'd forgotten—ambitious in my pursuit of proving it—gave way to another set of memories I promised myself I wouldn't go over during flashes of anxiety or late at night or when I felt I'd disappointed someone anew. I saw myself, maybe in my late teens or early twenties, in the corner of a kitchen I'd only been in once, with someone's mom's cookie jar on the counter, quietly pleading with this person I loved to not hurt himself, as he reminded me that, if he did, it'd be all my fault. My mind flashed back again to another "please don't," in a car where someone locked the doors and grabbed me—my chest, the button on the stretch jeans from American Eagle I'd felt so fancy in, the back of my neck—as I leaned hard against the car door. I screamed, for the first time I could recall, shrill and insistent. And then a dozen little blips, flashing to childhood and all the situations my ten-year-old hands couldn't put back together again, to being sixteen and the doctor prescribing antidepressants I was too scared to take, to all the ways I've failed and the line around the block of people I've let down and all the things I can't control and—

And with the same energy level of someone ordering a pizza that only half-sounded good, I picked up the phone and called a therapist's help line. I needed a stranger, someone guaranteed not to tell me they knew I could do it when I felt I couldn't; someone I didn't have to fear letting down by falling apart. My coping mechanism—work—had broken down when I needed something to carry me, and as I recounted the strain of my mind's uncontrollable rumination, hypervigilance, and obsession, it came out to a stranger on the phone as, "I don't think I'm ambitious anymore."

It's OK if you rolled your eyes there. It reads as superficial, which is why my more ambitious self was tempted to leave this out, to make it more palatable. But what I meant was: I was sinking, and the grabbable things weren't grabbable anymore. My mind, once obsessed with *proving it,* was splintered into a cluster of shards that sliced me at every turn—whether I could trust my own memory, whether I could believe myself. My body, once semicontent to work at desks all day and exercise nonstop at night, was giving out. What I thought was the only good thing about me was giving up on me. Without that, what was I good for anyway?

Not long after, I recall telling a therapist about this moment. Everything wrong in the world and here I was, so fragile and selfish, sad about ambition. Sad because I was pretty sure I could purchase self-worth for the off-the-rack cost of a gold star, being told I was good at work or had tried hard or had, lord help me, gone above and beyond. "Have you ever thought," the therapist asked me, "that you believed all that striving would keep you safe?"

Every teetery accomplishment block stacked on top of the next is taken as proof that we are, in fact, doing OK after all. A study of ten thousand students aged twelve to twenty-one found that perfectionism predicated better academic achievement—better grades and higher GPAs.[5] As we know from research on work, the "ideal worker" paragon idealizes someone whose work comes ahead of their other interests, other relationships, or even their own personal health; they're the people who get the results, the saying goes. For some people, that's the case: having a goal, a sense of purpose, a sense of meaning matters. It can help save us. But I thought back to that research on extremism and harmonious passion—that sense of purpose stops being helpful when it cancels out all our other needs.

When ambition externally serves us, it's harder to link it to the sensation of internally breaking down. But those high-achieving perfectionists in the study were also found to experience significant psychological distress.[6] We know the impact of overwork—the destruction of mental and physical health. Perhaps privately, we know that, at least sometimes, we're sitting in the middle of things we wanted and strove for and fought for and find ourselves sad. Or lonely. Or unable to exist in our own skin. So, feeling like we're losing ambition—our capacity to keep going, to strive, to chase—feels more like losing a piece of ourselves.

I scraped whatever was left of myself off the underside of achievement: Who was this person so stuck on the belief that the best things about her were the ones she earned? I didn't know how to ask to take a step back or ask for help, because I'd never explicitly done it before. I didn't know how to confess I wasn't fired up and ready to tackle each week with godforsaken #MondayMotivation, and no, I really didn't have any ideas about that pitch someone asked me to Zoom about. My mind zipped from being panicked, looking for ways I'd done something wrong, to blank in a way that felt more unmoored than restful. If I'd lost ambition, how was I going to take care of everyone I felt responsible for even when I was exhausted? How was I going to prove I was capable at work? If I wasn't ambitious, what was I?

I thought of how other people framed it: the stay-at-home mother of two who told me she was ambitious about "going to bed," the thirty-one-year-old who'd held a slate of high-level positions and explained that her ambition was rooted in needs of steadiness and self-reliance after a childhood punctuated with instability, the man who described his ambition as wanting to save the world one minute and leave it the next. Someone explained that they "distrusted" their ambition, fearing it would lead them to compromise themselves. While it's obvious how ambition manifests in work, what's striking is how many people aligned their sense of ambition with their safety and security, their mental health, their sense of self, and even their capacity to take care of others. Losing ambition was never just about losing work. Ambition is always wrapped up in all the rest of us.

"Is there such a thing as ambition without dissatisfaction? Like, does ambition exist in a world where everybody has what they need?" Mikey asked during our call. "What does ambition allow us to ignore? What holes do we use ambition to plug?"

When I asked Ettinger about their own relationship with ambition, they said, "I think that ambition is great, but it has to be paired with a big amount of imagination." Sure, drive is good; yes, maximize your own potential. "All those things and also, why are we choosing to live the way we are?"

I sat with the question, trying to answer for myself. Was it fear that changing course meant dropping a ball, and dropping a ball spelled doom? That if I stopped I wouldn't start again? But imagination is what I'd lost, saving up my brainpower for worst-case scenarios and striving *away* from them, rather than fixating on what was worth striving *for*. Ettinger referred to it as queering ambition—not clinging to the norms of heteronormative, capitalist systems of social behavior or accepting the terms of discussion as laid out by the "cis, hetero, capitalist kyriarchy." We don't *have* to live by the so-called norms or standards of what it means to be ambitious. In fact, we don't have to live this way, Ettinger said. "Why don't you be ambitious in ways that allow you to make your own rules, and dream for yourself?"

We could add on: What hold does ambition have on our imaginations that striving is the only way? I thought for sure hustling could save me, and maybe it did. But when I slipped through a fault line of my own ambition, what saved me when my brain was too overwhelmed for me to open my eyes and my body felt like it was eating itself and when I was good for nothing and no one, wasn't what I assumed would. What did come through, quietly, as if scooting aside all the broken pieces to sit in the silence, was care. Soup my family left on the warming burner. Texts from friends offering up chances to *not* talk about anything, humor, dinner recipes botched, and pet videos. Doctors who listened and looked again. Me, looking again.

There's no world in which I think these alone are the solutions to health crises, or crises of ambition, for that matter. To suggest that rejects everything we know about how our structures lift this sort of self-reliance and individualism up and give them a gold star for effort.

Instead I wondered: if those were the things that protected me, that cared for me, that imagined a fuller me, where was my ambition for *that*?

9: Good for Something

As much as I was still trying to cling to my ambition, I knew it wasn't the same as it had been before; I'd been emptied out, and for the first time, I was coming to terms with everything I was instead of ambitious.

I was *angry,* a sensation I hadn't thought I was allowed to feel, so I kept the cap screwed on tightly even as I shook the bottle.

I was *grieving,* for losses I assumed shouldn't have hit me as hard as they did and felt uncomfortable expressing because they weren't clean cut or outright bereavement.

I was *lost,* because the path I'd clung to by my fingernails seemed to have guided me directly toward a dead end.

There was a lot simmering under my ambition, nestled into the embers of what I would've called passion or hustle, a lot of me I had never gotten to know because I centered the one good thing I thought I was. Even when my ambition was too much—too pushy, too big, too forceful, according to people who wanted me to be a little quieter—it was *mine.* Yet these other feelings swam in the same blood as the sensation that I'd give it all I've got until I had nothing left to lose. All while I was losing my ambition, as I'd half-jokingly phrased it, so many *other* things were happening: the gutting clarifier that is true heartbreak; being shoved into confronting one demon that opened the door to invite in all the others I'd locked out for so long; navigating my physical and mental health.

But it wasn't all bad. I might have been drained of everything that shined, but in the absence of reaching for goals, I reached for others. Or, more accurately, I reached back. Not only did it change the shape of my life—from a pointy star to a circle, where there is much more room—it squeezed the way I thought of ambition like silly putty, reshaping it and me along with it. At the time all I thought was: Will I ever strive for anything again? Will anything be worth it?

Spoiler: a lot will be worth it.

In the second chapter of this book, I referenced a study drawing a connection between self-worth, self-discipline, and self-reliance, among other elements, and how the Calvinist doctrine and capitalism uphold that. For longer than I care to admit, my calculations of "worth it" didn't exist outside what I thought of as an ambition: I'd ask if extra work was worth the time and sacrifice. I'd ask if going to dinner with a friend was worth the medication it took to get me there. I'd ask if a goal was worth the striving. But never once did I consider whether so many of my dearly held ambitions were worth all of *me*.

One humid summer morning, Dr. Meag-gan O'Reilly, staff psychologist at Stanford University, joined me on Zoom to discuss self-worth, identity, and ambition. I tried to recall the first time I was ever praised for being a hard worker, for earning it, and took that to mean "you're good for something."

O'Reilly first began by talking about a psychologist named Carl Rogers who believed that, in order for a person to grow, they needed a self-concept, defined as "the organized, consistent set of perceptions and beliefs about oneself."[1] This is the stuff we know makes us, us: the ways we think about our communities, what we value, how we spend our time, whether we consider ourselves a kind friend, a great baker, or a good listener.

Unsurprisingly—but perhaps sadly—two primary sources of influence on our self-concept are our childhood experiences and our evaluation by others. Evaluation: ambition's sidekick. O'Reilly sees ambition as falling under a condition of worth, not better or worse than any of the others. "They're all just selling the same thing: that you need to do something to be valuable," she said, "which is a great business model, selling something that you already have." We'll always be repeat customers, bargaining our way into worth. Of course, striving isn't always a negative. Neither is goal setting, prioritizing, or being proud of what we're good at. But it so rarely comes with the countermessaging O'Reilly described: you're worthy even if you *aren't*. The absence sets us up for a life of proving.

O'Reilly pointed out to me that when her clients, who are often millennials or younger, hear the word *ambition* they register it as achievement. What comes to mind for O'Reilly when she hears ambition is the "natural side of striving when you're curious or interested and engaged, [and] really alive in whatever you're pursuing," she told me. Achievement, on the other hand, is an outcome, and even achievement has been warped, favoring certain achievements as more desirable than others. By default, we become desirable by associating ourselves with those achievements. That's where, she said, ambition and achievement get "a little entangled in a way that I don't think [is] helpful for the soul."

I wanted to sit with the heft of it. These words—*worth, value, soul*—were much deeper attributes than what I'd ascribed to ambition. What are the systems and structures in play that tell us what kind of accomplishment has value? I asked. Because by now, we know what's considered ambitious or accolade-worthy isn't value neutral. You don't earn gold stars in a vacuum. This is what she'll often find herself sitting under a tree thinking about, O'Reilly told me, because "I always tell my clients and myself—especially any marginalized [clients], my gay clients, my trans clients, people of color—you've got to ask, Who benefits from you believing a certain way?" This isn't just how things happen to be. "They've all been constructed, meaning they can be deconstructed," O'Reilly said.

O'Reilly told me about cultivating inherent self-worth, and one of the things she talks about is to become self-defining. "We have this small voice inside of us that knows a little bit better or has our best interests in mind," she explained, and we ignore that voice often. (Or blast over it with expectations, ambitions, and the reality that most of us have far more people to answer to in a day than just ourselves.) Her work looks at the three s's: stillness, silence, solitude. On the one hand, that sounds like the opposite of striving: We're supposed to get what we want by holding still? No! We're supposed to ask for it; demand it! But that dictate, ambitious as it might be, doesn't hold up if we don't know what we want or need to begin with. And that's where shifting our personal definitions of ambition comes in.

Eventually, after we spend enough time asking the important questions—What matters to us? What fulfills us? What could we choose if we could choose anything at all?—we move closer to clarity on our own internal benchmarks, as O'Reilly called them. It's not that we should abandon all external benchmarks; it's that personal benchmarks are fuller, more robust, more meaningful. O'Reilly offered up her own life as an example: she's currently considering whether or not to have a second child. "I'm holding that, and that label of 'advanced maternal age,' but some of my internal benchmarks around family [are]: I do want my [older] one to have a sibling," she told me. Another example can be found in all the things she wants to do that don't show up on her résumé, such as wanting to return to her dance practice. "So, I talk about the unrésuméd self quite a bit," she said. "What are the things that actually fill you up that no one cares about, or you can't put on your résumé?" For that matter, what's an activity or pursuit you'd regret not having in the narrative of your life? she asked. Her career began in gerontology, meaning that her clients were often eighty or ninety-year-old adults—who rarely mentioned spreadsheets or job titles. "They talked about relationships. They talk about places they wanted to see, skills they wanted to acquire that they didn't devote time to, conversations they wanted to have. It's always experiences or relationships, always," O'Reilly told me.

I'd met myself in versions of this place a million times before—atop my mound of broken promises that I'd drink more water to help my body, find a new therapist to help my brain, refocus my day-to-day on the glimmers of peace or humor or joy. Fall short, get frustrated, repeat. That's where I was going wrong: I wanted to *achieve* these things so I could say I'd done them and felt better because of them.

There is no tiny, personal dismantling of ambition that replaces the structural. But I wondered if reframing my own ambition could be a way of thinking about being compassionate. At its best, ambition had clarified what mattered to me; at its worst, it impressed upon me what I *should* do, not what I might want to do. For a while, the counterpoint to ambition felt like ceasing aspiring toward *anything*. After all, I thought, that's being present and still. I don't need more than I have right now. This is enough.

And even in the enoughness, I still had dreams, even work-related ones. I aspired to be a good listener to my friends and a good community member. These aspirations are ambitious in the sense that there's a goal (learning, showing up, and being part of someone's life) and effort put into reaching that aim (time, attention, and various batches of cookies in the mail). I strove to rediscover parts of myself I'd forgotten: I had a sense of humor, I used to make a mean pumpkin loaf, I liked making new friends. I wanted to be able to imagine how much could be different.

What I am less ambitious about, though, is the trope that there's only one kind of striving worth doing. That's why, I realized, I'm ambitious about hearing what other people are striving *for*.

10: Pal Around

"It's really *fun*."

That's how Emiliana, a fifty-two-year-old in the Midwest, described artistic swimming—previously known as synchronized swimming. She picked up the sport despite never considering herself an athlete—or an especially good swimmer—over a decade ago, when her father died. At the time, part of her rationale was that if she was crying, it wouldn't matter, because she'd be in the water. But synchro, as she called it, combines dance, which she's long loved, with music, swimming, and choreography. The kid who failed the swim test at her all-girl summer camp every single year became an adult who routinely tells her coworkers at the journalism nonprofit where she works: "OK, guys, it's Wednesday. I have swim practice. You can Slack me all you want, but I will literally be underwater." A good boundary if there ever was one.

The group is based at a trade school and practices twice a week, which bumps up to three times in the summer leading to a big competition in the fall, when the group commutes in rented vans, stays together in one house, eats plenty of food, and drinks lots of wine. One of things Emiliana loves about the sport is that any person of any age, size, or shape and any skill level can join. When the group competes, there is an eighty- and ninety-year-old division. "Hitting meno-pause, getting older, I'm in this body that I'm not used to," she told me. "It's very strange to me, and in the water, you don't feel that."

Beyond the personal benefit, Emiliana stressed that you have to get out of your own head and focus on what's hap-pening with the group as a whole. Once a week she truly can't think about anything else. When she was doing group fitness classes before the pandemic, she'd pick up the cho-reography and then feel her mind wander. "When I'm in the water, I'm either thinking: How do I breathe through this? Or, OK, I need to move over or I'm gonna kick that person, or all right, if this is the little part where three of us are doing something [and] we all have to be together, what's that beat?" she explained. It's clearly something she practices and wants to get better at, but it's also fun. "You have to get out of your head and just be in the moment," she added.

A few days after we spoke, I opened up an email from Emiliana. During our phone call, I'd asked how she'd de-scribe artistic swimming: Was it a hobby? Hobby felt too minimizing, but commitment, which was what she'd used on the phone, made it sound like a task. Via email, she'd landed on a better descriptor: promise. "It's a promise to my-self to keep trying new things," she wrote. "It's a promise to keep moving as I age and my body changes. It's a promise that there's something to be passionate about after ballet gets too painful. It's a promise to build new relationships."

A promise might not be the first thing that comes to mind when thinking about fun or the ways we have it—the activities we pursue and the people we spend time with—but it felt novel. When I think of promises I make to myself, I think of goals: I promise that I'm going to write five hundred words by the end of this hour, so I don't just sit and make prolonged eye contact with a blinking cursor. I promise I'm going to move my laundry off the chair in the corner of my room before it's time to wash it again. But fun? I can't remember the last time I made a promise to myself to have fun. Which is a shame, because it turns out that's a promise that really matters.

First, just like our personal definitions of ambition shape how we use it, our personal definitions of fun shape how we experience it. But to get technical, some research describes fun as "enjoyment of one's activity, potentially spanning affects that range from quiet joy to active elation."[1] A goal of this research—which looked at how fun is experienced—was identifying the "affective state" that fun evokes in day-to-day life, and it showed that fun is associated with both high activation (like being excited about plans you have later) and low activation (like enjoying every minute of a book you love). Fun can occur through pleasure, adventure, play, entertainment, amusement.

It won't be surprising that some research, putting forth a psychological theory of consumer fun, pins the "emergence of fun as a societal phenomenon" to the Industrial Revolution: as working-class people endured rigid, monotonous work, interest jumped in consumable entertainment, not unlike the rise of the hobby and the need to fill leisure time.[2] Relatedly, a major theme these researchers noticed in accounts of fun is a "sense of liberation," which they defined as a "temporary release from various forms of internalized restrictions, such as professional obligations, parental duties, schoolwork, financial constraints, and a range of self-imposed disciplines."[3] Fun: take it seriously.

What all this backstory to something seemingly simple tells us is that the word *promise* isn't too far off what it means to emphasize fun in our lives. (Easier said than done, I know.) Maybe we can't be *ambitious* about fun, but we can certainly be motivated to engage and excited to participate and keep a promise. And maybe that's what it takes to be ambitious about prioritizing fun: making consistent promises to participate.

Speaking of participation, every time Hailey, a twenty-six-year-old software engineer, picks up her double bass in rehearsals for the community orchestra, she feels like a kid again. First, there's the instrument itself. She played the viola growing up but took a break from music in college. Once she graduated, the desire to do something just for fun was strong, which is how she wound up taking double bass lessons. Eventually, she found her community orchestra. "It's nice having this thing that's solely dictated on the premise of me wanting to do it because I enjoy it," she explained. She sent me a video, wearing an N95 mask with the neck of her bass leaning on her shoulder, playing the opening of Hugo Alfvén's *Swedish Rhapsody No.1*. The music is whimsical and sweeping, like it might convince you to get up and dance in spite of yourself. The music itself *sounds* like fun.

Another part of that fun is the community in which it's unfolding. Her community orchestra is diverse, Hailey said, from music students and young adults to professional

musicians to older adults who are just starting out. The
French horn player is a dentist; the cellist is a teacher; the
second violin is a nurse. But every week, around eighty people with their own individual lives, work schedules, aspirations, and pressures come together to play music. As Hailey
puts it, playing in the orchestra is a team sport. Individually,
their parts might not sound like much, but when they come
together, everything clicks. "This orchestra presents a moment of relief from that need to work for monetary survival,"
she said, "and it provides that relief within a moment of music making with fellow community members who, like me,
love music and are doing the best they can every day."

Earlier in the year, Hailey got a job offer and turned it
down because she realized it wouldn't have allowed her to
attend orchestra anymore. It was at that moment she knew
her orchestra—this community—was too important to give
up. It made me curious: Is she ambitious about orchestra?
She is: she pours work into it; she sets goals around it. Hailey
aspires to work her way up to principal for the bass section;
next year, she's planning to audition into a higher seat because she knows she's capable. Ambition can exist beyond
work and achievement, she told me. "The place where people get caught is when ambition becomes external," Hailey
shared. "Somewhere along the line your goals become somebody else's story."

My relationship to ambition had changed shape, but the
plot of my story hadn't quite caught up yet. I kept to myself, quiet and watchful, sure that if I wasn't sure of myself,
people wouldn't want to be around me, which made it incredibly easy to convince myself not just to stay home—it's a
pandemic, after all—but to quit reaching out. I checked the

boxes of doing what I was supposed to do in my career, and I quit aspiring to *anything*.

I got a text from a high school friend I'd seen a handful of times over the years because we'd moved to different cities. Was I home? And if I was, did I want to go on a walk? I did not. I wanted to burrow underground, and if that wasn't feasible because I didn't have the energy to dig the hole, I wanted to pull the covers over my head and turn my phone off. This is *caring for myself*, I protested. I am *taking time for me*. In the shower, I argued that this was the antidote to hyperambition: pausing to reflect on what I wanted was a form of self-care, and that required being alone. But the part I was dodging during those internal arguments was how *lonely* the fixation on hustling had made me, how selfish my sense of achievement had become.

Then came the hard questions. I never missed a deadline, but how many messages from friends did I inadvertently forget to reply to? At one point, I chased down goals like they were a seasonal Trader Joe's product, but how often did I apply that tenacity to showing up in ways beyond work? For all the pressure to do more and be more and earn more, having such a one-track view of ambition made me less of the things I wanted to be the *most* of—a good friend, a good listener, a good community member. And yes, it almost certainly made me less fun.

What Hailey and Emiliana both described, in different contexts, was fun—but it was also participating. They were showing up for something that benefited them and brought joy to their lives personally, but they were also part of groups in which showing up for each other *added* to the fun. Other people narrated similar desires, playing out in domains we typically wouldn't articulate as accomplishments: they were ambitious about staying in touch with friends, prioritizing their relationships, communities, and group activities with the same level of enthusiasm, thoughtfulness, and planning one would expect from someone pursuing a dream. They sought outlets where accomplishment was ongoing rather than zeroed in on completion—where projects or participation required renewed commitment to showing up, like in a community garden or book clubs, where the success wasn't just growing the tomato or finishing a novel but, rather, in the act of participating itself. Commitment to participating, rise! Commitment trophies for all. There was persistent striving—to learn the best means of showing up for a friend, whether it was dropping off lasagna or a long phone call. It showed up in ways that were playful and imaginative and in places where people weren't going it alone. As I listened to people describing the communities, groups, or relationships in which that unfolded, I found myself aspiring to *that*.

One example that stayed with me was how Kal, a thirty-year-old working for a journalism start-up and living in Los Angeles, explained the crash and burn of one ambition and the birth of a new one. As he put it, he's still ambitious, but now he's ambitious about the life he wants to live. In 2019, Kal's dad was hospitalized for three and a half months as doctors attempted to diagnose a neurological condition, and Kal moved in to be his father's caretaker. He figured out how to keep his dad's flower shop afloat and eventually sold his dad's house to ensure they had money to live on. He managed the housekeeping and care and continued working because he couldn't afford not to. "I just did what I had to do to get a paycheck and survive," he told me.

So, "my ambition totally got eclipsed by just like real-life shit—basically disease, illness, financial stressors."

Initially, Kal's ambition had a "singular, laser focus" on succeeding as a screenwriter, but then after a few years of working in Hollywood and in the aftermath of the 2016 election, he zeroed in on journalism. He is innately a little ambitious, he thinks, but also believes ambition is shaped by cultural forces surrounding what's expected of us—in his case, the child of an immigrant single father—but also more generally. "I think everything feels so precarious that we're pushed to be ambitious and exceptional and really, that's sort of messaged to us, that that's one of the few ways to succeed and be stable economically," he explained. He absorbed it all, so much so that he described having a chip on his shoulder and a fantasy of going to his high school reunion to "show people how successful I'd become, like some crap like that." (I wish I could study how many revenge fantasies motivate ambition; I've certainly had some of my own.)

But that changed. "When you're watching your dad scream in pain in a hospital bed and the same day you have to try to sell his house and make sure that the money doesn't get screwed up or make sure all these different things happen, and you try to keep him alive, who cares about your job at that point?" he asked. To him, ambition became a privilege—but, he pointed out, for most people taking care of a child or parent, working multiple jobs to get by, or otherwise struggling, often ambition doesn't even feel like an option.

Recently, Kal's father passed away, and his own relationship with ambition continues to evolve. He still cares about doing a good job at work and even about advancing, but he's ambitious about other parts of life, too. Six months ago, Kal and his girlfriend moved in together, and that's the first ambition he mentions: "I'm ambitious to be present and show up for her regularly," he told me. "I'm ambitious to maintain my friendships," even if that means calling friends out of the blue and rediscovering how to connect in person following the pandemic, a recent move to a new apartment, and his dad's passing. And it's aspirational right now, but he has big ambitions to get involved in his community: he wants to volunteer for community organizations and spend time getting to know his neighbors in his new apartment complex. Of course, these things—community, friendship, being part of a neighborhood—are either dismissed as givens, like a natural by-product of being a human and not practices that require care, attention, and commitment *or* dismissed as easy parts of life we should automatically know how to do. But like all goals, they take practice, patience, and a willingness to show up. We're not really taught to value things like this, Kal mentioned, so "I'm still kind of trying to teach myself or remind myself that I should put myself out there in these ways that are important to me and not just try to climb a career ladder."

That can be a goal: to keep showing up. It makes effort around fun and friendship less transactional—putting in X effort to get Y outcome—and more about sustained action and commitment.

Dr. Robyn Gobin, author of *The Self-Care Prescription* and a licensed psychologist whose research focuses on interpersonal trauma, post-traumatic stress disorder, cultural diversity, and resilience, said her work involves helping people view self-care as expansive and sustainable throughout their lifetimes. That's how I was thinking about ambition, as an engine for prioritizing community, fun, and even friendship. How do we actually broaden the definition and expand it outward instead of upward, like a ladder?

Caring Is the Main Event

The first time I spoke to Gobin, she noted our achievement-focused society makes it difficult to check in with ourselves or slow down—something that particularly impacts parents, caregivers, front-line workers, and people of color, especially during the pandemic. Workplace cultures that center productivity and capitalism often punish people who *do* attempt to take care of themselves or set boundaries. Women in particular struggle with taking time for themselves without feeling guilty, Gobin told me. She explained that people even experience negative reactions at work because they become less "productive" when they start to implement care regimens. "We run ourselves into the ground trying to prove our worth or trying to prove our value, but the benchmarks [are] always changing, and so the bar keeps being raised higher and higher because once you achieve this next level, then it's, like, oh there's something else to be achieved," she told me. "You can never be good enough and never reach that mark."

Just like the arrival fallacy tells us we're one Big Accomplishment away from our happily ever after, treating fun, care, and fulfillment as treats that happen *after* we've achieved enough to take our eye off the ball is a false promise.

At its worst, modern packaging of self-care is one more get-out-of-responsibility-free card for exploitation. One example are the emails that people received from workplaces, reminding them to "take care of themselves," followed by notices that calling out sick hurt the rest of the team, nudges on deadlines, or a mental health training they were expected to complete during off-hours. Take care of yourself—but only to the extent that it doesn't inconvenience anyone else. (This is a stark contrast, obviously, to actually meeting material needs—ensuring workers have comfortable wages and good work conditions in the first place, as well as the ability to take time off.)

The expectation that self-care is a stand-in for abolishing exploitative systems—where the goal isn't care but, rather, to keep being productive—is a stark contrast to the actual origins of the practice. "The origins of today's self-care industry are deeply embedded in the Black Power movement of the 1960s and '70s, in underserved communities across the country," wrote Lenora E. Houseworth for *Teen Vogue*,[4] writing that former Black Panther leaders Angela Davis and Ericka Huggins took up mindfulness techniques while incarcerated,[5] and in the 1980s, activist and writer Audre Lorde wrote specifically of self-care in the book *A Burst of Light and Other Essays*. Self-care's origins are entirely different— more substantive, more centered in community, and more radical—than much Instagram marketing would encourage us to believe.

My own personal version of self-care featured scream-singing Britney Spears with the windows rolled up in the grocery store parking lot while passersby looked at me out of the corners of their eyes—the almost thirty-year-old who was so overprepared she was having her midlife crisis early. Fortunately, Gobin pointed out a much more practical approach: first of all, self-care doesn't look like any one thing, and of the multitude forms it can take, other people are actually a pretty significant part of it.

Walking me through the domains of self-care detailed in her book, Gobin said that because commodified self-care has been presented as lavish vacations or luxury products, people often think they simply don't have the time and resources to take care of themselves, but in reality, self-care can be far more realistic and dynamic. In Gobin's work, she cites six domains: *intellectual self-care*, strengthening our brains to think in different ways that help us be better problem solvers and creative thinkers; *social self-care*, being in community with other people and the relationships that build out our lives; *spiritual self-care*, recognizing we exist beyond what we see in the mirror, whether that's connecting with a higher power, existing in nature, or connecting with people who have similar values; *physical self-care*, or feeding, moving, and resting our bodies in ways that make sense for us; *vocational self-care*, which means finding a balance between our work identity and personal identity; and *emotional self-care*, tending to, acknowledging, and processing our feelings.

If this sounds like a ton to start doing all at once, Gobin's advice is to pick one area that feels out of balance for you and ask: "How can I just take one courageous step, one small step, one tiny step, to help me to feel more in balance in this one area of my life?" For me, the one tiny step was going on the aforementioned walk with my friend, which made me curious to know about social self-care. "We are not born to do life alone," Gobin said. "We thrive when we are in community and when we have people who we can turn to in moments of grief and moments of sadness—when life is exciting, too. We thrive when we have people in our world who we can share that with."

"When you take better care of yourself, then you are a better member of the community," she continued. "You can be more empathetic, you can be more supportive to people, you have more energy, more effort to offer people." It also helps communities to organize in ways that are important, Gobin said. "The collective can be more powerful than our individual efforts," she explained, and because of that, taking care of ourselves can be part of taking care of a larger whole. That means our broader communities, but it also means our friendships.

Just Showing Up: Spontaneous Fun

OK, but how? When I'm too sick to leave the house, I'm supposed to be social and have fun, how? Or when my priority has been rent, not activities, how am I supposed to plan anything? The world is on fire, and you expect me to focus on *having fun?*

Asking what we're curious about, what brings us joy, or what feels playful—separate from the outcomes of those things—is a rarity, but it's also a habit we can practice even if the answer changes every day. I bristle at turning fun into a Personal Development Project, which is what some of this language sounds like. But at the same time, sometimes we need a way to jump-start ourselves. There's an unquestionable fullness you can hear in people's voices when listening to them describe their fun or their friendships—and it sounds like an invitation.

T., a thirty-seven-year-old from Minnesota who works in the nonprofit space, told me about "friend dates," a way she spends time with different pockets of friends. What sparked friend dates, she told me, was the realization of how much lighter she felt after having spent time with friends with whom she can talk about the silly things *and* the heavier things, depending on how everyone is feeling on a given day. With one friend, who T. hasn't met in person yet but used to work with, they bonded over needing to work to make a living but knowing you don't have to love your work. They sent T. and a couple of other friends stickers and a keychain they made that said "work is a scam," and the group exchanges memes on Instagram, which is an outlet of joy. With another friend, T. went to an adult day camp at an alpaca farm, where the plan was to spend the day petting alpacas and fluffy Highland cows and eating the included lunch from Jimmy John's—only to realize spending the day on a farm included doing farm chores. T.'s friend dates include an awesome, actionable way to prioritize friendship: she thinks of something she'd like to do for herself anyway but would put off if she was going alone, like getting a pedicure or trying a new Filipino restaurant. Then, she makes a date with a friend around that activity.

T.'s commitment to friend dates is part of a larger practice. She cited Mariame Kaba, organizer, educator, and author of *We Do This 'Til We Free Us*, among other works, whose work focuses on dismantling the prison industrial complex and transformative justice. T. said she had "learned . . . about hope as a discipline, that it's not a feeling, but it's a practice that you have to do every day and it's showing up for yourself, showing up for your community." Shortly after we spoke, T. sent me a zine her partner had created, quoting bell hooks and Kelly Hayes, among others, on finding hope, resistance, and possibility. T. thinks about what Kelly Hayes has said about fatalism and despair, "How our fatalism is often more harmful to the people around us," she told me. "I think about what that means; I think about my parents having basically survived the end of their world."

T. is the child of refugees; her family was one of the first to resettle in Minneapolis back in 1975. "They had to leave their country with literal go bags and their kids in tow and left their home and never went back and started over in a completely different place where they didn't speak the language." They found systems of support and navigated communities that built care around them, she added. "It'd be selfish of me to not allow myself to find some joy, to find the laughter, to find those spaces with friends or family, with even my parents, because it's, like, why did they go through all of that for us?" T. told me. "I know we shouldn't have to go through hardship to earn or deserve joy, and at the same time, I know making those pockets of joy makes navigating the world a little less lonely." Friendship, in this context, is fundamentally an act of hope—of reaching out and reaching back, not an afterthought but a foundation of what it means to live fully.

In addition to asserting friendship and fun as inherently hopeful, what I loved about friend dates is that they felt practical: It underscores how different ways of participating work for different groups of friends. What if the things we'd never do for ourselves—or the things we have to do, like grocery shopping or painting a bedroom—could become opportunities to literally phone a friend?

Borrowing this idea, rather than making an activity a whole production, I attempted to build it into the mundanities of everyday life: the bakery across town that I never would've justified a visit to became an outing, where a friend and I drove there and consumed our chocolate croissants in her car. I texted a friend that I needed to do an hour of emails in the evening, and we sat together at the library to do our work and spent an hour in the library's green space afterward. It didn't happen every week or weekend, but the feelings of peace, wholeness, and joy sustained me. Without realizing it, I'd developed a checklist:

What's something I've been putting off doing despite it sounding like fun, whether it's sitting in a park, watching a show, or eating something new and delicious?

Does the activity make me feel good? Not productive, not accomplished—but curious, happy, or relaxed?

Who can I invite to do whatever that activity is with me, even if it's sitting on a porch sipping coffee?

In my small example of the friend who invited me to go for a walk, she introduced something to my routine, while giving me space to build out a new part of one: we now meet up to walk frequently and don't typically text much in between or beforehand. It's a quick "Hey, want to walk tomorrow?" and if the answer is no, we find a different time and try again. It's just the right amount of spontaneous. Speaking of spontaneity, Denali, who lives in Chicago, messaged me about something her mutual aid group instituted: the Rolling Hang. The group has a designated spot in the park where they converge, usually on Sundays, no planning required. "As a parent with young children, this is the everything way to do nothing," Denali told me. The Rolling Hang is exactly what it sounds like: "If I'm doing something and want company, I will ask, and it's OK to say yes or no," Denali told me. They also have a Slack channel called Rolling Hang where people can drop what they're doing—an errand, a walk, a trip to the park—and others show up to join them. It's created an accessible way to show up and have fun in community without the stress of making firm plans. And that low barrier to entry has been key, especially as people figure out the safest and most sustainable ways to socialize during a pandemic that requires immense amounts of planning and coordination. "So many of us are ready for something, but we need to be asked, reasked, encouraged, and warmly welcomed," said Denali. And as wild as it feels to my introvert self, who is convinced every invite she extends must be annoying, wherever and however we can, *we* can be the reaskers—the ones who ask again.

Put It on Your Calendar: We're Phoning a Friend

In their book *Big Friendship: How We Keep Each Other Close*, Aminatou Sow and Ann Friedman coined one of my all-time favorite definitions in how they describe their own friendship: a big friendship, they wrote, is "one of the most affirming—and most complicated—relationships that a human life can hold."[6] In the book, Sow and Friedman detail going to therapy together to save their friendship: something they acknowledge isn't an option for everyone, and noting that earlier in their lives, they wouldn't have been able to afford it. "As humans, we are all thoroughly shaped by the people we know and love," they wrote. What struck me (in addition to sobbing during a passage toward the end of the book in which they underscore the importance of saying, with your words, out loud, that you value your friend's presence in your life) was that friendship takes work. And time. And practice. Cornerstones of ambition in an area we're not typically encouraged to be ambitious about. Being "ambitious" about friendship usually gets contextualized as networking. It sounds a little clinical to schedule time on the calendar to phone a friend, and our stressed-out, maxed-out mentality makes it feel maybe not *urgent*. There's always next time, right?

Yeah, maybe. But I also know how many weeks on my own calendar I let flip by, year after year, promising to reach out when things calmed down, when this week was over, when that project was wrapped up. That's not to say the stressors of workdays or family or health weren't there and that there aren't valid excuses to reschedule. But it was jarring how willing I was to put off fun because "when things calmed down" never occurred. Without fun, without friendship, without the robust hope these connections and experiences provide, what was I moving forward toward that was so urgent, so valid?

"I think we expect that our friends will be there, and that [friendship] doesn't require watering like a plant," Danielle Bayard Jackson, a friendship coach, told me. "So, the idea of working to maintain it just kind of goes against all of the fantasy stuff we've been consuming about friends forever and having friendships with ease, and if it's a real friendship, it should be organic." Jackson's career started as a high school teacher, where she found herself inadvertently doubling as an unofficial friendship counselor for young people, seeing firsthand how the social issues and bonds they were experiencing impacted the joy they had in class and how they focused. After six years as a teacher, she shifted into public relations, where she once again noticed a pattern: her clients were high achieving and charismatic and described struggling to connect with friends. There's research that suggests our social networks expand until around age twenty-five, Jackson explained, at which point they begin to decrease. It makes sense: for a lot of twenty-somethings, that coincides with leaving college, if you attended, and not having the built-in support structure of an institution. But the tough part is that later in adulthood, "friendship, we kind of push to the margins of our lives," Jackson told me. "We invest time into the things that are rewarded." And the stuff that gets gold stars doesn't include friendship bracelets.

There's pressure—especially for cisgender, heterosexual women—to be partnered or dating and have a certain kind of relationship on a certain timeline. Then there's pressure to make it in a career or field or reach a point of financial stability, so sometimes, interpersonal relationships get booted to the trunk, the baggage we'll get around to unpacking once we've hit our final destination. Parents and caregivers have schedules that are not entirely their own, which makes building in extracurricular time trickier. The obligations mount right as time dwindles. There's also, Jackson noted, a culture around what we celebrate. "Congratulations when you're married! And there's a congratulations when you get a promotion," she continued. "Are we patting each other on the back for sustaining a friendship or nurturing a meaningful friendship over time?" Think about it: if there isn't even institutional support for families or health care, it's hard to fathom having structural support to maintain friendships. It pushes us a little further apart.

There are people I've grown apart from less because of distance or time and more because we see the world in different ways and lack shared ideas. But I was more concerned about the friendships I'd inadvertently let fade because I'd assumed the ones I needed would last. It feels selfish even to type it: I wouldn't assume that this book would write itself, would I? It looks like being intentional, Jackson said. "I always joke, it's very unsexy advice—but to say, 'OK, Thursday at six, me and you, we're catching up,' and I'm gonna honor that the way I would anything else on my calendar," she explained.

The immediate rebuttal might be that this is treating friendship like a transaction—too calculated, too scheduled, too close to what we do at work all day. But it's really just prioritization, and we're not going to get it perfect all the time. "What's the thing that we can commit to doing every week or every month?" Jackson asked. The key thing about scheduling—whether it's a phone call on your way to work, a monthly coffee catchup, or something else altogether—is that it takes the last-minute guesswork out. There's less bantering about where to go, what to eat, or what someone feels like doing if the plan has been set and stands in advance.

That also means not trying to maintain twenty friendships at once. That's bad news for the "squad" culture that swept celebrities and Instagram alike circa 2014, where the friendship du jour was having a wide but somehow close-knit collection of pals, but better news for our intentionality and vulnerability. Jackson said to settle on three to five people (which, gotta be honest, feels like a lot to me!) who both affirm and challenge you, while taking into consideration how comfortable you are with them and how pleasurable your experiences are together. It is a detriment, she said, to maintain friendships in which you have to constantly walk on eggshells or are continuously being hurt by someone.

There's a distinction, though, between that and hitting a rough patch with a friendship the way we might hit a slump at work. "I think a lot of our friendships end prematurely because we do not have an example of what it looks like to push through a tense moment," Jackson said. What a lot of us want is platonic intimacy, but "platonic intimacy often lies on the other side of having a tense moment or working something out because it creates a better shared understanding, and now we feel closer to each other," Jackson explained.

She cited a couple of qualities that make a good friend: first, being reliable, and I cringed thinking about the plans I'd made only to back out later because my stomach was doing some sort of god-awful experiment *or* because I just didn't feel like being social. Then, I flipped the script and thought of the friendship that'd been extended to me during the former scenarios: one friend, in particular, always let me know my health came first—that there was no pressure to perform or push through. When we spent time together, she always thought about where we went, sometimes even pointing out bathrooms along the way because she knew it'd make me more at ease. That's the kind of reliable I aspire to—the person who follows through when they can and gives others grace when they can't. Jackson also noted that trustworthiness makes a good friend and—surprisingly—confidence.

Wait, we have to be vulnerable *and* confident?

"If you don't believe that you have anything worthy to offer a friendship, how does that affect how you show up to
other people?"

That's the first time I'd heard confidence phrased in that
way, as silly as it sounds. "What can I bring to other people?"
feels a whole lot more manageable than my usual standby
of "I shall fix myself, heal myself, and organize my sock
drawer, *then* I will be worthy of friendship and care." Ultimately, Jackson encourages people to question any messages
we've consumed over the course of our lifetimes about what
friendship should be and challenge those. That includes the
idea that "we don't have time to play; I've got business to attend to," she noted, explaining that friendship isn't just a fun
respite from daily life—it's part of the whole.

That's where I decided to start. Especially as someone
who lives fairly far away from a lot of her friends, during
a pandemic where travel feels iffy if not impossible, I knew
if I kept waiting for ideal conditions, the moment—all of
them—would've passed. So, I searched for ways to prioritize
friends in different ways: every time my friend and I are in
the same place, we walk, usually the same route, with different stories to bring to the conversation every time, and
a couple of times, we've popped our respective earbuds in
and talked via phone when apart during the morning walks.
Another friend and I experimented with baking the same
recipe at the same time via Zoom to mixed results—her final
product looked like it belonged on a food magazine cover; I
ate a lot of batter. (A win both ways, really.) Other friends
and I routinely take turns sending each other meal deliveries or twenty dollars to cover coffee and a pastry for no
reason other than adding a bit of levity to the other's day. I'm

working on reconnecting with friends I've lost touch with—hearing about their toddler's first steps or the elderly rescue dog they adopted, while sharing that my greatest ambition right now is to adopt a cat and name him after one of my favorite snack foods. Slowly but intentionally, I am building a foundation of friendships and, in turn, hopefully being part of that foundation, of joy, of care, of a safe spot to vent for others, too.

And the good news? It only grows from here.

Why Play?

Participating—showing up as a friend, showing up as a community member, showing up to care—takes a bunch of different forms. And just like fun matters, turns out, so does an offshoot of fun: play. In fact, the earlier research we looked at on fun underscores play as part of the essential definition. When was the last time you played? Not planned, perfected, or practiced—but played? (Don't ask me to answer this.)

Childhood play is considered essential for brain development,[7] is characterized by fun and spontaneity,[8] and is considered to be a way we make sense of the world.[9] But the benefits of play—empathy, resilience, communication, creativity, and imagination[10]—sound like the qualities that would enrich our adult lives, too. When I first started wondering about adults and play, I winced: the world is hard, impossible, and cruel, and the solution here is to go down a slide or something? It isn't, unquestionably, and when someone is strapped for time and resources as it is, "just have some fun!" is about the least comforting platitude they could be offered.

But it felt worth looking at how these small possibilities—small outlets—could offer respite, even occasionally, which is how I wound up on the phone with Kathryn Hirsh-Pasek, professor of psychology at Temple University whose research examines the development of early language and literacy in addition to the role of play. She was telling me how—starting young—we're tasked with school and extracurriculars, and then as we age, we lose the habit of playing or doing activities that are engaging, meaningful, usually joyful, and performed with others. "You're writing a book on ambition, so you obviously have the ambition to write the book," she told me. "So here's the question when it comes out: Do you take a moment to celebrate it? Or are you going to go, 'Oh thank God I sent that in—next.'"

"Oh no," I joked. "I'm scared to answer this honestly."

Because I not only knew what my response would be, I was borderline notorious for it, fueled partially by a belief that if I looked any good thing in the eye for too long, I'd realize I never deserved it to begin with and partially because "onward" was my default setting. Play brought up something else; namely, that my child self would be super into "the person I had grown to be" relearning how to play.

In turn, I asked Hirsh-Pasek why play is so important for adults—a simple question, but I couldn't remember the last time I *played* to the extent that I struggled to describe it. Hung out? Yes, I blew through season two of *Bridgerton*. Had a good time? I saw a friend for coffee and belly-laughed until I could feel my ribs creaking. But was I missing something? "The first thing is, I put curiosity in there," Hirsh-Pasek said. If we don't have curiosity to look beyond what we know, she continued, we'll never have the imagination to think of something beyond it. The second is that we've been taught to live in a tunnel—thinking that we have to do produce something to be valued, she explained.

Envisioning Gobin's domains of self-care, I thought of how many of them included fun for me: For physical self-care, I genuinely had fun smacking a tennis ball around with a friend, even if I had to chase after it, and I genuinely had fun throwing sticks for another friend's dogs and watching them successfully chase their tails. For social self-care, I loved being in the company of people I care about—even via text and Zoom—because getting to recount the highs and lows of the week inevitably leads to gossip, pep talks, fury and sympathy when needed, and laughter.

What awed me about others, the more I thought about it, was how much care, commitment, and imagination people poured into the world in ways that could never be quantified or measured. They did so in the face of tremendous pressures—true structural challenges that aren't going to be dismantled because we decided to goof off, as joyous as that is. But these relationships, this fun, *did* make the days a little easier, a little fuller, a little more supported. If these small acts can bring us this much to strive toward—connection, community, awe—then we need more of them.

11: Worked Up

By now, I would've thought I'd taken time off. (I haven't.) I would have liked to say I stopped working in the evenings. (It is currently 9:51 p.m.) I hoped that I would've recalibrated my relationship to work enough to confidently report that balance is *mine*. (There is at least one task I've forgotten and won't remember until midweek.)

But what *has* changed isn't some newfound work-life balance or work-life integration or whatever we're calling it now. It's the knowledge that I can care about my work *and* not have it be all of me. Because of the way my work functions—something I credit to luck and privilege more than my own skill—I'm practicing how to say no to extra projects, which gives me the chance to recommend someone else. I'm talking about salaries and payment with coworkers or peers, and we're helping each other negotiate. I'm forcing work out of the center of my life by adding more in. That hasn't changed the fact that my insurance is tethered to my job, and I worry incessantly about being laid off, but it's helped remind me that, sometimes, it's enough to do the task and move on, and my ambition doesn't have to belong to my job. But I'd be lying if I said I wasn't ambitious about my work; this book is an example of how meaningful my work sometimes feels. I'm holding two seemingly conflicting pieces of knowledge: Overwork made the book, I have dreams around it, and there's meaning, at least to me, within it. *And* this book will not make me, it doesn't hold all of me, even as deadlines creep up and threaten to take a little more. Part of my work *is* something to me, but it isn't—it can't—be everything. As Sarah Jaffe wrote in *Work Won't Love You Back*, "Work will never love us back. But other people will."[1]

That's part of imagination to me: not denying that some of my work holds meaning but daring to imagine everywhere and everything that creates meaning—all that work alone can't hold. After all, the most ambitious changes to work aren't going to come in a tool kit on how to hack our time or even personal affirmations that we're more than our jobs. Rather, the structural changes to work are the ambitious ones.

"I've learned lately that I'm no longer interested in ambition," Kendra, thirty-two, wrote to me a few months before we spoke on the phone, providing me with a line I will perhaps be borrowing as an email signature.

Kendra has always been working, since she was sixteen years old and legally could. She worked full-time in college and, after finishing a bachelor's degree in English, described how she "slipped and fell into public policy." She loved focusing on doing good things through work: it wasn't about the prestige or credit; it was about trying to improve communities she cares about. In 2017, she wound up getting a job in New York at what she described as an "elite" nonprofit, and that was when the pressures of ambition came to fruition. She was surrounded by people who prioritize their careers above all else—above relationships, above friends, above their own well-being. "I think some people kind of pigeon-hole themselves in that isolation because they're so focused on their career," she told me. People kept leaving the organization, so she kept advancing.

Not only was Kendra supposed to be ambitious about work, her workplace presented an even more sinister version of ambition, framing overwork as her employer being *ambitious* about her. "I was getting extracted from, and that was getting reframed as, we're just ambitious about you," she explained. She was made to feel like she was an integral part of the organization. And suddenly, she was down a hole, with no idea how she got there.

By the time 2020—and the start of the pandemic—hit, Kendra's struggles with anxiety and depression were hitting a fever pitch. She began thinking she didn't want to manage a whole team and be responsible for all those people. She didn't want to lead big strategy conversations. Rather than the workload slowing down to account for a deadly virus, her workload increased as she worked from home with the company of her cat. "I just started to self-medicate. I didn't even have the energy to address what was going on," she said. "I was drinking beyond excess."

When she thought she needed to go to rehab—"I really, really needed help," she told me—instead of her employer sitting with that conversation, they pivoted. They said her team needed her. They doubled down on her work. "Well, if they need me, I'm not going to be helpful if I die," Kendra recounted.

That was her "I'm done" moment: the great quit. After all, she told me, our dreams might need us, but if we cease to exist, they don't exist. The self-sacrificing in pursuit of a dream—a goal at work, a certain title, a specific job—lets us skim over a fundamental question. In Kendra's words: "So what were you ambitious *for*?"

When I first began reporting on whether work will *always* be the primary home for our ambition, the individualism frustrated me even as I accidentally slipped all over it myself. Some of the solutions referenced most often carry all the weight of a Hallmark card we forgot to sign: parents are advised to look for jobs with flexible schedules; those who feel their humanity is being encroached upon are told to get a hobby to restore it; chronically ill or disabled workers who ask that flexible work arrangements, made possible during the pandemic, continue are met with "Well, we'll cross that bridge when we get there," ignoring that people *are* there; those barely scraping by on unreliable contract work or freelance projects are told to apply for full-time jobs. Sure, great in theory!

But meanwhile, work is swallowing people whole and spitting the remains out. "I think in the same way that individualistic tendencies or structures lead to this idea of ambition being like such a small, close-minded thing, I think that the opposite of that is collectivity, which is imagination, right?" Nat Baldino, the labor expert who took us through overwork's relationship to ambition, told me. "Being able to empathize with your coworkers and not be isolated from them. That's a form of imagination."

We need structural changes to work that, first, don't force us to be ambitious about something as basic as having our basic needs met; second, don't rely on overwork as a driver of security *and* self-worth; and third, create collective power for workers so that people have more agency and autonomy in their lives. If it sounds too idyllic, the continuation of these fights is ongoing: according to data from the National Labor Relations Board, released in July 2022, growing numbers of workers are showing interest in joining unions;[2] a CNBC poll found the majority of workers in the United States (59 percent) across all sectors of work said they support increased unionization in their *own* workplaces.[3] A 2021 survey by Paid Leave for All Action showed that bipartisan support for paid leave is overwhelming—84 percent of voters support it.[4] People want more time, more resources, and more support, and they are sticking together to demand it. Being ambitious about work looks like being ambitious about each other— the collective power it takes to truly change a workplace and protect life beyond it.

In an effort to capture the layers, I wanted to hear about actions people were taking in their own work lives to wrestle back power and redirect their ambition elsewhere; how organizing efforts in workplaces or enacting new, collective models of work were changing *how* people worked; and any examples that existed of *how* a workplace prioritized the well-being of workers—that last one with the caveat that even relying on individual employers only helps that particular workplace because there isn't one solution. Changing work ambition means changing, well, everything.

"I Quit": How We Move On and Why We Need More

For some workers, like Kendra, quitting is a starting point. She instantly felt "so fucking relieved" she had the ability to breathe again. But it took time to adjust. She launched her own consulting firm but eventually decided to close because she got "way too ambitious about that"—she couldn't say no to anything. Eventually, Kendra found her way into a different nonprofit, one that prioritizes being more liberatory both in their mission to build the power of people of color to transform the economy and in their day-to-day options. Kendra sent me an essay she cowrote with her colleague, Azza Altiraifi, organizer and strategist, where they note they are Black women working to undo structural inequities at the intersections of white supremacy, capitalism, cis-heteronormativity, ableism, and patriarchy. During our conversation, she described how part of their process is to actually make work collective, meaning her team has conversations together with a collective decision-making process about strategy, outcomes, and shaping projects. They are intentional, she said, about stopping the power hoarding of decision-making. Even beyond that, Kendra imagines a nonprofit with no hierarchy: no executive director, all staff on the same level, with the same pay. In the essay, Kendra and Azza wrote, "Ambition creates the necessary space to imagine alternative economic arrangements, to experiment daily with liberatory ways of relating to each other and the natural world, and to reclaim the ancestral wisdom that colonialism sought to bury."[5] It echoed what Kendra had mentioned to me on our call: her first instinct was to abdicate her ambition. But really, she expanded it. What she is ambitious about changed, and she thinks ambition needs a reclaiming.

"I'm really ambitious about doing the least," she told me. "I just want to be ambitious about caring for myself and caring for the people I love." Though ambition is often tied to material things, she said, she's getting more ambitious about her values. One example that comes to mind is when she was recruited to lead communications for a huge organization, a role that came with a significant title and, in theory, a bigger role. The answer was a hard no.

No is terrifying. No is enough to stand my hair on end. Not the receipt of no—I've amassed enough rejection letters to design viral Instagram wallpaper. But saying: No, I won't do this. No, I can't meet that deadline. No, I don't want that anymore. That's scary. Because most of my working life has been collecting jobs or projects and assuming I'd be let go at some point and need a plan B, the thought of saying no felt like the equivalent of turning down stability. But is it actually stability if we're constantly anxious about having it taken away? Also, ironically, no.

More recently than I would care to admit, I waffled on taking an extra project, one in addition to this book and to my job. It was a good opportunity, I told myself, but really, I was scared to say no. I might not get asked again. It felt irresponsible. I probably *could* manage it, right? The reasons not to say no felt obvious, until a friend messaged me: *OK, but what does saying no give you the chance to say yes to?*

Saying no to another project meant saying yes to other parts of me, the nooks and crannies of my life that were cloaked in cobwebs because work was at the center of the room every time. It meant saying yes to prioritizing my health and not canceling a doctor's appointment. It meant saying yes to baking cookies for neighbors who just had a new baby. It meant saying yes to prioritizing the parts of myself that will remain when I'm too sick to work, when I get fired, and when I yearn to be someone who is more than the last task they completed. Saying no to something at work was, in reality, saying yes to so many other things.

Remy, who spoke about ambition and ideas of worth in the second chapter, has also funneled ambition that used to belong to careers into other areas of life. After taking time off to treat severe burnout—funded by savings and severance from a layoff—Remy found a new job. They purposefully avoided applying to positions that emphasized mission-driven work because they didn't want to be tempted to fall back into old habits. "My hope is to do enough at this job to rebuild a solid nest egg, and maybe be able to either quit tech forever, or establish a strong enough boundary that my job is just the job I do, and I can redistribute my wealth to communities with less access, and draw my little pictures and read my little books," Remy wrote me after our conversation. "And maybe not be so goddamned intense about my life's purpose or my legacy or anything, and chill."

Now, there aren't necessarily dream jobs; just dreams. Remy wants to write and draw a graphic novel; they want to grow their friendships into closer relationships and community. She wants to explore creative activities that she can learn and get better at, just for herself—woodwork, ceramics, playing guitar and piano, and printmaking are all on the list. "And on a personal level, frankly, doing the work I've needed to outgrow and unlearn the things I learned in my childhood in favor of healthier self-worth is going to be the most ambitious thing I do in my lifetime," Remy added. "And I want to be freed of feeling beholden to dreams. We'll see."

But of course, that's one individual solution in one individual circumstance. Saying no when we can and quitting if we can matters. I believe we ought to have celebratory cards for quitting like we do for promotions. But it's also not enough on its own.

Within a span of thirty-six minutes while writing this section of this chapter, I saw three different references to the Great Resignation: one in a headline, one in an email about millennials who quit their jobs to pursue travel via yacht full-time (who among us?), and one that was—surprise, surprise selling me something, in this case an athleisure blazer I will "never quit." Most reporting on the term itself credits it to Anthony Klotz, an associate professor of management at Texas A&M University, who coined "the great resignation" and took it mainstream after mentioning it in a viral 2021 story published by Bloomberg.[6] "Workers saw that quitting their jobs gave them a chance to take control of their personal and professional lives," Klotz told *Texas A&M Today* in a 2022 interview.[7] For a while, it was framed as an overdue rallying cry: people have *had it* with work, and after spending two years having priorities rocked by mass death and chaos, they were ready to hang up their bootstraps for good and embrace the sweet freedom of quitting. In so many of the instances of "I quit" announcements that went viral, the tone was unwaveringly that of a success story, the opposite of how quitting usually gets positioned in American society, where pushing through, powering onward, and fulfilling commitments are worn like merit badges.

While it's been termed the Great Resignation (or the Great Rethink, the Great Reshuffle, the Great Realization), the framing of workers leaving their jobs often felt more like a great oversight. What about everyone who *can't* quit? It's what I think of when I see remarks on how a new generation

is "rethinking the workplace!" In that assessment, are undocumented workers, workers supporting families, workers
juggling multiple jobs, and/or workers who can't afford to
leave a job before finding another included? While quitting
might spell individual freedom, announcing quitting as the
most ambitious version of changing work ignores everyone
left behind.

Jhumpa Bhattacharya told me that a lot of people in the
workforce development space, which broadly focuses on
helping individuals gain skills and the creation of "good
jobs," emphasizes exactly this: they want to "upskill" people,
giving them more education so they can move up the ladder
to a better job. Sounds good, right? This is one solution to
being overworked or in a job that's toxic: find a new one.

Except when that is presented as *the* key solution, it ac-
cepts a backward argument: that some jobs are inherently
"better" than others, which means accepting some people
will inevitably be in jobs that are inherently exploitative, abusive, or unwilling to meet the basic needs of workers. When
we think only some people deserve good jobs—meaningful
work—we're telling on ourselves about where we derive our
own meaning and how we measure that in others. "What
if we just didn't have shitty jobs?" Bhattacharya said. "How
do we accept that there's going to be a subset of jobs that are
underpaid, that strip your dignity, where you have no control
over your schedule?" She uses the example of a home health
aid worker, someone who comes into a home to provide care.
Wouldn't you want your relative or yourself to be taken care
of by someone who actually wants to be there? Someone
whose basic needs are met and who is treated well and supported in their work, so they can do a good job?

A version of that is present in office jobs, too, albeit to a less dire degree. Overwork is popcorned from person to person because rather than implement policies that stand to improve quality of life—paid leave, flexible schedules and reasonable hours, paid overtime—it's easier to just fire someone or find the next person in line willing to do the work. To use an example from a former job, I was handed a task at the last minute that involved extra, unpaid, after-hours labor for a nonemergency and so stretched my scope of work it threatened to pop at the seams. Feeling quite tickled with myself, I set a boundary: I was at the hospital with a grandparent, and so no, I wouldn't be able to complete this task. (It's startling that this felt like a victory, given the circumstances.) Afterward, I found out that my coworker did it instead, while she was technically out sick. My boundary became her burden, and I've thought about that nearly every day since. In some instances, I can't set boundaries if my coworkers aren't able to set boundaries, either. Sometimes, the situation is *so* bad, and the harm to mental and physical health is so great, that quitting is the best, if not only, option. But if we offload changing work to quitting and quitting alone, eventually we'll run into the same problems at our next job, and even if we don't, a friend, neighbor, or coworker will because, ultimately, "it's not you," Baldino told me. "It's the nature of work itself."

I spoke with Elizabeth Gedmark, vice president of A Better Balance, a national nonprofit advocacy organization that uses the law to advance justice for workers and tackles issues including paid medical leave and paid sick time, pregnant workers' fairness and breastfeeding while working, fair and flexible work arrangements, fair and equal pay, abusive attendance policies, and recognizing all families.[8] She pointed to the impact this work attitude has on independent contractors, too. "We are seeing more folks who are becoming independent contractors or starting their own businesses, finding ways that they can make income," she told me. Often, that's spun as a positive for entrepreneurship—work on your terms, make your own schedule, do work you like. And sometimes, it is. "But the thing that's important to remember is that oftentimes that was not really a choice—that was a necessity because the workplace was so hostile to their needs or their families that they really didn't have any choice but to try and find something completely different," she told me. Part of A Better Balance's work, Gedmark said, is looking at a future of work that ensures independent contractors, self-employed, or nonstandard workers have access to the same laws and benefits as full-time counterparts. (Anyone who has ever attempted to find health insurance as an independent contractor knows it's a job in and of itself. And no one pays you to do it.)

Via A Better Balance's free, confidential work-family legal helpline,[9] Gedmark told me she sees how workers spiral into economic insecurity when they become pregnant, get a medical diagnosis, or need to care for a sick or disabled loved one. "Improving work in our country means guaranteeing benefits like paid family and medical leave and paid sick time for every worker, passing stronger protections for pregnant and breastfeeding workers, and ensuring fair and flexible workplaces that are free from abusive attendance policies," Gedmark added. "It means ensuring independent contractors have the same protections as other workers, so our laws reflect the reality of today's workforce."

What We Deserve

"They don't actually care about us," Joselyn, a twenty-seven-year-old former Starbucks worker and union leader told me. Though initially most workers at the Starbucks store where Joselyn worked were on board to form a union, they voted not to unionize—following what she describes as union-busting tactics on Starbucks' part. (Starbucks has denied claims of union busting or any other wrongdoing.) Shortly after the union effort, Joselyn said she believes the company then tried to make it appear that workers have more of a voice than they do, by conducting more staff surveys and sponsoring activities, like an art night. Joselyn described these efforts as "some bullshit" because she felt Starbucks was avoiding addressing workplace concerns, such as safety on the job and low wages. She told me the store she once worked at has been trying a new approach to recruiting, asking people to join the Starbucks "family." "I'm, like, this sounds cultish," she told me. "What do you mean, family? This is a workplace."

In 2022, Starbucks announced it would not offer enhanced benefits, including higher wages and additional training, to stores that voted to unionize.[10] Joselyn told me she heard similar things—other stores would get wage increases, not unionized stores—during her time there. She also claimed Starbucks told other employees she was being paid by the union and slashed her hours. (If proven, this could be considered retaliation and possibly illegal.) To Joselyn, the reasons for unionizing are straightforward: "We just deserve to have rights, and we deserve to have our needs met." She believes that's what is driving unionizing in workplaces—people demanding a say.

"Almost everyone has at one point felt unheard or power-less as an employee," states a report from the Economic Policy Institute on how unions help working people.[11] Collective power for workers means having the power to shape working lives—like a collective version of the self-determination that ambition alone is thought to afford us. Through collective bargaining, workers negotiate for better working conditions, better benefits, and higher wages. As of 2019, union workers earned about 19 percent more than nonunion workers.[12] These are fundamentals every worker deserves.

Joselyn was inspired by the unionizing efforts of employees at a Starbucks store in Buffalo, New York, which became, in December 2021, the first unionized Starbucks in the United States. Before coverage of Starbucks' Buffalo location unionizing hit national news, Joselyn told me she didn't have a firm grasp on what unions were or what rights she deserved as a worker. She felt her work conditions weren't ideal, mentioning that the wages paid by Starbucks didn't align with the cost of living and saying she had worked while sick even throughout the pandemic. But it wasn't until she began talking to the Buffalo union that she started realizing the path to holding her workplace accountable began with collective action. So, she started talking to her coworkers about their respective experiences. She formed an organizing committee of coworkers who were interested in helping with the unionization efforts. And it all started with conversations about what would makes everyone's work lives better.

Organizing a workplace, or really any sort of collectivity, runs counter to individualized ambition, Nat Baldino said. When Baldino was a barista leading the organizing drive at their coffee shop, they'd call their mom at the end of the day with an update on how the union was going. "She'd be, like, 'What if you get fired? Aren't you going to risk your job? Can you afford to risk your job?'" At the time, Baldino had negative $300 in his bank account. "I could not afford to be fired, but I was compelled to take collective action to form a community, and that ran directly counter to my own personal ambition," Baldino explained. An instinct might be to cling to what you have. It's a by-product of how work is designed. "How can we get as much productivity out of our workers as possible, while ensuring that they don't talk to each other enough to figure out what's going on?" Baldino said. But the facts tell us we get more when we stand together; we go further when we prioritize one another. We need empathy—empathy to keep our worlds from becoming small and insular and so tangled up in our personal dreams and ambitions and the daily grind that we lose everything else.

Throughout history, some sources say, unions have been central in industries like manufacturing and transportation,[13] as well as fields including public administration, education and health services, and construction.[14] But unions are expansive, not contained to a single industry. As labor journalist Kim Kelly wrote in the prologue of *Fight Like Hell*, "From fast food to education to museums to mines to digital media to tech, workers in industry after industry are taking control, forcing bosses to the table, and fighting for their piece of the pie." And as Kelly notes, it's often those with the most to lose, including "poor and working-class women, Black people, Latino people, Indigenous people, Asian and Pacific Islander people, immigrants of all backgrounds, religious minorities, queer and trans people, disabled people, the sex workers and undocumented people whose work is criminalized, and people who are incarcerated," who have fought harder than anyone else.[15]

Whether someone is in a truly bad job—one that exploits and harms them—or one in which expectations of their working life implodes, unionizing is the collective opportunity to halt feeling replaceable in your workplace, get more than the bare minimum, set better, structural boundaries around work with clearer scheduling, and have a say in what your work conditions are actually like. But even the right to organize isn't spread equally across workers: for example, independent contractors and gig workers aren't all protected by the Fair Labor Standards Act[16]—meaning they have less protection than full-time employees, which we also see in lack of benefits afforded to part-time or contract workers.

"It's all about being collective and having a greater say within a larger group," Joselyn said. "I feel like if we were all to collectively get together and just fight for what we believe in, what rights that we need—because they aren't wants, they're needs, right—they can't ignore us." For Joselyn's part, she thinks now is a good time for people to realize we don't have to deal with exploitation and the profits-over-people approach many of us feel at the mercy of in our workplaces. Standing together collectively is her solution to that. She told me that she doesn't think people view baristas as ambitious or hardworking; they see them as the people who pour the milk in their coffee. But she's going to school while working. She has a massive role in raising her niece. The people she worked with are artists, parents, and students, as well as being baristas committed to doing a great job. "I think forming a union is ambitious," she added.

From the Ground Up

In addition to unionizing, part of being ambitious about reimagining work means creating better structures that don't involve feeling like we're trying to wrestle our lives away from the jaws of our employment. For some, that includes cutting off exploitative systems at the root, before we've technically begun working. For example, for Carlos Vera, cofounder of Pay Our Interns, unpaid internships aren't only about internships, they're also about systemic inequities that often define work trajectories and who gets to be in the room making policies that impact work, education, and life in general.

Unpaid internships connect to far more issues within our workforce than those of us who aren't interns might initially realize. First is the idea that if we love something enough, we'll find a way to do it for free—which often means the people who end up in a given field, be it media or public service, are the ones who can *afford* to work for free. Vera explained that frequently nonprofits focused on solving big, save-the-world issues exploit their own staff: they underpay or do not pay their workers, operating under the assumption that people in those roles want to make the world a better place and that's the reward. Similar logic pops up every time "passion" is used as an excuse to talk someone out of negotiating for a higher salary or to guilt them for complaining about their workload if they are technically in a job they love. But dream jobs are ultimately still jobs. Even work we love doesn't deserve to take everything from us. As Vera pointed out, this isn't just in industries like media or politics; much of the care economy is also structured on the assumption of unpaid labor from the start. In certain professions, including teaching or social work, students are required to work a number of unpaid practicum hours to complete credentials that allow them to enter the field.

Second, much of the way our current job market and society interacts with work dates back to the 2008 economic and housing crash, Vera said, where pay started going down and job qualifications shot up, thanks to mass job loss within the Great Recession.[17] (That's one reason for the increase in internships.) Because of a lack of oversight from the Department of Labor, internships "are jacking up the entry-level job market," Vera said, which is why we see job listings where applicants need five years of experience for an entry-level position or the endless list of prerequisites that seem related to several different jobs. Plus, despite the myth that every intern is a college student who is having their rent paid by their parents, that's not who today's interns are. "Today's interns are more than likely to be a thirty-year-old, a single mom, a veteran that's trying to enter a new career," Vera said. Regardless of age, when the assumption is that the more we want a job, the more we'll be willing to devote our time for nothing, everyone loses—except the employers profiting off someone following their dreams instead of paying their bills.

Pay Our Interns is working to abolish unpaid internships by 2030, but bigger picture, they are trying to create equitable pathways across all sectors, and the solutions they see for internships mirror a solid solution for work overall: "I know that seems like a no-brainer, but literally, just pay people directly," Vera said. "Don't give them financial aid workshops and how to manage it, just give people money. It works wonders. We saw it with the Child Tax Credit." What would *you* do if you knew you could fail at work or lose a job and not be in fear of falling behind on student loan payments, missing a car payment, or otherwise?

Having to hustle for basic standards of living isn't ambitious and means our best, most imaginative selves are so wrapped up in productivity that we miss everything else. We also miss one another.

Even in individual workplaces, there are changes that are working and that chart a better path forward, prioritizing the well-being and lives of workers ahead of their work. For example, Sadé—who spoke about her former workplace being unwilling to accept that she needed time off to care for her mother who had a heart attack— now works at Caring Across Generations, a campaign that doesn't just tolerate her responsibilities but makes them a priority. She was frank in interviews: she needed a workplace that was comfortable with her needing to prioritize her mom and daughter. "I thought it was being super brave by saying it," she explained. "I think a lot of jobs would have said 'No, you can't, you have too many conflicting priorities.' Caregiving takes up a lot of your time." Instead, she was exactly what the campaign was looking for, and now Sadé's work focuses on ensuring others have the same support she does: she has a job that allows her to say "Hey, I need four hours in the middle of the day just to care."

"And my job is one of the minority, unfortunately, that allow for that sort of flexibility," she said. "Part of the issue is that there are no sort of regulations or large-scale standardizations around leave." It's not enough to offer people remote workdays if there's no infrastructure ensuring they can take them.

Meanwhile, others use new models of work to meet the needs of their communities. Cassia, an organizer, writer, and community development specialist in Kentucky, had secured a space for the catering business she'd started out of her house: she wanted to serve low-income seniors in her community and needed a little kitchen in the back of a building. During an open house at the space, around forty people indicated they wanted to have a conversation about a co-op, defined as a "user-owned and controlled business," where benefits are distributed equitably and controlled by people who own and use the services.[18] At the time, Cassia was reading *Collective Courage* by Jessica Gordon Nembhard,[19] focusing on the history of Black cooperative economic thought and development. That gave way to conversations with friends and monthly meetings with different neighborhoods, trying to figure out what people would want to see if they had the chance to create their own grocery store. "I've never been into a Kroger where I met a shareholder," Cassia told me. In a co-op, "the owners are the community and the community of their owners." That means there is more ownership and investment in the success of the store. Nobody is getting rich, Cassia explained, but they have the opportunity to help their worker-owners and consumer-owners create wealth. They share values, prioritize transparency, and center shared power and responsibility. "This kind of work is—you're in the work; you're rolling your sleeves up and getting it done," Cassia told me. "A large part of our work right now is really helping our community understand and identify their superpowers and helping move them to action based on the things that they know best," she said. Then, the organizers help community members find resources to support in helping enact whatever they want to do around the business itself.

"It was hard to get out of bed some days," Cassia told me about 2020. In addition to the pandemic, Cassia was in Louisville, Kentucky, at the epicenter of protests calling for justice for the murder of Breonna Taylor, watching her community be directly impacted. "And it was the co-op work that allowed me to get out of the bed because it was a space where I was able to imagine a different world," she said. We don't have the time or ability to imagine for a lot of reasons, Cassia added, but the grocery store is an impetus to allow other people to dream about what's possible. "We can create the kind of world that we really want to be in," Cassia told me. "And it's messy, and it's unclear, and it's great. And it's uncomfortable." She knows firsthand how much there is to eradicate, including systems that dictate what success looks like and who it is supposed to belong to. "But there's joy in waking up and imagining a different world; there's joy in actualizing the dream that you've never seen," she told me. "We have to have wild imaginations, and then we've got to work towards actualizing that other future that we believe to be true."

It's a means of striving toward the future we want—the lives we want, the work we have to do. Reconsidering what that model of success is at work reminded me of something Carlos said. He's an immigrant from Colombia and carries the weight of not just his own hopes and dreams but those of his parents. He interned at Congress and the White House, only to realize "it did not bring me any happiness or any fulfillment." When he helped organize custodial workers at the university he was attending, that made him happier than anything else. Later, when he quit a prestigious job to start Pay Our Interns, people thought he was "stupid . . . I think awards and honors can be like a drug," he told me. "[You] get a high, but the high wears off a couple days later, then what do you have to stand on?" His observation and query— *What do you have to stand on?* —expresses perhaps the most terrifying aspect about work: the abyss that opens up when we center all our hopes and dreams and our well-being in our work and on ephemeral external rewards. A collective ambition is a chance to reclaim our hopes and dreams.

I Hope This Email Never Finds You

"[There] will never be a replacement for structural, systematic change," Maryana Arvan, an industrial, organizational psychologist, told me about three minutes into our conversation on enacting work boundaries, echoing what I've turned over and over in my head every time a conversation on rejecting ambition and embracing work-life balance flits across my Twitter feed. I don't know where you'll be when you put this book down, but I know I'll turn it in and have to go to work tomorrow. I'll talk to my coworkers about the boundaries we want to see around our jobs, serve as a reference for the colleague who is quitting. I'll try to turn my computer off at a reasonable hour, and I'll wonder whether I've done enough to pick the knot that is my work and my individualistic ambition. And it made me wonder what else I could be doing to ease the sensation that no matter how hard I work, it's not enough.

Some of the suggestions Arvan offered, she said, are in the absence of larger structural changes—including federal legislation that would make it feasible for work not to be the centerpiece of people's lives. "I'm a little bit cynical about the

US and our willingness to challenge the great capitalist machine," she told me. For example, paid leave—paid sick leave, parental leave, care leave, paid time off in general—shouldn't be a luxury. Ultimately, workers shouldn't have to rely on having a "good job" or a "good boss" to have a good standard of living and not be overworked. There will be no change in the workplace without management buying in and changing the culture, Arvan said. It doesn't matter if a workplace offers sick days, if the implication is that you're slacking if you take them or you'll have to work double to compensate for time off; workers won't feel safe taking any time off. Arvan also noted that the public accountability some workplaces are facing, amplified on social media—including walkouts over low wages or being forced to come back into an office after having successfully worked from home for two years—are a good thing. "To me, the biggest movement has been around workers and society continuing to pressure companies to do the right thing," she told me.

Short of wider structural solutions, Arvan pointed to practicing psychological detachment, or refraining from work-related thoughts, as a personal tool to help counterbalance work's grip on our identities and time. Practicing detachment is going to vary based on the person: for people who don't have the option to work from home, a detachment routine might look different than it does for a remote peer. There are varying abilities of people to engage in hobbies, distance themselves from work, or utilize time outside work, depending on how long their hours are, Arvan said. "But basically, the idea is that all of these small, incremental changes will add up to a more psychologically healthy state," she said. And the goal is to build routines and structure around them.

First, Arvan suggested that if your job has any virtual or remote component—including emails that follow you around—turn it off, literally. Not checking emails or Slack after a certain hour sounds simple, but it can be effective in helping our minds truly separate from work. If you're working in person, another version of this looks like setting clear expectations with your managers and coworkers about your work hours. That "just one more little thing" can stack up to one hundred little things. If you find that your boundaries are constantly being encroached upon, first talk to your coworkers to assess whether this is a widespread problem. That way, when you approach a supervisor, you can do so with others, and frame it as coming together to work out collective solutions to ensure everyone has actual downtime.

Second, try not to ruminate on work, which is where the "refrain from work-related thoughts" comes in. (This, apparently, includes me spending a Friday evening pacing back and forth worrying that an impending performance review will lead to me being fired *and* me obsessing over whether I remembered to edit that typo out of chapter three.) Especially if your work feels closely connected to your identity—or you enjoy it—drawing lines between work-thoughts and life-thoughts matters. "It's also important to ensure you're giving yourself space and time for different activities that make you feel good about yourself," Arvan said. And activities don't have to be organized hobbies, though they could be. It also means downtime, cooking (or ordering) something that feels nourishing, or spending time with loved ones. Altogether, these small choices add up to make us feel more detached from work by attaching ourselves more to the life unfolding around us. "They help us focus on other identities besides our work identity," Arvan said of these activities. "That's so key because we're more than our work."

For those of us who feel that some of our performance at work—or our ambition—is the most valuable, worthiest, and most significant part of us and, thus, the most important part of our lives, Arvan shared a word of caution: "I think that what you lose is yourself at the center of your story."

"We're such complex things: what we want now and what motivates us now and what makes us want to get up every day in the morning now—it can change from all sorts of transformative experiences," she explained, mentioning the pandemic, loved ones getting sick, meeting the right person, time, travel, and more among the reasons our needs or desires might change. My mind shuffled through the flipbook of how profoundly my wants and needs and aspirations had changed even over the past few years. Grief clarified them and sharpened all the urgency I was spending trying to catch up to some unknown starting line, sweating and ashamed that I was moving too fast to notice all that was right in front of me. My own health grabbed my warped notions of "productivity" and shook them hard. Heartbreak spun my life around like the board in the game of Twister, and I landed on prioritizing family and friendship in ways I'd let lapse more than I wanted to admit.

"When you make work the center of everything, you're centering all of your resources in one spot," she told me. It makes the shifts—a layoff, priorities changing, it could be anything—that much harder to navigate. Arvan even gave me a personal example: she had devoted so much of herself to her career in academia, she lost herself, and when her father was diagnosed with Alzheimer's during the pandemic, her priorities changed instantly, sharply. "You can't predict the future. You can't predict how you might change," she added. "You don't know what your future self is going to need and care about. So, don't pigeonhole your present self."

At the outset of reporting this chapter, I was convinced that a solid individual solution to work overtaking too much—for myself—was to be less ambitious. If I was less ambitious about it, I figured, work would consume less airtime. But in addition to that not being any sort of tangible solution to work precariousness, I wasn't sticking the landing. In spite of myself, there were projects I wanted to try; there were experiences through work that I wanted. But I also wanted a life beyond work and ambition outside it. Those shouldn't be at odds. They are part of the same ambition. My big shift hasn't come in the form of ditching work-related ambition altogether, but rather the more complicated business of reckoning with the fact that even achievements I yearned for had, in some ways, limited staying power. By thinking about ambition less in the vein of accomplishments and more about being part of a whole, it expanded. Hearing about how people are reimagining their relationships to work reminded me of something Bhattacharya said, about how collective organizing thwarts the mentality that we're supposed to be in competition with each other. We have common goals. "You actually start to see how your fates are tied to one another," she told me.

12: Take Good Care

The biggest limit of my ambition—of my imagination—
was believing I needed to do everything alone and that my
aloneness, my self-reliance, my couching of every problem
someone offered help for with "no worries, I've got it" was
an opportunity to be the kind of ambitious I'd heard about:
capable, confident, and composed in spite of everything. I
knew, logically, how much my life depended on other people; the fact I make it out the door in the morning, write a
single word, or have friends are direct results of the care I
have received. But I am sheepish in admitting that I thought
I wasn't supposed to *need* anybody; my need not to come
across as needy was a backward kind of ambition all on its
own, one that takes individualism I reject and makes it a
self-imposed standard.

When I was in the emergency room and needed help to
get to the bathroom, I repeatedly apologized to the nurse
as if I'd insulted her entire family, until she told me to stop.
When someone tried to take care of me—sending me dinner when I was too sick to cook for myself, picking up my
over-the-counter medicine when they saw it on sale—I

panicked and attempted to fend off guilt by returning the favor, kind in practice but more transactional than it should've
been. When I asked friends for advice, I'd hedge—*only if
you have time, it's truly no big deal, you don't owe me anything.*
"Actually," a friend told me once, "I hope we owe each other
a lot." We owe each other everything that matters.

This feels like a backward way to open a conversation on
how inherently ambitious the act of caring for each other
is—to tell you that as much as I want to care for others,
I've spent most of my adulthood so far thinking I didn't deserve it; as if rigidity would keep me on track and gentle-
ness would let me off too easy. To care for one another, to
make one another's lives better, is the ultimate ambition, the
heartbeat that creates the rhythm for everything else. When
we believe it's all up to us, it's all on us, it becomes too easy
to cut ourselves out of interdependence.

As my physical and mental health made new needs
known, it required new practices from me: when I was too
fatigued to go up stairs, saying "I can do it" didn't cancel
out that I couldn't. When I had to push back deadlines because I couldn't maintain the same workload—or could, but
at what cost?—persistent patience and asking for patience
got me through. I had to square the fact that no amount of
self-oriented striving made the humbling dent in my life
that the empathy of others did. At my most ambitious, I'm
someone with a strong desire to be *part* of a whole, not stand
alone, and the ways I practice care come from that desire.
That's why it felt urgent to explore care within the context of
ambition. Nothing can happen without care and without one
another, and just like ambition manifests in different ways,
care and community also take on many different forms.

Janice, seventy-one, and Brandon, forty, who are writing about their experiences with receiving care and caregiving together, know firsthand why prioritizing community is important—in part because of the differences their communities have made in their own lives. Early in the pandemic, Janice's cousin in Florida invited her to a nonviolent communication group that met via Zoom, and these women, all around Janice's age and living several states away, embraced her. As time went on, what started as an emotionally supportive community branched into a book group that tackled important subjects, including how to take antiracist action and how to face the challenges of aging. The group's facilitator, Stephanie, a teacher, family mediator, and caregiver herself, became a friend, mentoring Janice and Brandon through times of crisis. In turn, Janice is committed to being a mentor in support of other people with Parkinson's. "I hope I can reach people who need the things I have needed help with," she said. "It's difficult to face illness alone and honestly accept the consequences of a new situation. We grow by sharing."

Meanwhile, Brandon described how he and Janice, who share a household, had an isolating few years. There was a terrible situation with financial elder abuse that impacted Janice's options for care, followed by the pandemic, which heaped on health risks, exacerbated the caregiving crisis, and made it more challenging for Janice and Brandon to venture out. "You do get through that with your diehard friends, your diehard people," Brandon told me. "Sometimes family is community, but other times it isn't." Seeking out more community, a turning point for Brandon was joining a Facebook group for millennial caregivers, Caregiver Collective, in December 2017. Later, Brandon became one of Caring

Across Generations' 2020 Care Fellows, a cohort seeking to change the way caregiving is valued and supported in the United States. "It goes back to the idea of your individual goals and then this idea of collective goals," Brandon explained to me. "How can we meet up with that stream and swim with it and propel each other?"

In a report by Caring Across Generations, I noticed that—as they detailed the creation of a universal care infrastructure—they highlighted values that most of us share: love, care, community, family.[1] If we think of ambition as an opportunity to invest energy, effort, and imagination into what we value, then it's hard to fathom a list more foundational to how we move through the world, more robust in how it molds and shapes us, and more aspirational than the above. In their day-to-day and their collaborative writing, Brandon said, "If we're getting anywhere, it's because we're pouring energy into each other."

As Mia Birdsong illustrated so beautifully in the book *How We Show Up: Reclaiming Family, Friendship, and Community,* "We need a vision of community that is relevant and future-facing. A vision that brings us closer to one another, allows us to be vulnerable and imperfect, to grieve and stumble, to be held accountable and loved deeply. . . . We need models of success and leadership that fundamentally value love, care, and generosity of spirit."[2] Ambition doesn't cancel out our fundamental needs, nor can we out-ambition them. Loneliness, our fundamental neediness, our yearning for compassion and care, persist. In searching for how to highlight that caring for one another *is* inherently something we strive for, I wanted to speak to people who were seeing care and community manifest in their lives in different ways—because, in some form or fashion, we all need each other, at different times, in different ways.

The great fallacy here is that this knowledge—that we have all received care and will in the future; that we all want somewhere we can belong and feel held—situates itself in opposition to nearly everything we're told about striving. We've seen it in the myth of meritocracy that instructs that hustle in school or a job or hard work in general is the price of entry for each individual good life lived. We've seen it in how timelines that attach worth to age diminish the value of how our dreams change. We've seen it in work that seeks to keep us isolated because collective power disrupts a broken status quo. "Going it alone" isn't just a mood; it's a dictum, one that cheerleads optimization and the bootstraps mentality that make putting our goals first seem almost *noble*, somehow. Put yourself first, love yourself first, be responsible to yourself first have become the mantras of the age. What likely started as a well-intentioned means of reclaiming one's own agency and power has puffed up into individualism, amplifying self-reliance as a virtue and dodging fear of neediness, which is like attempting to move between raindrops—pointless. We're inevitably—just by the nature of rainfall—going to get soaked. In life, we're needy, even if we fear that fact.

I say that with confidence because *I* had that fear: that I would ask for too much from a friendship and then it would end; that needing help picking up a prescription from the pharmacy would inconvenience someone in a way they'd never forgive; even that living in an intergenerational household meant I wasn't doing enough to stand alone. Thank God for realizing I was reaching toward the wrong things, and instead of searching deep within myself for the little spark of hustle that made me a self-starter, I listened to people who focused on reaching *out* instead.

"Dependence on care has been pathologized, rather than recognized as part of our human condition," wrote the authors of *The Care Manifesto*.[3] They explained that "care is our individual and common ability to provide the political, social, material, and emotional conditions that allow the vast majority of people and living creatures on this planet to thrive—along with the planet itself." In the manifesto, care doesn't necessarily refer to explicit care or the act of caregiving. Rather, it has sustained focus on how living *itself* is about interdependence. The most ambitious thing we can do is care for each other.

On Caring for Each Other

As the report from Caring Across Generations noted, care being positioned as an individual responsibility—not a communal one—underscores the mentality that "if you struggle, there's something wrong with you."[4] It's isolating and individualistic, and in large part, it is there by societal design in the United States. To zoom out, first, there's what we know about caregiving itself: the history of devaluing family care work is a direct result of how white lawmakers excluded care workers from labor protections and fair wages. That's left caregivers underpaid or totally unpaid, and individuals without resources needed to live safe, fulfilling lives. Taking care of each other, a necessity, is also not an excuse for politicians and power brokers to sit passively and watch as people struggle to get by.

Prioritizing care also means advocating for infrastructure that supports caregivers and care workers: one example of this is Caring Across Generations' plans for universal long-term services and supports, universal childcare, paid leave for all, support for family caregivers, and raising wages and standards to ensure dignity for domestic and all care workers. Brandon and Janice still don't have access to a home health aide, which would provide real respite. Brandon has been certified as a home health aide and is paid for those hours, which helps. But later this year, they hope to transition to having a person from the home health agency take Brandon's place for about eighteen hours a week, he said. He told me about seeing a meme float around the internet that, if all caregivers went on strike for a day, life as we know it would essentially shut down. "But that's the thing: we're not going to do that," he told me. If all caregivers walked off to prove a point, Brandon said, Janice could fall and break bones, choke, or miss medication; people would suffer and die. "Our culture knows that we have no bluff to pull there, that there are enough people who won't let those things happen, to their own detriment," he continued. "Our culture knows that there will be people who care and who step up and do what has to be done; it's taken for granted." Having tangible support—both from the community and through resources and infrastructure—ensures that Brandon and Janice have the opportunity to live full, dignified lives on their own terms. As a report by Ai-Jen Poo and Sade Moonsammy stated: "We must begin to see care as a public good rather than a personal burden, and care failures as system failures rather than personal failures, worthy of public intervention and investment."[5]

Because Brandon and Janice share a household, they see each other's needs firsthand. Intergenerational living was presented as a pandemic-pod fad, with countless stories accompanied by photos of adults in their childhood bedrooms. Data from the Pew Research Center from September 2020[6] shows an increase in American young adults between the ages of eighteen and twenty-nine living with their parents. Many questioned whether those adults would ever "catch up" (think back to timelines and the marker of moving out on one's own being inherently hitched to the economy and class). But that misses the mark on how many communities have always prioritized multigenerational, more collectivist approaches to home and family, sharing resources like food, rent, housing, and utilities, but also easing the labor of childcare and eldercare, meal preparation and grocery shopping, cleaning and household maintenance, and the effort that comes with day-to-day living communally.

Even in the United States—where it seems independence is always the ultimate endgame—2016 numbers show that roughly 20 percent of the population in the United States was living in a multigenerational household already[7] and that Asian, Hispanic, and Black people were more likely to live in multigenerational households. In more recent data from Pew—which explains that multigenerational living has risen significantly in the United States over the past five decades and shows no signs of slowing down—people say finances are one significant reason for living together.[8] (A third of adults in the United States in multigenerational households say the cost of care is a major factor: about 25 percent cite adult caregiving, and 12 percent cite childcare.) But people also pointed to "an emotional component," according to Pew, including companionship: 23 percent said living in a multigenerational household is stressful much of the time, while 54 percent said it's rewarding mostly or always.[9] (Not unlike other relationships, it seems like living with other people is probably both stressful *and* rewarding—the stuff being in community with others is made of!)

This isn't to say living in an intergenerational household is the best choice for everyone, but for some, it creates a built-in support system. Syeedah, the twenty-three-year-old mother and graduate student who talked to me about parenting while in school, mentioned that no matter how many times living in an intergenerational household might frustrate her, "I feel like I would have had to give up so much if I didn't have that built-in support." There are six people in Syeedah's household, including her and her daughter. Syeedah's mother, siblings, and grandmother all live in the house, too, and the family, especially Syeedah's mom and grandmother, rotate to help with childcare. They take Syeedah's daughter to martial arts on Tuesdays and Thursdays while Syeedah goes to night school. Syeedah's younger cousin and her daughter attend the same school and often convince her grandmother to take them to McDonald's. Syeedah's boyfriend, her daughter's dad, is often over at the house too because their daughter lives with Syeedah most of the time. Her aunt lives five minutes away, and so Syeedah and her daughter are often there on weekends.

"Even after school," Syeedah told me of her daughter, "she's home with my grandma, my mom, so there's always somebody home." Her community is wider than her family, too. She used "like a family" to describe Generation Hope, the nonprofit that ensures all student parents have opportunities to succeed. In addition to the academic support, financial support, career services, and mental health support that Generation Hope provides, Syeedah talked about the nonprofit's "family dinners," where scholars, as Generation Hope calls young people in their programs, sit down together once a month for dinner. The kids all play together, and parents enjoy a meal, camaraderie, and guest speakers. "At the time, that was like the only social interaction I was really getting, because I was so busy with school and work. I had no money, so I couldn't really go out with my friends," Syeedah told me. There was also comfort in this community, specifically, because they were all similarly aged parents, and understood one another's experiences. They shared advice and motivated one another to keep going when school, work, and parenting felt overwhelming. While not as literal, it felt like another version of "there's always somebody home." What a way to describe knowing we have people, that a community is in our corner.

Having lived alone, with roommates, and with a significant other in the past, I'm now living in an intergenerational household with my family, in part because of the pandemic. With a remote job, at least some flexibility in my schedule, and the desire to focus less on, well, me, it made sense that I was in a position to do tasks like going to the grocery store during the day when it's less crowded and help coordinate care for my grandparents. Are these ambitious actions? I don't know. What I know is that they require patience, consistency, and the ability to move in alignment with a larger whole than my immediate desires; it means learning how to care for my own needs alongside those of others—meaning that I'm consistently motivated to be more thoughtful in my actions, take more initiative, and seek out where I can be most useful. And through that framing, it certainly doesn't feel *unambitious.* "Oftentimes, caring ambitiously is part and parcel of loving someone, but it doesn't have to be," wrote Julia B. Bear and Todd L. Pittinsky, authors of *The Caregiving Ambition: What It Is and Why It Matters at Home and Work.* "Many people are driven by a strong caregiving ambition, an individual's aspirations to nurture and care for others above and beyond any obligation."[10] Some would argue that's part of what being in a community is: the obligation exists because it matters enough for us to choose it.

And as we know, family and community are ever-shifting and personally defined. Much of the phrasing used to describe the communities we are part of and families we create, including "chosen family," have deep histories—they aren't new terms to explain celebrating Friendsgiving. By definition, "chosen families are nonbiological kinship bonds, whether legally recognized or not, deliberately chosen for the purpose of mutual support and love," according to *The SAGE Encyclopedia of Marriage, Family, and Couples Counseling.*[11] Some research connects the term *chosen family* to anthropologist Kath Weston's *Families We Choose: Lesbians, Gays, Kinship,* published in 1991, in which Weston examined the role close friends and communities played in the lives of queer people who endured homophobia and rejection from their biological families.[12]

"Caregiving in the LGBT community follows a very different pattern that reflects the importance of 'chosen family' in the lives of LGBT+ older adults," Nancy J. Knauer wrote, noting that rather than relying on biological relatives, LGBT+

older adults care for each other.[13] Knauer noted that other researchers suggested high levels of eldercare in the LGBT+ community connects to the "culture of care" that started in the 1980s during the early years of the HIV/AIDS pandemic "when the LGBT community mobilized to provide informal care and services in the face of governmental indifference and societal condemnation." Caring as fulfilling a need, yes, but also caring as an act of community in and of itself.

"While 'chosen family' is not an exclusively queer experience, the phenomenon of caregiving outside the bio-legal family framework has been shown to run parallel along multiple, intersecting lines of social disenfranchisement," wrote researchers of "'We Just Take Care of Each Other': Navigating 'Chosen Family' in the Context of Health, Illness, and the Mutual Provision of Care amongst Queer and Transgender Young Adults."[14] (Again, the devaluation of care work silos care, prioritizing heteronormative concepts of family and privileging those who can be "ideal workers" in service of capitalism.)

When we think of policy that's necessary to helping us support communities, this is a big one: according to a 2021 report by the Center for American Progress, data from 2020 shows that only 18.4 percent of American households follow a traditional, nuclear family structure.[15] That means more and more people are taking care of one another without blood or legal ties—from partners who aren't legally married, to roommates who contribute to the same household, to neighbors who pop by to help with mowing the grass. Expanding access to paid and medical leave is critically important, the report states, but that policy has to be reimagined to let workers use paid leave to care for loved ones who aren't necessarily biological relatives or legally related.[16] Another example seared in my brain is that most human resources policies in the United States offer one to five days of bereavement leave—if they offer it at all—and three is the average.[17] But even more grimly, some reports[18] assess that the number of *days off to grieve* tick downward depending on biological and legal ties, meaning someone might get three days for the death of a biological family member and zero days for the loss of a friend, a profoundly dark assessment of how much we're supposed to care. How we provide care—and who we are encouraged to care for—is constricted by America's legal, work, and education systems.

Including and beyond chosen family, people have poured compassion and commitment into their communities throughout history. Understanding why and how chosen or found families are created feels key to emphasizing how much ambition these relationships consist of—an enduring commitment with the goal of care that isn't reinforced by biological obligation.

In her book *Essential Labor*, Angela Garbes wrote of interdependence: "Building relationships can be messy and awkward. Interdependence requires real communication, empathy, sorting through calendars and logistics."[19] Via phone, she told me we *are* interdependent; we actually want to take care of one another and want to be taken care of. That can look like sharing a household, but it can also just mean sharing time, attention, and care. Garbes mentions needing a return to a commons, including spaces like community centers, where generations can interact with each other. We're interdependent because we must be, but it also just feels good. And yes, this is about a feeling.

"American life is really hard," Garbes explained. "It's only working for a very small percentage of people. And even people who are financially successful or more stable—a lot of people just feel like something's missing," she added. No one feels especially happy. Everything feels scarce and hard. We don't think about the intangible, emotional parts of community. The first thing that comes to mind is usually coordination and logistics because time is so scarce. But pursuing community ultimately makes life easier. You ask people what makes life worth living, Garbes said, and it is always closeness, friendship, other people. It's us that make it worth living for each other. And that's ambitious. "One of my ambitions is to be like a good friend, a good community member," Garbes added. "That's a goal for me, and it feels more in line with my values and just who I am as a person."

When Annie Zean Dunbar, AM, a PhD candidate at the University of Denver's Graduate School of Social Work, thinks about *why* we care about each other, "It's a human imperative to hopefully bring goodness into the world because that's what we want in return," she told me. "We want that sense of reciprocity." Dunbar, who moved to the United States when she was a child, is conducting doctoral research around the experiences of immigrants with marginalized experiences, as well as on community practices and mutuality of care systems. She sees care as expansive: feeding your family is a form of care and teaching your neighbors new skills, like cooking or gardening, is a form of care. We often engage in small forms of care without even realizing it. But care gets relegated as something menial because of two key factors, she explained: First, the patriarchy maligns care and care work as inconsequential—the opposite of what it is.

Second, socialization in the United States sets many of us up to feel like we're removed from what is happening to others and what's happening in the world. "It makes it a lot harder to understand care as a weaving project," she explained. "When we choose to give energy or time or resources to things, that is a form of care—what you nurture grows."

Spaces, Places, and People Within Them

"Community sucks sometimes," Dunbar told me, laughing. "But the fun has to outweigh the suck, right?" We don't have to individually, personally love every single person in our community, "but you can honor the fact that they're a person, and you can honor the fact that they deserve to have a life that is fulfilled and happy with as minimal suffering as possible," she added. While some versions of community might only be people in our immediate orbit, I was curious about what it looks like in practice to expand community to include a larger group.

We can start this in small ways, Dunbar explained, telling me to think back to primary school. What are some of the first things a new class does? They introduce themselves. "During the first day of school, everybody gets to know each other," Dunbar said. "These are extensions of how do you show up." The hard part is defining community because community can mean *everything*, Dunbar told me, from our social positions, to our identities, to shared spaces. Citing the work of her mentor Dr. Ramona Beltran, a scholar who describes herself as a mixed-race Xicana of Yaqui and Mexica descent, Dunbar now makes it a point to introduce herself by saying who she is and who her people are. "I think

that that's such an important shift from, 'This is what I do,'"
Dunbar explained. Thinking of herself, Dunbar said that she
does lots of things: she's a grad student, which means most
days she "suffers and cries" about her work, and she's a parent, a partner, a youngest sibling. "We totally lose all of the
nuances when we ask people what their title is, as opposed to
who they are," she said.

Dunbar is especially trying to think of this with regard
to intergenerational spaces. She recalled being fourteen and
attending open mic nights, full of eighteen- to twenty-two-
year-olds to fifty-year-old beat poets, where she learned to
be a good listener and to accept feedback. Now, she wants
more of those spaces, where people of all ages can show up
safely. "I want us to really think about it, as we imagine futures, as we imagine mutual aid, how we invite young people
to show up, how do we invite elders and older people to show
up, how we invite children to show up," she said, adding that
there has to be intention to include the experiences, voices,
and desires of all types of people.

Danielle Littman, PhD candidate at the University of
Denver's School of Social Work, is part of a research team
looking at mutual aid, which Dunbar is also part of, and has
also seen those effects in her own life, finding ways to proactively, safely connect with neighbors. "Some of the most
meaningful interactions I've had [are] when I'm, like, 'I just
made extra banana bread that I'm not going to eat all of, will
somebody help me eat it?'" she said. It's about recognizing
that every day, we could be more connected than we are.
Littman's work focuses on creating spaces of belonging and
healing for people who experience marginalization from societal structures, and she said there are true negative health

impacts to being isolated and disconnected.[20] Right now, two of the environments where she's conducting research are a program that brings artistic programming to incarcerated individuals in Colorado, and another is a supportive housing program for young adults who have previously been unhoused or unstably housed. In both instances, connection matters and is more feasible when spaces themselves are designed with communities in mind.

"We think of our first place is our home, our second place is school or work, [our] third place is community settings, socially engaged settings," Littman explained, places where we can interact socially and all belong. In theory, these third places—a term coined by Ramon Oldenburg and Dennis Brissett,[21] Littman told me—could include libraries, parks, or even coffee shops. But we know not all those so-called common spaces are accessible. For example, the impacts of existing in public spaces are inequitably oppressive, Littman said, pointing to how queer young people and young people of color are treated for hanging out in stores or other public areas for too long. Another example would be community spaces not being accessible to people who use mobility equipment, including wheelchairs or canes, or public spaces not including places to sit. "We all deserve to have that feeling of connection; we all deserve to have a sense of belonging," she told me.

Littman used to live on the South Side of Chicago and pointed to what's happening in old school buildings. They're being repurposed into community makerspaces—third places. "I'm really interested in this idea of repurposing and reimagining, through community-led design processes, what could become a space that is able to foster and celebrate what it is

that we need in this neighborhood or in this community," she
told me. For a fellowship project, she also assembled a future
map of a park in Denver—of what it could look like in ten
years—including a neighborhood tool library, food exchange,
childcare spaces, vast community gardens, and safe injection
sites. That's the goal: "Third places become the spaces where
you can relationally connect to one another, but also tangibly
meet one another's needs," she explained. "It brings me hope
to think about the fact that the more our structures fail us, the
more we will recognize that we need each other."

What We Share

In a Zoom meeting with me from their living rooms in Chicago, Denali, thirty-nine, and Sarah-Jayne, thirty-six, talked
me through the development of their neighborhood's mutual
aid group—the same group that started the Rolling Hang.
During the start of the pandemic, Sarah-Jayne saw that an
organizer, writer, and abolitionist she admires, Kelly Hayes,
shared a project that aimed to have autonomous mutual aid
in each neighborhood. She already had to work in person
and closely mitigate her risk factors and was ready to drop off
prescriptions or provide groceries where needed. Eventually,
she ended up creating a flyer and going around her neighborhood, essentially saying: "Hello, I'm your neighbor. This is
terrifying. Here's my number. I made a Facebook group. Do
you want to take care of each other?" she told me, laughing.

In addition to the Rolling Hang, the group has provided
cash aid, including helping keep a neighbor in her home,
has helped people schedule vaccine appointments, and has
represented their neighborhood at the local food sovereignty

coalition, which works to rebuild local food economies. The food sovereignty coalition brings a bunch of mutual aid groups together, working via WhatsApp, a Google Sheet, and a warehouse space, where people bag food and groceries that have been collected from venues. Denali described it as "moving at the speed of people, but it's also getting a shit-load done. . . . It's shared ambition."

Sarah-Jayne is an abolitionist and thinks of the work in terms of world building—practicing being the person you want to be, imagining the world you want to bring into being. As a *New York Times Magazine* feature on Ruth Wilson Gilmore and Gilmore's work stated, "Abolition means not just the closing of prisons but the presence, instead, of vital systems of support that many communities lack," including education, housing, and health care.[22]

Sarah-Jayne pointed out that they don't have to invent anything. "It's existed for much longer than capitalism has existed," she said of mutual aid. "And we can look to communities that know exactly how to do this—Indigenous communities and the Black radical organizing tradition," she added. None of what they are doing is the first time it is being done, she said, and they are continuously learning. "It's the organizing version of the beautifully exquisitely ordinary," she added. One of the elements that Denali loves the most is that it gives everyone the ability to say "I need something" or "thank you." She describes it as gentle, forgiving, and fun. But they also hold each other accountable, including one time they all sat down together and named something in their own life they wanted others to hold them accountable for. They've elevated the idea of what a neighbor is and what it means in practice.

According to the work of Tyesha Maddox, PhD, mutual aid is when "a group works together to implement collective strategies and pool resources to meet the community's needs when there is a lack of government assistance."[23] It's not charity—usually, charities have boards of directors and make decisions informed by boards or donors, focused on one area of need. With mutual aid, there is no hierarchy. As Mariame Kaba told the *New Yorker*, mutual aid is "not community service—you're not doing service for service's sake. You're trying to address real material needs."[24] As one commentary stated, "A long history of reciprocal caring relationships that seek to survive and resist white settler colonialism/capitalism exists in Indigenous and other marginalized communities,"[25] a stark opposite to the "survival of the fittest" mentality, privatizing and profiting from caregiving, and emphasis on the individual.[26] (The term *mutual aid* is credited to Peter Kropotkin, a nineteenth-century anarchist who used examples from humans and animals to show that its actually cooperation—not competition—that's the most important factor for survival.[27])

Research by Maddox states that among the Black American community, mutual aid societies were established back in the eighteenth century, and Maddox's work specifically mentions the New York African Mutual Relief Society in 1808, which was "organized around the principles of mutual interest, mutual benefit, and mutual relief." In "What Is Mutual Aid?," Maddox's slide-show presentation, she also highlights early Chinese family associations in San Francisco that connected immigrants to employment and provided payment of medical bills, burial expenses, and funds for travel, among other needs, and *landsmanshaftn*, which were benefit societies for Central and Eastern European Jewish immigrants that pooled resources. In 1892, there were about eighty-seven *landsmanshaftn* in New York City. More recently, the Black Panther Party for Self-Defense, which Maddox's work details, included survival programs with free clothing, legal aid education, free breakfast programs, and early childhood education programs.[28]

Because the West's imperialism, colonialism, and capitalism continue to harm communities, community care and reciprocal needs persist. It's the sustained investment, imagination, and generative nature of mutual aid that feels so ambitious. Britney, who I spoke to about overwork, thinks that mutual aid is one of the most ambitious movements happening in the United States right now. She thinks that a lot of young people, in particular, were activated by the events of summer 2020 and are "just over a political system that continually fails to meet our people's basic needs." What draws her to mutual aid is that it's accessible to participate wherever you are and however you can, something she hasn't experienced before. It isn't a nonprofit, a religiously affiliated group, or anything involving a hierarchy. "If you have money, you can use it to buy groceries for food distribution. If you have time, you can actually distribute the food. If you have neither, you can repost social media mutual aid requests," she explained. "Mutual aid meets people where they are, and I love it for that."

"First, there has to be a sense that it's not a zero-sum game," said Dunbar, who is part of a research team that looks at the values and beliefs underlying mutual aid throughout the pandemic. It's not about us doing something and then waiting for payback: "There are going to be times where you have more to give, there are going to be times where you have nothing to give, and sometimes you're going to need something." Dunbar told me it's about shifting our understanding to know anyone can be a giver and receiver at the same time. Throughout the pandemic, Dunbar said, there was a surge of people who identified as apolitical—or didn't have any sort of more radical orientation—latching onto mutual aid practices, wondering how to show up for neighbors or community members. "I think that it's been really cool to see this larger conversation emerge around care systems," Dunbar told me. "I'm hoping that as we move along, we really develop an understanding of the fact that mutual aid emerges because systems leave people out, sometimes intentionally."

"When we think about mutual aid, that's where we're starting from: people *deserve*," Dunbar said. Using an example of American policy, Dunbar flagged the distinction: political parties start from the presumption that we can't give everyone health care, as opposed to the starting point that "everyone deserves health care." "People deserve housing, people deserve food, people deserve community, they deserve wholeness—those are the ways that mutual aid orients us to think about the world," Dunbar added. When we enter mutual aid as a practice, "we have to say that that should be the starting point—we all fundamentally deserve to have whole happy lives," Dunbar said. "And that for each person requires different things."

Both Dunbar and Littman point out a key way to get started. "My first suggestion would be: look to what already exists," Littman said. Often, she sees people want to get involved, and the first instinct is to create something. But *contributing*, rather than creating, is often crucial, where we're diverting our resources to an existing network. Dunbar said we can throw a stone and find a mutual aid group or network in our communities, and social media is flooded with guides and tool kits that can offer starting points.

In addition to where we show up, equally important is how. We can slow down—if everyone is burnt out in six months, nothing is going to get done, Dunbar pointed out—and be intentional. For example, if your neighborhood has a community fridge, maybe you can't afford to buy anything for it, *but* you might be able to take an hour every other week and help clean it out. "It's not [just] the big gestures," Dunbar said. "Part of it is figuring out what your role is." If you're good at talking to your neighbors, to get them to come together on an issue, that's your role. If you have resources—food, funds, time—that can be your role. "You can't be everything, and it doesn't have to happen all right now," Dunbar said. "It's not just about me. It's all of us."

In Our Communities

Meeting people where they are is a form of community care. For Samantha, a thirty-year-old, her changing relationship with ambition coincided with her introduction to community care, which she characterized as shifting away from "being totally reliant on the self and more reliant on the idea that we do actually owe each other something." For all the talk of personal responsibility that propels ambition—all the "make it happen" and "believe in yourself"—the other side is discussed far more rarely and without the same rah-rah, motivational undertone: we owe each other; we have a responsibility to each other.

Samantha was an ambitious kid who was hyperinvolved all through high school and recalled a period of time in the early aughts and late nineties where girls being perfectionists was a *moment*. In her senior year of high school, after a lifetime of being fairly sick off and on, she was diagnosed with Crohn's disease. Later, in Los Angeles in her early twenties, with a dream of working in television writing, she has a vivid memory of noticing what one of her LA roommates wrote on a chalkboard in the apartment: *Good things come to those who hustle.* It was a motto for the era.

It wasn't until the move to LA that Samantha's Crohn's disease became a "central figure," as she put it, in her life. During a weekend her dad happened to be visiting, she ended up with severe rectal bleeding and had to go to the hospital. By the time she was discharged, it became clear she wasn't going to be able to stay in LA: she had no support system, the Crohn's was getting worse, and she was taking a biologic medication and pain medication. She moved home and returned to her old job. "There was no ambition involved. It was just like survival," she said.

Over the course of two years at home, she started writing a blog about being sick. "I feel like if I start a blog about my experience, my family will read it, and then I won't have to say these things to them," she said. "I historically had a hard time asking people for help." But starting the blog and being more open about the realities of being a sick person gave her loved ones an entry point, she said. Now she thinks about it as: How do we show people that we'll show up for them, even if we don't have to? There are all kinds of layers to community care, Samantha told me, from volunteering at a soup kitchen in your neighborhood to checking on a neighbor during a heat wave. "When your best friend's mom dies and you bring her a lasagna, that is community care. When your friend is in labor and you go watch her dog, that is community care," Samantha continued. When you're someone's ride home from a medical procedure or bring them groceries when they have COVID, that's community care. "I think that community care is the idea that we are able to form those networks for each other, even in the absence of structural or maybe familial bonds," she told me. "Not only can we be that for each other, but like we have to be that for each other because those structures have failed us."

It's not that Samantha considers herself some sort of community care expert—she said she wasn't aware of the concept until later in her medical journey—but she's witnessed firsthand how her friends, family, coworkers, and neighbors have created a community that improves her quality of life. "I have had dozens of phone calls with friends in their midtwenties who are transitioning off of their parents' health insurance and don't know what the hell to do and so they're calling me for advice," Samantha said. When she got sick, "I didn't know anyone who was living in this weird gray area of, like, I'm really, really sad that I'm in pain all the time, but I also have to go to work," she told me. Finding people in her community to walk through those experiences with her was a game changer.

"I think that that kind of digital, virtual community is what disabled people like myself have built," Samantha explained. She has a few people she could call if she needed someone to drive her to an appointment; she has more people to lean on for emotional support. Sometimes, the two coincide: when COVID-19 vaccines first were released in her city, Samantha said it was a *"Hunger Games*-style lottery" just to get an appointment. At eight o'clock in the morning on a Friday, around twenty of her loved ones gathered on a Zoom, all trying to secure an appointment for her at once. It was chaotic, helpful, and *fun*.

I thought about how this has gone down in my group chats—usually comprised of friends from different locations—over the past couple months alone: crowdsourcing the best way to shop your own health insurance; a script to help someone negotiate a higher fee for their work; coordinating grocery and food deliveries when someone was sick with COVID; advice on finding a new doctor; lists of reproductive justice resources and direct services by locale. You do it because you care. And it works like a cycle because we're all in different phases of our lives, which bring about different needs at different times.

Sometimes, those different needs bring about opportunities to create communities. When Fiona Lowenstein, now a twenty-eight-year-old journalist and author, was in their early twenties and living in New York, they'd gotten an entry-level job in publishing a week after graduating college. Without the groups that defined their academic life— a feminist comedy troupe and feminist publication, among others—they were lonely. At the time, they relied on movement and time at the gym to help balance their mental health and found themselves going to fitness classes and meditation classes that were technically helpful to them but expensive and "also really exclusive, shitty environments." "I'm a thin, white person, I'm cis-passing, and I just had a lot of friends that were Black or fat or plus-sized or trans and do not pass as cis, who were, like, 'I just can't go into that space,'" Fiona explained. Some of their friends were interested in trying boxing classes or learning about breath work, but most offerings felt exclusive, Fiona said.

That's how the first iteration of Body Politic, originally a queer feminist wellness collective and now a grassroots health justice organization, began. Fiona invited a group of friends to their home, encouraged them to invite their friends, and started an informal conversation about what queer feminist wellness meant to them. "How can I create a space where we can do some of this stuff and talk about some of this stuff but not separate from its political implications and cultural histories?" Fiona said. "And in a place where everyone can really feel safe."

Body Politic's work—and the way it has bloomed—is an incredible example of community that's changed shape as the community itself evolves. Originally, events were held in person at community spaces that had sliding scales for room rentals, and everyone— from organizers, including Fiona, to speakers, to workshop leaders—volunteered. Then, at the start of the pandemic, Fiona and their friend contracted COVID—during the time in New York when no one could get a test and the inaccurate assumption that people in their twenties wouldn't be badly affected was prevalent. They began experiencing symptoms they weren't seeing on the news or CDC list; they felt isolated from their roommates and friends, who didn't seem to understand what they were going through.

Fiona was hospitalized and wrote an op-ed for the *New York Times* on the health crisis that is long COVID, linking to an online support group they'd created.[29] Two thousand people signed up overnight. They outgrew Instagram Messenger. They got too big for WhatsApp. The group ended up on Slack, and they started noticing that people were organically becoming leaders within the community.

Fiona stepped down from Body Politic as president toward the end of summer 2021 and now considers themself an ally of the organization, thinking of engaging in community building through their journalism work. The pandemic coincided with a time when there was massive upheaval in Fiona's life and family, including deaths, divorces, and moves. Whatever plan had been laid out, whatever they expected of themself, was no longer. "As bad as that is, in the rubble, [there are] a lot of other paths you can take," they added. Fiona is discovering different forms of community, including joining more LGBT+ communities and witnessing how queer elders have radical, communal approaches to life. That's helped them think more creatively, too. "That is the most important thing—creating the life that works for you over what people might have expected you to do when you were twelve or twenty," they noted.

That also means creating spaces that are responsive to community needs and even communities within a larger whole. Angela Meriquez Vázquez, MSW, Body Politic's interim president, told me that the priority is bringing people into conversations in a way that's equalizing and helps people find commonalities, rather than emphasizing hierarchies, whether that be in education level, income, race or ethnicity, gender, or ability. Angela is Latina and grew up working class and has devoted her life to grassroots movement building. "I am trying to soak myself [in] and do more thinking and learning from other grassroots organizers," she told me. "Immigrants' rights organizers here in LA, Black Lives Matter movements, even youth-led movements," in addition to AIDS activists, ME/CFS (myalgic encephalomyelitis/ chronic fatigue syndrome) activists, and disability rights activists who have been doing the work for a long time. She doesn't want to make long COVID advocacy out to be so unique "because, really, we're yet another symptom of how white supremacist capitalism doesn't work for most people."

Interdependence is my ambition—one that, perhaps ironically for the softness and grace care evokes, takes discipline. My default setting remains that I am responsible for myself, or should be, even as I am proven wrong every day—and glad to be. Rewiring that has meant changing both how I show up and how I let others in. In showing up, it means doing so proactively instead of reactively. To be invested in my communities, causes I care about or my neighborhood, means no longer waiting for someone to send me an invitation. In opening the door, it means that when someone extends me grace, I don't rebuff them with a chipper, "Oh, thank you, but I've got it." I don't "got it." But what we do have is each other. I am still learning that: that people won't leave when you ask for too much, that I have something worth sharing with them too.

We all have needs that are going to change as we grow and meet different parts of ourselves, our bodies, our minds, our circumstances, and our surroundings. The way we think about caring for our communities, our families, and our loved ones is an extension of how we must think about caring for ourselves: worthy of time, worthy of resources, and worthy of striving toward something we've built together.

13: All That Glitters

I have a confession to make. (Yes, another one.)

I was on a work Zoom that didn't require my attention—just my attendance—so I was dialed into the chat of an initiative I volunteer for. Toggling between laptop and phone screens—like a living, breathing cautionary tale of too much screen time—I was bouncing from project to project. Then, boom, in my inbox: the marked-up first draft of this book, ready for me to take it apart and put it back together again.

My first impulse was to slash everything: to cancel the tennis balls I promised myself I'd go hit, to postpone a catch-up call with a friend a third time, to nix the early night's rest I'd been looking forward to all day. If there was ever a time to be ambitious, this was it! Phone on do not disturb! Writing playlist on, volume up! Writing candle lit! And after this big lift is done, won't it feel great to have earned time off, to experience such joy, to give myself grace, to hug someone I love?

Then I realized I'd have to look myself in the eye at some point. I'd have to emerge from behind my screen and earbuds and hear the voices of the people who took time out of their days—their own striving—to share their stories with me. I'd have to sit with the people who sat with me when it all fell down in my life, my health, and my ambition. I'd have to let go of these pages that have shaped my days and my thoughts for more than a year.

With ambition, there is never a tidy "after" or endpoint; it's generative, because aspirations build on each other. There is never a single fulfilled moment because as we aspire, we expand: it makes fulfillment a process, a practice, not a grand finale. There is, as we know, always more. Was I going to have written this many pages about the fallacy of ambition and the flaws of earning gold stars and the dire straits of living a life rooted in earning—and still make my own ambition the star of every single show?

My overzealous reaction is to take a sledgehammer to benchmarks and tear the gold stars in half. I'd like to announce I am not ambitious anymore, and you know, in a way, I think I'm not. I thought about the glory of working around the clock, the big finishes and grand finales—and how they just didn't feel the same. When I first began publishing my writing, I celebrated every single time, whether it was grabbing discount flowers in line at the grocery store or ordering a pizza. Somewhere along the way, I lost the habit when the giddiness expired. The celebration was replaced with "thank God, one thing completed," lapped by fear over what would happen next. I wonder about what got lost when celebration stopped: when it was the next thing, then the thing after, and . . . why not one more after that.

Celebrating meant acknowledging. It meant a pause—not for the accomplishment but for noticing that ambition in the context of a whole life happening around it. It was an important thing but not *the* thing.

And what I've learned is that I am ambitious for the pauses.

—

At the start of this book, we talked about the idea of spending a lifetime proving yourself—that worth is the thing we earn at the end of the story. I've thought about it nearly every day since: the relentless *more* of ambition, hustle's attachment to our basic needs and scarcity of time and resources, the individualism that instructs we must keep going at all costs, all focus on the endings: what we will have completed, who we will have become, what we will have earned. Rather than landing on a single new definition of ambition, I found a stratosphere of everything I missed when I thought ambition was only one thing.

I'm ambitious about being a friend. My goal is to follow up with friends like I follow up with pitches. My motivation is to become someone on whom others depend, who listens, who shows up, not when it's convenient but when it's needed.

I'm ambitious about imagination. My goal is to move away from what I know I can get right and sit in everything I've been too scared to try. My motivation is to not edit my imagination down to what I would change about my life, my dreams, or my circumstances, but rather, what I can see even beyond them.

I'm ambitious about interdependence. My goal is to contribute: to mutual aid groups and folks doing good work in my area, to care I provide my communities and friends. My motivation is that to care for others, I have to practice asking for care myself.

I'm ambitious about this pause. Not the future I can envision; not the deadline I've met. This second, the only one I get for sure.

I read a quote where someone mentioned not letting the world place limits on your ambition. That could be read a multitude of ways: refusing to allow the world to tell you what matters, taking back your time and how you spend it, rejecting the idea that failure is final and our missteps make up the heft of it. But I also choose to read it as refusing to let the world limit our imaginations. That defiance—that our efforts, time, imagination, and care can be oriented toward what matters to us most deeply in the face of a world that's screaming to-do lists at us—feels ambitious. I noticed the more imaginative I got about my ambition, the more I felt my dreams stack up around me. It was such a difference from the striving of before—where I'd worked so hard to stay on track that I hadn't realized the track was gone. Trying so forcefully to strive toward what I thought would hold me up guided me away from everything else: everything I could've tried, everything I am still learning, everything I am practicing letting myself want.

A few weeks ago, a friend gently bulldozed me into sending them a list of dreams. No way, I balked initially. Right now, I want to aspire to nothing. But I thought about it as I walked, and realized the aspirations—which ranged from "do one in-person bookstore event" to "adopt a cat"—had a shared set of standards by which I was subconsciously checking them. Maybe it's not a new definition of ambition so much as a new framework to hold it: Who came up with this aspiration? Is it my idea or something random I thought I should aspire to? What resources does it take to be ambitious about this, and is it worth it? What does this ambition serve? Is it me, a loved one, or something I care deeply about, or just an arbitrary marker of success? How can the personal definitions we have of ambition expand?

A personal rethink isn't going to singlehandedly detangle ambition from capitalism; they run off each other. It also feels relevant how much energy, aspiration, effort, attention, time, and care do the truly gritty work of imagining a new and better world beyond oppressive systems. Whether that's ambition or not isn't a clear-cut answer, but it's the kind of aspiration backed by action I want to learn from and practice.

We may not all consider ourselves ambitious, running on a treadmill toward success that keeps scooting us backward with every stride, but I think it's safe to say we all want better lives. We want to feel fulfilled, connected, and like our worth isn't dependent on the last project we handled or task we did. If ambition is going to persist—and given how long it's been part of the cultural, political, and societal makeup, we can safely bet a version of it will—that's how we reconsider it. We imagine it not as striving for a goal that dematerializes as soon as we reach it but more an investment in our imaginations. In who we are. In what matters to us. In what we're striving toward together.

Acknowledgments

Getting to write this book changed the way I see and experience the world. I attribute that entirely to the brilliant people who made time to share their knowledge and experiences with me, and the people in my own life who show me, time and time again, what it means to be ambitious about each other. It takes so many people to make a book. The writing and reporting that appears in this book is so much bigger than me. It's the sum of people's stories, their time, and their work that shaped both the pages you read here and my thinking in too many ways to name. To everyone who spoke with me for this project, my thanks will never be enough. The opportunity to hear these stories is the honor of a lifetime.

To Mollie Weisenfeld, the book editor of my dreams: You took a book that I thought was about *losing* ambition and somehow made me more ambitious about writing than I've ever been. I learned so much by working with you (specifics, specifics, specifics), and that's such a gift. I'm not sure Mollie remembers it, but on our first call, I rambled about how my life had fallen apart, and for the first time, my ambition hadn't saved me. Well, my ambition may not have come to the rescue, but having the chance to work with Mollie on this book certainly did. Mollie, you deserve a whole sky of gold stars for your editing, your patience with my emails, and for being the best partner in this project.

To Jamie Carr, my agent and friend: I can't imagine writing with anyone else. At every turn, your sense of humor, your advocacy, and your thoughtful thinking make you the best agent and an even better friend. It's hard to fathom that this book began as a one-line email about how I'd been thinking a lot about ambition lately. Only you could've seen what I was really trying to say in those first shaky pages I'd written just for myself, and only you could bring it to life this way. From emailing you while crying in an airport to celebrating every win, big and small, I am endlessly grateful for you. None of this would have happened without you.

To Katie Walsh, who fact-checked this book and pushed my thinking at every turn: I'm so honored to have gotten to work with you on this project, and am so grateful for the skill, attention to detail, and care you brought to these pages. I learned so much working with you, and getting to do so was such a gift—both personally and professionally.

To the incredible teams that have worked on this book: I'm so grateful for the support of The Book Group, and for the brilliant Hachette Books team, especially Lauren Rosenthal, Michael Barrs, Fred Francis, Amber Morris, Kate Mueller, Sara Pinsonault, Amanda Kain, Melanie Schmidt, and so many other incredible people who brought their skill to this project.

To my family: I lucked out. A million times over. My mom remains the person I run everything by, the person who believes in me when I certainly do not, the one who taught me from my earliest days that I was—that we all are—worth more than any gold star or grade or single accomplishment. My dad endlessly encourages me to go for it—even when I'm tired, even when I'm frustrated, and never doubts for a second that things will turn out alright in the end. They remain the best teachers I've ever had. I'm the oldest—and least cool—sibling of four, and Luke, Matt, and Annie are my best friends. I learn from *their* ambition: Luke's tenacity, Matt's innovation, Annie's brilliance. I learn from the patience and strength of my grandparents. (To top it off, the family pets, Tom Hanks, Butters, Rory, and Margo, remain the *real* stars of our family's show.)

It's difficult to articulate just how profoundly my life has been impacted by the extraordinary people I've been fortunate enough to work with, but I'm going to try. Over the course of the past couple of years, I'm so lucky to have worked with editors who have helped me grow as a writer and given me chances I couldn't imagine. To name a few: Allegra Kirkland, for letting me turn my thoughts on work into a column and for being one of the best people and editors I've ever gotten to know; Brittney McNamara, for letting me pitch a dream three-part series and letting me learn from your incredible edits; Ko Bragg, one of the greatest writers, editors, and human beings around, for time spent helping me develop a dream project centering youth and for sharing such deep expertise with me; Lovey Cooper, for the endless time, support, and skill poured into that project, and for believing in stories that center young people; Leah Johnson, who let me write a "gold stars" column and taught me a million things in the process; Stella Cabot Wilson, who edited the first essay I ever wrote about writing this book; Jennifer Reitman and Clare Murphy for letting me think big on the page. To Dr. Alexis Redding, whose support and kindness have meant the world. To the Carter Center, and particularly to Katie Hawkins-Gaar and Dr. Kortni Alston, who I am so honored to learn from. To the Kentucky Student Voice Team—and especially to Norah, Ramona, Cadence, Esha, Minhal, Connor, Raima, Sara, Pragya, Rachel, Ian, and Andrew, who teach me so much every single day.

I'm so fortunate to have been buoyed by incredible friendships throughout the course of writing this book, and beyond it. I'm in the lucky position of having too many loved ones and not enough space. So, endless thanks to, to name a few . . . Madysen Luebke, who read my crappiest drafts, listened on the phone as I cried, and is one of the greatest writers and editors I know—I'm thankful a million times over. To Abdullah Shihipar, for Dunkin' and text gossip; to Sonia, for all our walks and all our memories; to Becca Andrews, whose work and presence inspire me and pushed me as I wrote the first draft; to Chloe Angyal, whose advice is gold-star-worthy; to Fiza, Fortesa, Chelsea, and Julie, for the ultimate freelancers group chat; to Nikhil Goyal, for constant words of wisdom, personally and professionally. To Lexi McMenamin and Mary Retta for their endless amazing work and for building space for community in journalism through Zenith—and to Serena, an incredible friend I've made as a result, and to Elly Belle, who I've been fortunate to know throughout many chapters of life. To so many new friends I've been fortunate enough to make over the past year, including Casey, Savannah, Kelsey, and Alana: you brought me back to life.

I joked throughout this writing process that I was *most* ambitious about getting a cat. Well, I adopted two, so thank you to Harry and Fig Newton for laying directly on my laptop keys when I need to take a break.

Ultimately, I'm ambitious about paying forward the extraordinary amounts of kindness, patience, and compassion that have been shown to me, both in the creation of this book and otherwise. That'll be the ambition that lasts for the rest of my days.

Notes

I'll Go First: An Introduction

1. Timothy A. Judge and John D. Kammeyer-Mueller, "On the Value of Aiming High: The Causes and Consequences of Ambition," *Journal of Applied Psychology* 97, no. 4 (July 2012): 758–757, http://www.timothy-judge .com/documents/Ambition-JAPINPRESS.pdf.

2. Chardie L. Baird, Stephen W. Burge, and John R. Reynolds, "Absurdly Ambitious? Teenagers' Expectations for the Future and the Realities of Social Structure," *Sociology Compass* 2, no. 3 (2008): 944–962, https:// its.fsu.edu/sites/g/files/imported/storage/original/application/a994acf2 df39d64e299a41b65281d389.pdf.

3. KFF, "Global COVID-19 Tracker," updated daily, https://www.kff .org/coronavirus-covid-19/issue-brief/global-covid-19-tracker/.

4. Adewaie Maye, Asha Banerjee, and Cameron Johnson, "The Dual Crisis: How the COVID-19 Recession Deepens Racial and Economic Inequality Among Communities of Color," CLASP: The Center for Law and Social Policy, November 19, 2020, https://www.clasp.org /publications/report/brief/dual-crisis-how-covid-19-recession-deepens -racial-and-economic-inequality.

5. Catarina Demony, "Disabled Workers Fear COVID-19 Silver Lining to Fade as 'Old Normal' Returns," Reuters, July 26, 2021, https://www .reuters.com/world/the-great-reboot/disabled-workers-fear-covid-19-silver -lining-fade-old-normal-returns-2021-07-26/.

6. Oksana V. Barsukova, "Psychological Characteristics of Ambitious Person," *Journal of Process Management: New Technologies, International* 4, no. 2 (2016), https://scindeks-clanci.ceon.rs/data/pdf/2334 -735X/2016/2334-735X1602079B.pdf.

Chapter 1: So You're Calling Me a Striver, and Some Thoughts on Sin

1. Andreas Hirschi and Daniel Spurk, "Striving for Success: Towards a Refined Understanding and Measurement of Ambition," *Journal Vocational Behavior* 127 (June 2021), https://doi.org/10.1016/j.jvb.2021.103577.

2. Hirschi and Spurk, "Striving for Success: Towards a Refined Understanding and Measurement of Ambition."

3. Deborah L. Rhode, *Ambition: For What?* (Oxford University Press, 2021).

4. *Merriam-Webster*, s.v. "ambition," https://www.merriam-webster.com/dictionary/ambition#:~:text=The%20Latin%20word%20for%20this,in%20the%20late%20Middle%20Ages; and William Casey King, *Ambition, A History: From Vice to Virtue* (New Haven, CT: Yale University Press, 2013), 19 (in ebook), https://books.google.com/books?id=UElGCn0QN3gC&pg=PT7&source=gbs_toc_r&cad=4#v=onepage&q&f=false.

5. King, *Ambition, A History*.

6. Genesis 3:6 (1599 Geneva Bible), https://www.biblegateway.com/passage/?search=Genesis%203%3A6&version=GNV#en-GNV-62.

7. J. M. Opal, "Review: As American as Ambition," *Reviews in American History* 41, no. 4 (December 2013): 614–619.

8. Opal, "Review: As American as Ambition."

9. Jamila Osman, "What Is Colonialism? A History of Violence, Control and Exploitation," *Teen Vogue*, October 11, 2020, https://www.teenvogue.com/story/colonialism-explained.

10. *Britannica*, s.v. "capitalism," https://www.britannica.com/topic/capitalism; and Kim Kelly, "What 'Capitalism' Is and How It Affects People," *Teen Vogue*, August 25, 2020, https://www.teenvogue.com/story/what-capitalism-is.

11. *Britannica*, s.v. "predestination," https://www.britannica.com/topic/predestination.

12. Max Weber, "The Religious Foundations of Worldly Asceticism (Part 1, Calvinism)," chap. 4 in *The Protestant Ethic and the Spirit of Capitalism* (London and Chicago: Fitzroy Dearborn, 2001), first published 1905, https://www.sparknotes.com/philosophy/protestantethic/section5/.

13. Errin Haines, "The New Deal Devalued Home Care Workers; Advocates Hope New Legislation Can Undo That," The 19th, October 6, 2021, https://19thnews.org/2021/10/home-care-workers-new-deal-reconciliation/.

14. Jo Littler, "Meritocracy as Plutocracy: The Marketing of 'Equality' Under Neoliberalism," *New Formations* 80, no. 1 (November 2013): 54.

15. Lisa Baer-Tsarfati, "Definitely! William Casey King argues . . . ," Twitter, https://twitter.com/baersafari/status/1248258966863446016?s=2 0&t=-7JELcYQC9m3u-_wWQpILg.

16. Caroline Bologna, "Why the Phrase 'Pull Yourself Up by Your Bootstraps' Is Nonsense," HuffPost, August 9, 2018, https://www.huffpost.com /entry/pull-yourself-up-by-your-bootstraps-nonsense_n_5b1ed024e4b0bbb 7a0e037d4; and Chris Waigl, "Figurative 'Bootstraps,'" August 11, 2005, https://listserv.linguistlist.org/pipermail/ads-l/2005-August/052757.html.

17. David Cooper, "Workers of Color Are Far More Likely to Be Paid Poverty-level Wages Than White Workers," Working Economics Blog, Economic Policy Institute, June 21, 2018, https://www.epi.org/blog /workers-of-color-are-far-more-likely-to-be-paid-poverty-level-wages -than-white-workers/.

18. Adewale Maye and Asha Banerjee, "The Struggles of Low-Wage Work," CLASP: The Center for Law and Social Policy, June 16, 2021, https://www.clasp.org/publications/fact-sheet/struggles-low-wage-work-0/.

19. Tressie McMillan Cottom, "Nearly 6 Decades After the Civil Rights Act, Why Do Black Workers Still Have to Hustle to Get Ahead?," *Time*, February 20, 2020, https://time.com/5783869/gig-economy-inequality/.

20. Frankie Mastrangelo, "Theorizing #Girlboss Culture: Mediated Neoliberal Feminisms from Influencers to Multilevel Schemes," PhD diss., VCU Scholars Compass, Virginia Commonwealth University, 2021, https:// scholarscompass.vcu.edu/cgi/viewcontent.cgi?article=7768&context=etd.

21. Samhita Mukhopadhyay, "The Girlboss Is Dead. Long Live the Girlboss," The Cut, *New York*, August 31, 2021, https://www.thecut .com/2021/08/demise-of-the-girlboss.html.

22. Mukhopadhyay, "The Girlboss Is Dead."

23. Mukhopadhyay.

24. Courtney L. McCluney et al., "The Costs of Code-Switching," *Harvard Business Review*, November 15, 2019, https://hbr.org/2019/11/ the-costs-of -codeswitching.

Chapter 2: Life's Good Behavior Chart

1. Courtney Tanner, "'We're Done Being Disrespected': Salt Lake City Teachers Walk Out of Meeting About Salary Increase," *Salt Lake Tribune*, June 4, 2019, https://www.sltrib.com/news/education/2019/06/05 /nearly-teachers-salt/.

2. Lindsay Lee Wallace, "The Real Villain in 'The Devil Wears Prada' Is Toxic Work Culture," Catapult, July 1, 2021, https://catapult.co/stories /the-real-villain-in-the-devil-wears-prada-is-toxic-work-culture -lindsay-lee-wallace.

3. Jennifer Crocker, Shawna J. Lee, and Lora E. Park, "The Pursuit of Self-Esteem: Implications for Good and Evil," in *The Social Psychology of Good and Evil*, ed. A. G. Miller (New York: Guildford Press, 2004), 271–302, https://ubwp.buffalo.edu/selfandmotivationlab/wp-content/uploads/sites/91/2018/05/Crocker-Lee-Park-2004.pdf; and Shuqi Li, Ashley A. Brown, and Jennifer Crocker, "Contingencies of Self-Worth (CSW) Scale," in *Encyclopedia of Personality and Individual Differences*, ed. V. Zeigler-Hill and T. K. Shackelford (New York: Springer, 2020), https://link.springer.com/referenceworkentry/10.1007/978-3-319-24612-3_1221#:~:text=Contingencies%20of%20self%2Dworth%20are,drops%20in%20state%20self%2Desteem.

4. Crocker, Lee, and Park, "The Pursuit of Self-Esteem."

5. Jennifer Crocker and Lora E. Park, "The Costly Pursuit of Self-Esteem," *Psychological Bulletin* 130, no. 3 (2004): 392–414, https://motamem.org/wp-content/uploads/2016/07/The-Costly-Pursuit-of-Self-Esteem-Crocker-and-Park.pdf.

6. Crocker, Lee, and Park, "The Costly Pursuit of Self-Esteem."

Chapter 3: Schoolhouse Rock (and a Hard Place)

1. Jenna Collins, "Merited Behavior: Rewarding the 19th Century Schoolchild," O Say Can You See? (blog), National Museum of American History, July 25, 2017, https://americanhistory.si.edu/blog/merited-behavior.

2. Kathleen O. Ryan, "'90s Family: Making the Grade," *Los Angeles Times*, December 27, 1995, https://www.latimes.com/archives/la-xpm-1995-12-27-ls-18127-story.html.

3. Book It!, "Mission Statement" (webpage), n.d., https://www.bookitprogram.com/about.

4. "Book It! Buttons and the Symbol of Reading Progress," Busy Beaver Button Museum, http://buttonmuseum.org/content/book-it-buttons-and-symbol-reading-progress.

5. Leah Y. Latimer, "Pupil Prizes Also Reward Big Business," *Washington Post*, November 28, 1987, https://www.washingtonpost.com/archive/local/1987/11/28/pupil-prizes-also-reward-big-business/52e0db94-2f10-4a6b-bab3-3d422a7e5f76/.

6. Whitney Pirtle, "The Other Segregation," *The Atlantic*, April 23, 2019, https://www.theatlantic.com/education/archive/2019/04/gifted-and-talented-programs-separate-students-race/587614/.

7. Pirtle, "The Other Segregation."

8. The Education Trust, "Black and Latino Students Shut Out of Advanced Coursework Opportunities" (press release), January 9, 2020, https://

edtrust.org/press-release/black-and-latino-students-shut-out-of-advanced -coursework-opportunities/.

9. Wayne Au, "Hiding Behind High-Stakes Testing: Meritocracy, Objectivity and Inequality in U.S. Education," *International Education Journal: Comparative Perspectives* 12, no. 2 (2013): 7–19, https://files.eric.ed.gov /fulltext/EJ1017702.pdf.

10. Abigail Johnson Hess, "College Costs Have Increased by 169% Since 1980—But Pay for Young Workers Is Up Just 19%: Georgetown Report," Make It, CNBC, November 2, 2021, https://www.cnbc.com/2021/11/02 /the-gap-in-college-costs-and-earnings-for-young-workers-since-1980.html.

11. Melanie Hanson, "Student Loan Debt by Generation," Education Data Initiative, updated October 12, 2021, https://educationdata.org /student-loan-debt-by-generation.

12. Santul Nerkar, "Canceling Student Debt Could Help Close the Wealth Gap Between White and Black Americans," FiveThirtyEight, May 31, 2022, https://fivethirtyeight.com/features/canceling-student -debt-could-help-close-the-wealth-gap-between-white-and-black -americans/.

13. Lumina Foundation, "Today's Student" (webpage), n.d., https:// www.luminafoundation.org/campaign/todays-student/.

14. Institute for Women's Policy Research, *Parents in College by the Numbers*, 2017, https://iwpr.org/iwpr-issues/student-parent-success-initiative /parents-in-college-by-the-numbers/.

Chapter 4: Parental Guidance Suggested

1. Sarah Jaffe, *Work Won't Love You Back: How Devotion to Our Jobs Keeps Us Exploited, Exhausted, and Alone* (New York: Bold Type Books, 2021), 26.

2. Stephanie Coontz, "Can the Working Family Work in America?," *American Prospect*, May 17, 2016, https://prospect.org/power/can-working -family-work-america/.

3. Rebecca Sear, "The Male Breadwinner Nuclear Family Is Not the 'Traditional' Human Family, and Promotion of This Myth May Have Adverse Health Consequences," *Philosophical Transactions of the Royal Society B* 376, no. 1827 (May 3, 2021), https://royalsocietypublishing.org /doi/10.1098/rstb.2020.0020.

4. Sophie Lewis, "The Family Lottery," *Dissent*, summer 2021, https:// www.dissentmagazine.org/article/the-family-lottery.

5. Jocelyn Frye, "On the Frontlines at Work and at Home: The Disproportionate Economic Effects of the Coronavirus Pandemic on Women of Color," Center for American Progress, April 23, 2020, https://www .americanprogress.org/article/frontlines-work-home/.

6. Nina Banks, "Black Women's Labor Market History Reveals Deep-seated Race and Gender Discrimination," Working Economics Blog, Economic Policy Institute, February 19, 2019, https://www.epi.org/blog/black-womens-labor-market-history-reveals-deep-seated-race-and-gender-discrimination/.

7. Banks, "Black Women's Labor Market History."

8. Meg Conley, "What the Conversation Around the 'Great Resignation' Leaves Out," *Harper's Bazaar*, Jan. 31, 2022, https://www.harpersbazaar.com/culture/features/a38941844/what-the-conversation-around-the-great-resignation-leaves-out/.

9. Angela Garbes, *Essential Labor: Mothering as Social Change* (New York: HarperCollins, 2022).

10. Katie Bishop, "The Parental Shame That Haunts Working Parents," BBC, January 25, 2022, https://www.bbc.com/worklife/article/20220121-the-parental-shame-that-haunts-working-parents.

11. Ellen Ernst Kossek, Matthew Perrigino, and Alyson Gounden Rock, "From Ideal Workers to Ideal Work for All: A 50-Year Review Integrating Careers and Work-Family Research with a Future Research Agenda," *Journal of Vocational Behavior* 126 (April 2021), https://www.sciencedirect.com/science/article/pii/S0001879120301299#!.

12. USDA: Food and Nutrition Service, "SNAP Work Requirements," May 29, 2019, https://www.fns.usda.gov/snap/work-requirements.

13. Elisa Minoff, "The Racist Roots of Work Requirements," Center for the Study of Social Policy, February 2020, https://cssp.org/wp-content/uploads/2020/02/Racist-Roots-of-Work-Requirements-CSSP-1.pdf.

14. Madison Allen, "Racism in Public Benefit Programs: Where Do We Go from Here?" (blog), CLASP: The Center for Law and Social Policy, July 23, 2020, https://www.clasp.org/blog/racism-public-benefit-programs-where-do-we-go-here/.

15. Minoff, "The Racist Roots of Work Requirements."

16. Chabeli Carrazana, "America's First Female Recession," The 19th, August 2, 2020, https://19thnews.org/2020/08/americas-first-female-recession/.

17. Amil Niazi, "Losing My Ambition," The Cut, *New York*, March 25, 2020, https://www.thecut.com/2022/03/post-pandemic-loss-of-ambition.html.

18. Lauren Bauer, Sara Estep, and Winnie Yee, "Time Waited for No Mom in 2020" (blog), The Hamilton Project, July 22, 2021, https://www.hamiltonproject.org/blog/mothers_time_use_update; and Chabeli Carrazana, "Moms Spent the Equivalent of a Full-time Job on Child Care Last Year—While Working at the Same Time," The 19th, August 3,

2021, https://19thnews.org/2021/08/moms-child-care-pandemic-full-time-job/.

19. Shauneen Miranda, "For Many Dads, the COVID Pandemic Brought New Perspectives on Fatherhood," NPR, June 19, 2022, https://www.npr.org/2022/06/19/1105442434/dads-work-from-home-covid-pandemic-new-perspective-fatherhood-children; and Pew Research Center, "Shares of Working Parents Who Report Difficulty Handling Child Care Responsibilities Have Changed Little Since 2020," February 23, 2022, https://www.pewresearch.org/fact-tank/2022/02/23/many-working-parents-with-young-children-say-finding-backup-care-would-be-very-difficult/ft_2022-02-23_childcare_01/.

20. Gretchen Livingston, "Growing Number of Dads Home with Kids," Pew Research Center, June 5, 2014, https://www.pewresearch.org/social-trends/2014/06/05/growing-number-of-dads-home-with-the-kids/#:~:text=The%20number%20of%20fathers%20who%20are%20at%20home%20with%20their,spanned%20from%202007%20to%202009.

21. Rebecca L. Stotzer, Jody L. Herman, Amira Hasenbush, "Transgender Parenting: A Review of Existing Research," October 2014, https://williamsinstitute.law.ucla.edu/publications/transgender-parenting/.

22. Siegel, "Trans Moms Discuss Their Unique Parenting Challenges," *The Conversation*, May 20, 2021, https://scholars.org/contribution/trans-moms-discuss-their-unique-parenting.

23. Kenzie Bryant, "'Operation Varsity Blues' Is the One Scam to Rule Them All," *Vanity Fair*, March 12, 2019, https://www.vanityfair.com/style/2019/03/lori-loughlin-felicity-huffman-college-cheating-scandal.

24. Zulie Rane, "The Terrifying Rise of the Child Influencer and the Parents Who Profit," OneZero, October 25, 2021, https://onezero.medium.com/the-terrifying-rise-of-the-child-fashion-influencer-e7b03278d887.

Chapter 5: "Just" a Hobby

1. Steven M. Gelber, *Hobbies: Leisure and the Culture of Work in America* (New York: Columbia University Press, 1999).

2. Gelber, *Hobbies: Leisure and the Culture of Work in America*, 3.

3. Gelber, 28.

4. Corroboration on Gelber, 1.

5. The Serious Leisure Perspective (SLP), "Basic Concepts" (webpage), n.d., https://www.seriousleisure.net/concepts.html.

6. Serious Leisure Perspective (SLP), "Basic Concepts."

7. Gelber, *Hobbies*, 20.

8. Erin Cech, *The Trouble with Passion: How Searching for Fulfillment at Works Fosters Inequality* (Berkeley: University of California Press, 2021), 35.

9. R. N. Bellah, "Religion: Evolution and Development," and P. Demeu-lenaere, "Interests, Sociological Analysis of," in *International Encyclopedia of the Social & Behavioral Sciences*, ed. Neil J. Smelser and Paul B. Baltes (Oxford, UK: Pergamon, 2001); https://www.sciencedirect.com/topics/computer-science/protestant-ethic.

10. Elena Resta et al., "Marie Curie vs. Serena Williams: Ambition Leads to Extremism Through Obsessive (but Not Harmonious) Passion," *Motivation and Emotion* 46 (2022): 382–393, https://link.springer.com/article/10.1007/s11031-022-09936-3.

11. Paula Thomson and S. Victoria Jaque, "Personality and Motivation," in *Creativity and the Performing Artist: Behind the Mask* (London: Academic Press, 2017), https://www.sciencedirect.com/topics/psychology/harmonious-passion#:~:text=Harmonious%20passion%20implies%20that%20performing,they%20love%20into%20their%20identity.

12. Thomson and Jaque, "Personality and Motivation."

13. Susana Juniu and Karia A. Henderson, "Problems in Researching Leisure and Women: Global Considerations," *World Leisure Journal* 43, no. 4 (March 2011), https://www.researchgate.net/publication/241748588_Problems_in_Researching_Leisure_and_Women_Global_Considerations.

14. Juniu and Henderson, "Problems in Researching Leisure and Women."

15. Nichole Marie Shippen, *Decolonizing Time: Work, Leisure, and Free-dom* (New York: Palgrave Macmillan, 2014).

16. Shippen, "The Culture Industry: The Extension of Work, Disciplined Leisure, and the Deterioration of Culture," in *Decolonizing Time*, 115–138, https://link.springer.com/chapter/10.1057/9781137354020_6.

17. Robert J. Vallerand, "The Role of Passion in Sustainable Psycholog-ical Well-Being," *Psychology of Well-Being: Theory, Research and Practice* 2, no. 1 (2012), https://psywb.springeropen.com/articles/10.1186/2211-1522-2-1.

Chapter 6: A Ticking Time Bomb

1. Barbara Adam, *Time* (Cambridge, UK: Polity Press, 2004), http://wendynorris.com/wp-content/uploads/2018/05/Adam-2004PS-ENH-The-Quest-for-Time-Control.pdf.

2. Katrina Onstad, "It Took a Century to Create the Weekend—and Only a Decade to Undo It," *Quartz*, May 6, 2017, updated July 20, 2022, https://qz.com/969245/it-took-a-century-to-create-the-weekend-and-only-a-decade-to-undo-it/.

3. Reid Cramer, "Framing the Millennial Wealth Gap: Demographic Realities and Divergent Trajectories," New America, n.d, https://www

.newamerica.org/millennials/reports/emerging-millennial-wealth-gap /framing-the-millennial-wealth-gap-demographic-realities-and-divergent -trajectories/.

4. Abigail Johnson Hess, "Just 50% of the College Class of 2020 Had Traditional Full-Time Jobs 6 Months After Graduation," Make It, CNBC, December 10, 2021, https://www.cnbc.com/2021/12/10/50percent -of-the-class-of-2020-got-full-time-jobs-6-months-after-graduation .html.

5. Paul A. Laudicina, "Wages Have Fallen 43% for Millennials. No Wonder They've Lost Hope," World Economic Forum, January 15, 2017, https://www.weforum.org/agenda/2017/01/wages-have-fallen-43-for -millennials-no-wonder-they-ve-lost-hope/.

6. Hillary Hoffower, "Millennials' Life Stage Means They're Suffering the Most from Rising Prices," Insider, February 11, 2022, https://www .businessinsider.com/inflation hitting-millennials-hardest-buying-homes -cars-2022-2.

7. Fenaba R. Addo and William A. Darity Jr., "Disparate Recoveries: Wealth, Race, and the Working Class After the Great Recession," *Annals of the American Academy of Political and Social Science* 695, no. 1 (2021): 173–192, https://journals.sagepub.com/doi/full/10.1177/00027162211028822.

8. Alex Shashkevich, "Millennials Are 'Canaries in the Coalmine' for Toxic Economic Trends, Say Stanford Scholars," Stanford News, June 6, 2019, https://news.stanford.edu/2019/06/06/toxic-economic-trends -impacted-millennials/.

9. Nancy E. Hill and Alexis Redding, "The Real Reason Young Adults Seem Slow to 'Grow Up,'" *The Atlantic*, April 28, 2021, https://www .theatlantic.com/family/archive/2021/04/real-reason-young-adults-seem -slow-grow/618733/.

10. Paul B. Baltes, Ulman Lindenberger, and Ursula M. Staudinger, "Life Span Theory in Developmental Psychology," chap. 11 in *Theoretical Models of Human Development*, vol. 1, ed. Richard M. Lerner, of *Handbook of Child Psychology*, 6th ed., ed. William Damon and Richard M. Lerner (Hoboken, NJ: John Wiley, 2006), 569–664, https://www.imprs-life.mpg .de/25249/023_baltes-06a.pdf.

11. Baltes, Lindenberger, and Staudinger, "Life Span Theory in Developmental Psychology."

12. Baltes, Lindenberger, and Staudinger.

13. Rachel E. Friedensen et al., "Queer Science: Temporality and Futurity for Queer Students in STEM," *Time & Society* (2021): 1–23, https:// www.jefferson.edu/content/dam/academic/life-science/diversity-inclusion /journal-club/QueerInSTEM_Article%20(1).pdf.

14. Judith Halberstam, *In a Queer Time and Place: Transgender Bodies, Subcultural Lives* (New York University Press, 2005).

15. Gabrielle Kassel, "Teenage Dream or Teenage Scream? Why LBTQIA+ People Experience 2 Kinds of Adolescence," Healthline, 2021, https://www.healthline.com/health/healthy-sex/second-queer-adolescence #why-this-is.

16. Karin Ljuslinder, Katie Ellis, and Lotta Vikström, "Cripping Time—Understanding the Life Course Through the Lens of Ableism," *Scandinavian Journal of Disability Research* 22, no. 1 (2020): 35–38.

17. Ljuslinder, Ellis, and Vikström, "Cripping Time."

18. Ljuslinder, Ellis, and Vikström.

19. Ljuslinder, Ellis, and Vikström.

20. Anne Helen Petersen, "The Escalating Costs of Being Single in America," Vox, December 2, 2021, https://www.vox.com/the-goods /22788620/single-living-alone-cost.

21. Noémi Nagy, Ariane Froidevaux, and Andreas Hirschi, "Lifespan Perspectives on Careers and Career Development," chap. 10 in *Work Across the Lifespan*, ed. Boris Baltes, Cort Rudolph, and Hannes Zacher (London: Academic Press, 2019), 235–259, https://www.researchgate.net /publication/323309112_Lifespan_Perspectives_on_Careers_and_Career _Development.

22. *Express*, "33 Is the Age at Which We Peak—New Study," January 27, 2020, https://www.express.co.uk/life-style/life/1234225/age-ambition -life-peak.

23. A. C. Shilton, "You Accomplished Something Great. So Now What?," *New York Times*, May 28, 2019, https://www.nytimes.com/2019/05 /28/smarter-living/you-accomplished-something-great-so-now-what.html.

24. US Bureau of Labor Statistics, "Number of People 75 and Older in the Labor Force Is Expected to Grow 96.5 Percent by 2030," TED: The Economics Daily, November 4, 2021, https://www.bls.gov/opub/ted/2021 /number-of-people-75-and-older-in-the-labor-force-is-expected-to-grow -96-5-percent-by-2030.htm.

25. Michael Sainato, "'At 75, I Still Have to Work': Millions of Americans Can't Afford to Retire," *The Guardian* (Manchester, UK), December 13, 2021, https://www.theguardian.com/money/2021/dec/13/americans -retire-work-social-security.

26. Raqota Berger, "Aging in America: Ageism and General Attitudes Toward Growing Old and the Elderly," *Open Journal of Social Sciences* 5, no. 8 (2017), https://www.scirp.org/html/15-1761515_78445.htm.

27. Anti-Ageism Taskforce, International Longevity Center, *Ageism in America*, Open Society Institute, 2006, https://aging.columbia.edu/sites /default/files/Ageism_in_America.pdf.

Chapter 7: Nine to . . . Forever

1. John Ross, "Only the Overworked Die Young," Heart Health (blog), Harvard Health Publishing, Harvard Medical School, December 14, 2015, https://www.health.harvard.edu/blog/only-the-overworked-die-young-201512148815.

2. Frank Pega et al., "Global, Regional, and National Burdens of Ischemic Heart Disease and Stroke Attributable to Exposure to Long Working Hours for 194 Countries, 2000–2016," *Environment International* 154 (September 2021), https://www.sciencedirect.com/science/article/pii/S0160412021002208.

3. Harry Cheadle, "New Report Confirms Just How Shitty US Workers Have It," *Vice*, November 6, 2019, https://www.vice.com/en/article/ywajnj/new-report-confirms-just-how-shitty-us-workers-have-it.

4. Ryan Cooper, *The Leisure Agenda*, People's Policy Project and The Gravel Institute, 2019, https://www.peoplespolicyproject.org/projects/the-leisure-agenda/.

5. Malissa A. Clark, "Workaholism: It's Not Just Long Hours on the Job," American Psychological Association, April 2016, https://www.apa.org/science/about/psa/2016/04/workaholism.

6. Clark, "Workaholism."

7. Adewalé Maye and Asha Banerjee, "The Struggles of Low-Wage Work," CLASP: The Center for Law and Social Policy, June 16, 2021, https://www.clasp.org/publications/fact-sheet/struggles-low-wage-work-0/.

8. Adewale Maye, Asha Banerjee, and Cameron Johnson, "The Dual Crisis: How the COVID-19 Recession Deepens Racial and Economic Inequality Among Communities of Color," CLASP: The Center for Law and Social Policy, November 19, 2020, https://www.clasp.org/publications/report/brief/dual-crisis-how-covid-19-recession-deepens-racial-and-economic-inequality/.

9. EH.net, "Hours of Work in U.S. History," Economic History Association, n.d., https://eh.net/encyclopedia/hours-of-work-in-u-s-history/.

10. EH.net, "Hours of Work in U.S. History."

11. Kim Kelly, "How American Workers Won the Eight-Hour Workday," *Teen Vogue*, July 11, 2019, https://www.teenvogue.com/story/american-workers-eight-hour-workday.

12. Philip Sopher, "Where the Five-Day Workweek Came From," *The Atlantic*, August 21, 2014, https://www.theatlantic.com/business/archive/2014/08/where-the-five-day-workweek-came-from/378870/.

13. UMWA, "United Mine Workers of America History," n.d., https://umwa.org/about/history/#:~:text=The%20strike%20lasted%20just%20over,on%20a%2010%2Dmonth%20strike.

14. Sidney Milkis, "Theodore Roosevelt: Campaigns and Elections," Miller Center, University of Virginia, n.d., https://millercenter.org /president/roosevelt/campaigns-and-elections.

15. History.com editors, "Ford Factory Workers Get 40-Hour Week," History, November 13, 2009, updated April 29, 2020, https://www .history.com/this-day-in-history/ford-factory-workers-get-40-hour-week#:~:text=Henry%20Ford%20said%20of%20the,job%20had%20 decreased%2C%20they%20were; and Marguerite Ward, "A Brief History of the 8-Hour Workday, Which Changed How Americans Work," Make It, CNBC, May 3, 2017, https://www.cnbc.com/2017/05/03/how-the-8-hour -workday-changed-how-americans-work.html.

16. Jonathan Grossman, "Fair Labor Standards Act of 1938: Maximum Struggle for a Minimum Wage," US Department of Labor, n.d., https:// www.dol.gov/general/aboutdol/history/flsa1938.

17. Encyclopedia.com, "Fair Labor Standards Act of 1938," https://www .encyclopedia.com/social-sciences-and-law/economics-business-and-labor /labor/fair-labor-standards-act.

18. Meral Elci, Irge Sener, Lutfihak Alpkan, "The Impact of Morality and Religiosity of Employees on Their Hardworking Behavior," *Elsevier Procedia* 24, 2011, 1367-1377, https://doi.org/10.1016/j.sbspro.2011.09.135.

19. Ella Nilsen, "These Workers Were Left Out of the New Deal. They've Been Fighting for Better Pay Ever Since," Vox, May 18, 2021, https://www .vox.com/22423690/american-jobs-plan-care-workers-new-deal.

20. Krista Lynn Minnotte and Michael C. Minnotte, "The Ideal Worker Norm and Workplace Social Support Among U.S. Workers," *Sociological Focus* 54, no. 2 (April 2021): 120–137, https://www.tandfonline.com/doi /abs/10.1080/00380237.2021.1894622?journalCode=usfo20.

21. Erin Reid, "Embracing, Passing, Revealing, and the Ideal Worker Image: How People Navigate Expected and Experienced Professional Identities," *Organization Science* 26, no. 4 (2015): 997–1017, https://ideas .wharton.upenn.edu/wp-content/uploads/2018/07/Reid-2015.pdf.

22. Alex Lisitza, "17 Job Recruiters Who Somehow Thought They Could Demand Extra Work for Less Than Minimum Wage," BuzzFeed, September 15, 2021, https://www.buzzfeed.com/alexalisitza/reddit-job -listings-little-pay-salary.

23. Gillian B. White, "Black Workers Really Do Need to Be Twice as Good," *The Atlantic*, October 7, 2015, https://www.theatlantic.com /business/archive/2015/10/why-black-workers-really-do-need-to-be -twice-as-good/409276/.

24. Julie A. Kmec, Lindsey Trimble O'Connor, and Scott Schie-man, "Not Ideal: The Association Between Working Anything but

Full Time and Perceived Unfair Treatment," *Work and Occupations* 41, no. 1 (February 1, 2014): 63–65, https://journals.sagepub.com/doi /full/10.1177/0730888413515691.

25. Erin Cech, *The Trouble with Passion: How Searching for Fulfillment at Work Fosters Inequality* (Berkeley: University of California Press, 2021), 81.

Chapter 8: When Gold Stars Shatter

1. Thomas Curran and Andrew P. Hill, "How Perfectionism Became a Hidden Epidemic Among Young People," *The Conversation*, January 3, 2018, https://theconversation.com/how-perfectionism-became-a -hidden-epidemic-among-young-people-89405.

2. Thomas Curran and Andrew P. Hill, "Perfectionism Is Increasing Over Time: A Meta-Analysis of Birth Cohort Differences from 1989 to 2016," *Psychological Bulletin* 145, no. 4 (2019): 410–429, https://www.apa .org/pubs/journals/releases/bul-bul0000138.pdf.

3. Tanya Paperny, "Do Some Trauma Survivors Cope by Overworking?," *The Atlantic*, February 16, 2017, https://www.theatlantic.com/health /archive/2017/02/do-some-trauma-survivors-cope-by-overworking /516540/.

4. Eve Ettinger, "Have We Been Thinking About Burnout All Wrong?," *Bustle*, March 7, 2022.

5. Daniel Madigan, "Perfectionist Students Get Higher Grades, but at What Cost?," *The Conversation*, December 20, 2019, https://theconversation .com/perfectionistic-students-get-higher-grades-but-at-what-cost-126558.

6. OECD iLibrary, "Education at a Glance," 2019, https://www .oecd-ilibrary.org/education/education-at-a-glance-2019_f8d7880d-en.

Chapter 9: Good for Something

1. Saul McLeod, "Carl Rogers' Humanistic Theory of Personality Development," Simply Psychology, updated 2014, https://www.simplypsychology .org/carl-rogers.html.

Chapter 10: Pal Around

1. Harry T. Reis, Stephanie D. O'Keefe, and Richard D. Lane, "Fun Is More Fun When Others Are Involved," *Journal of Positive Psychology* 12, no. 6 (2017): 547–557, https://www.ncbi.nlm.nih.gov/pmc/articles /PMC5597001/.

2. Travis Tae Oh and Michel Tuan Pham, "A Liberating-Engagement Theory of Consumer Fun," *Journal of Consumer Research* (2021), https:// papers.ssrn.com/sol3/papers.cfm?abstract_id=3909337.

3. Oh and Pham, "A Liberating-Engagement Theory."

4. Lenora E. Houseworth, "The Radical History of Self-Care," *Teen Vogue*, January 14, 2021, https://www.teenvogue.com/story/the-radical -history-of-self-care.

5. Arturo Pineda, "Former Panthers Chart the Course to Revolutionary Education," Arts Council, Greater New Haven, September 11, 2020, https://www.newhavenarts.org/arts-paper/articles/former-panthers -map-a-blueprint-to-revolutionary-education.

6. Aminatou Sow and Ann Friedman, *Big Friendship: How We Keep Each Other Close* (New York: Simon and Schuster, 2020).

7. Sami Yenigun, "Play Doesn't End with Childhood: Why Adults Need Recess Too," NPR, August 6, 2014, https://www.npr.org/sections /ed/2014/08/06/336360521/play-doesnt-end-with-childhood-why -adults-need-recess-too.

8. Patty Obrzut, "What Is Play?," audio (mp3) video, 8:59, September 2016, Penrickton Center for Blind Children, Active Learning Space, https://activelearningspace.org/principles/what-is-play/#:~:text="Play%20 is%3A,and%20imitation%20of%20one's%20surroundings."

9. Harvard Graduate School of Education, "Pedagogy of Play," http:// www.pz.harvard.edu/projects/pedagogy-of-play.

10. Yenigun, "Play Doesn't End with Childhood."

Chapter 11: Worked Up

1. Sarah Jaffe, *Work Won't Love You Back: How Devotion to Our Jobs Keeps Us Exploited, Exhausted, and Alone* (New York: Bold Type Books, 2021), 329.

2. Dave Jamieson, "Union Elections Increase Amid Worker Organizing Wave," HuffPost, July 18, 2022, https://www.huffpost.com/entry /union-elections-jump-amid-worker-organizing-wave_n_62d59cfee4b0 e6fc1a9a045b.

3. Eric Rosenbaum, "The Amazon, Starbucks, Apple Union Push Is Capturing What a Majority of All American Workers Now Say They Want," CNBC, June 3, 2022, https://www.cnbc.com/2022/06/02/majority -of-american-workers-want-more-unionization-at-their-own-jobs.html.

4. Global Strategy Group & Paid Leave for All Action, "New Survey Shows Voters in Senate Battleground States Want Paid Leave Urgently, as Part of Infrastructure Package," May 2021, memo, https://global strategygroup.com/wp-content/uploads/2020/05/PLFA-BG-Press-Memo -F06.01.21.pdf.

5. Azza Altiraifi and Kendra Bozarth, "Practice, Practice, Practice," The Forge, June 1, 2022, https://forgeorganizing.org/article/practice-practice -practice.

6. Arianne Cohen, "How to Quit Your Job in the Great Post-Pandemic

Resignation Boom," Bloomberg, May 10, 2021, https://www.bloomberg
.com/news/articles/2021-05-10/quit-your-job-how-to-resign-after-covid
-pandemic.

7. Ann Kellett, "The Texas A&M Professor Who Predicted 'The
Great Resignation,'" *Texas A&M Today*, February 11, 2022, https://today
.tamu.edu/2022/02/11/the-texas-am-professor-who-predicted-the
-great-resignation/.

8. A Better Balance, "Our Issues" (webpage), n.d., https://www.abetter
balance.org/our-issues/.

9. A Better Balance, "Get Help" (webpage), n.d., https://www.abetter
balance.org/get-help/.

10. Amelia Lucas, "Starbucks to Hike Wages, Double Training for
Workers as CEO Schultz Tries to Head Off Union Push," CNBC, May
4, 2022, https://www.cnbc.com/2022/05/03/starbucks-to-hike-wages
-double-training-for-workers-amid-union-push.html.

11. Josh Bivens et al., "How Today's Unions Help Working People," Economic Policy Institute, August 24, 2017, https://www.cpi.org
/publication/how-todays-unions-help-working-people-giving-workers
-the-power-to-improve-their-jobs-and-unrig-the-economy/.

12. Abigail Johnson Hess, "Union Enrollment Has Declined for Decades, but Union Workers Still Earn 19% More," Make It, CNBC, February 5, 2021, https://www.cnbc.com/2021/02/05/union-enrollment
-declined-for-decades-but-union-workers-still-earn-more.html.

13. Kim Kelly, "What a Labor Union Is and How It Works," *Teen
Vogue*, March 12, 2018, https://www.teenvogue.com/story/what-a-labor
-union-is-and-how-it-works.

14. Bivens et al., "How Today's Unions Help Working People."

15. Kim Kelly, *Fight Like Hell: The Untold History of American Labor*,
(New York: Simon & Schuster, 2022).

16. Rainesford Stauffer, "What Is Retaliation in the Workplace? Here
Are Your Rights and What to Know," *Teen Vogue*, April 7, 2022, https://www
.teenvogue.com/story/what-is-retaliation-workplace.

17. Diane Whitmore Schanzenback et al., "The Closing of the Jobs
Gap: A Decade of Recession and Recovery," The Hamilton Project,
Brookings, August 4, 2017, https://www.brookings.edu/research/the
-closing-of-the-jobs-gap-a-decade-of-recession-and-recovery/.

18. USDA, "Cooperative Business Principles," Cooperative Information Report 45, Section 2, August 1994, revised April 2011, https://www
.rd.usda.gov/sites/default/files/publications/CIR_45-2.pdf.

19. John Jay: College of Criminal Justice, "Jessica Gordon Nembhard"
(bio), https://www.jjay.cuny.edu/faculty/jessica-gordon-nembhard.

Chapter 12: Take Good Care

1. Josephine Kalipeni and Julie Kashen, *Building Our Care Infrastructure: For Equity Economic Recovery and Beyond*, September 1, 2020, https://caringacross.org/wp-content/uploads/2020/09/Building-Our-Care-infrastructure_FINAL.pdf.

2. Mia Birdsong, *How We Show Up: Reclaiming Family, Friendship, and Community* (New York: Hachette Go, 2020), 13.

3. Andreas Chatzidakis et al., *The Care Manifesto: The Politics of Interdependence* (London: Verso, 2020), https://www.uhn.ca/Research/Research_Institutes/The_Institute_for_Education_Research/Events/Documents/Care-Manifesto-Readings.pdf.

4. Kalipeni and Kashen, *Building Our Care Infrastructure*.

5. Ai-Jen Poo and Sade Moonsammy, "The Care Infrastructure: Building Across Movements," *Generations Journal*, October 20, 2021, https://generations.asaging.org/building-care-infrastructure-across-movements.

6. Richard Fry, Jeffrey S. Passel, and D'Vera Cohn, "A Majority of Young Adults in the U.S. Live with Their Parents for the First Time Since the Great Depression," Pew Research Center, September 4, 2020, https://www.pewresearch.org/fact-tank/2020/09/04/a-majority-of-young-adults-in-the-u-s-live-with-their-parents-for-the-first-time-since-the-great-depression/.

7. D'Vera Cohn and Jeffrey S. Passel, "A Record 64 Million Americans Live in Multigenerational Households," Pew Research Center, April 5, 2018, https://www.pewresearch.org/fact-tank/2018/04/05/a-record-64-million-americans-live-in-multigenerational-households/.

8. D'Vera Cohn et al., "Financial Issues Top the List of Reasons U.S. Adults Live in Multigenerational Homes," Pew Research Center, March 24, 2022, https://www.pewresearch.org/social-trends/2022/03/24/financial-issues-top-the-list-of-reasons-u-s-adults-live-in-multigenerational-homes/#:~:text=Among%20the%20other%20reasons%20given,they%20live%20with%20family%20members.

9. D'Vera Cohn et al., "The Experiences of Adults in Multigenerational Households," Pew Research Center, March 24, 2022, https://www.pewresearch.org/social-trends/2022/03/24/the-experiences-of-adults-in-multigenerational-households/.

10. Julia B. Bear and Todd L. Pittinsky, *The Caregiving Ambition: What It Is and Why It Matters at Home and Work* (New York: Oxford University Press, 2022), 3.

11. Jon Carlson and Shannon B. Dermer, *The SAGE Encyclopedia of Marriage, Family, and Couples Counseling* (Thousand Oaks, CA:

Sage, 2017), https://sk.sagepub.com/reference/the-sage-encyclopedia-of-marriage-family-couples-counseling/i2967.xm.

12. Nina Jackson Levin et al., "'We Just Take Care of Each Other': Navigating 'Chosen Family' in the Context of Health, Illness, and the Mutual Provision of Care amongst Queer and Transgender Young Adults," *International Journal of Environmental Research and Public Health* 17, no. 19 (October 2020): 7346, https://www.ncbi.nlm.nih.gov/pmc/articles/PMC7579626/#B2-ijerph-17-07346.

13. Nancy J. Knauer, "LGBT Older Adults: Chosen Family and Caregiving," *Journal of Law and Religion* 31, no. 2 (2016): 150–168, https://papers.ssrn.com/sol3/papers.cfm?abstract_id=2721451.

14. Levin et al., "'We Just Take Care of Each Other.'"

15. Lindsay Mahowald and Diana Boesch, "Making the Case for Chosen Family in Paid Family and Medical Leave Policies," Center for American Progress, February 16, 2021, https://www.americanprogress.org/article/making-case-chosen-family-paid-family-medical-leave-policies/.

16. Mahowald and Boesch, "Making the Case for Chosen Family."

17. Society for Human Resource Management, *SHRM Customized Paid Leave Benchmarking Report*, 2017, https://www.shrm.org/Resources AndTools/business-solutions/PublishingImages/Pages/Forms/Edit Form/Health%20Care%20and%20Social%20Assistance%20All%20 FTEs%20Paid%20Leave%20Report.pdf; and Marguerite Ward, "Despite a Pandemic and Opioid Crisis, America's Bereavement Leave Is Still Causing a Grief Crisis," Insider, August 26, 2022, https://www.businessinsider.com/bereavement-leave-asking-time-off-work-funeral-2020-5.

18. Society for Human Resource Management, "2016 Paid Leave in the Workplace," October 6, 2016, https://www.shrm.org/hr-today/trends-and-forecasting/research-and-surveys/pages/2016-paid-leave-in-the-workplace.aspx.

19. Angela Garbes, *Essential Labor: Mothering as Social Change* (New York: HarperCollins, 2022).

20. Julianne Holt-Lunstad, "The Potential Public Health Relevance of Social Isolation and Loneliness: Prevalence, Epidemiology, and Risk Factors," *Public Policy and Aging Report* 27, no. 4 (2017): 127–130, https://academic.oup.com/ppar/article/27/4/127/4782506.

21. Ramon Oldenburg and Dennis Brissett, "The Third Place," *Qualitative Sociology* 5 (1982): 265–284, https://link.springer.com/article/10.1007/BF00986754.

22. Rachel Kushner, "Is Prison Necessary? Ruth Wilson Gilmore Might Change Your Mind," *New York Times Magazine*, May 17, 2019,

https://www.nytimes.com/2019/04/17/magazine/prison-abolition-ruth
-wilson-gilmore.html.

23. Tyesha Maddox, "What Is Mutual Aid?," slide show presentation,
n.d., https://www.tyeshamaddox.com/what-is-mutual-aid.

24. Jia Tolentino, "What Mutual Aid Can Do During a Pandemic," *New
Yorker*, May 11, 2020, https://www.newyorker.com/magazine/2020/05/18
/what-mutual-aid-can-do-during-a-pandemic.

25. Theresa Hernandez, Beryl-Ann Mark, Anne O'Connell, Ana Te-
resa Portillo, Nadia Rajaram, Bernadette Rilloraza, Mercedes SharpeZayas,
"Mutual Aid Parkdale," *Canadian Review of Social Policy* 81, Dec. 14, 2021,
https://crsp.journals.yorku.ca/index.php/crsp/article/view/40394

26. Tina Gerhardt, "COVID-19, the Climate Crisis, and Mutual
Aid," *Progressive*, December 19, 2020, https://progressive.org/latest
/covid-climate-crisis-mutual-aid-gerhardt-201219/.

27. Peter Kropotkin, *Mutual Aid: A Factor of Evolution* (Traverse City, MI:
Horizons Books, 1976), first published 1902, https://www.college.columbia
.edu/core/content/mutual-aid-factor-evolution-peter-kropotkin-1902-ce.

28. Maddox, "What Is Mutual Aid?"

29. Fiona Lowenstein, "I'm 26. Coronavirus Sent Me to the Hospital,"
New York Times, March 23, 2020, https://www.nytimes.com/2020/03/23
/opinion/coronavirus-young-people.html.